ILLUSTRATED
BIBLE STUDY
OUTLINES

ILLUSTRATED BIBLE STUDY OUTLINES

by
F. E. Marsh

KREGEL PUBLICATIONS
Grand Rapids, Michigan 49501

Illustrated Bible Study Outlines was formerly published as *Illustrated Bible Studies,* by Kregel Publications, a division of Kregel, Inc., under special arrangements with the original publisher, Marshall, Morgan & Scott, Ltd. London.

Library of Congress Catalog Card Number 79-125116

ISBN 0-8254-3245-6

First Kregel Publications edition 1970
Reprinted in 1978, 1984

Printed in the United States of America

Introduction

The teachings of our Lord and those of the Apostle Paul abound in illustrations, metaphors and similes. They were both keen in their observations in calling attention to passing events, and present objects. They used these to enforce the claims and character of Eternal verities.

When the Apostle Paul looked upon the religious objective of the Athenians and their erected altar to the Unknown God, he seized the opportunity to declare to them the True God. Can we not see the Apostle pointing with his index finger to the altar, and then looking up and pointing heavenwards and giving his testimony by saying, " Whom therefore ye ignorantly worship, Him declare I unto you " ? And as he does so, he proclaims God, in a masterly address, as the Universal Provider of things. He says :

He is the CREATOR of everything, for " God made the world and all things therein."

He is the POSSESSOR of all things, for " He is Lord of heaven and earth."

He is the GIVER of life to every one, for He "giveth to all life, and breath."

He is the DISTRIBUTOR of all things, for " He giveth to all . . . all things."

He is the UNITER of all men to one another, for He " hath made of one blood all nations of men."

He is the ALLOCATOR of all things, for He " causeth all nations of men to dwell on the earth, and hath determined the bounds of their habitations."

He is the ATTRACTION of all men, for they are made to " feel after Him."

He is the OMNIPRESENT ONE to all men, for He is not " far from every one of us."

He is the ENVIRONMENT of all men, " for in Him we live and move and have our being."

He is the FATHER-CREATOR of all men, for men are said to be " His offspring."

He is the GOD of all men, hence He " now commandeth all men everywhere to repent."

He is the JUDGE of all men, for " He hath appointed a day, in the which He will judge the world in righteousness."

He is willing to be the SAVIOUR of all men, and He has given " assurance " of this, for He hath raised up Christ from the dead.

He is the RULER of all men, for when it says He will judge the world it means He will administer for all men in a rule which will be a rule of righteousness.

What a simple, complete, and yet profound revelation of God we have in these fourteen particulars in Acts xvii. 22–31.

How full John's Gospel is of metaphors. Take but a sevenfold reference to Christ Himself as used by Him, in seven " I AM'S " :

" I am the Light," to illuminate.
" I am the Door," to give entrance.
" I am the Way," to lead to a destination.
" I am the Good Shepherd," to bestow.
" I am the Bread," to satisfy.
" I am the Resurrection," to raise.
" I am the Life," to quicken.

The plan of these Readings is along the line of my *Pearls, Points, and Parables.*

These readings are for busy Christian workers, that they may find in them suggestions and help in their testimony and work.

F. E. MARSH

London

Illustrated
Bible Study Outlines

ACCOUNTABILITY

" Give account."—Rom. xiv. 12.

A good steward glories in his master by his praise and service. Well did Adolph Monod say, " All in Christ, by the Holy Spirit, for the glory of God ; all else is nothing." When we seek God's glory we find our good. We find our-selves and all things when we find the Lord. Everything is a chaos without Him ; all is a kosmos (in order) with Him.

Stewardship means accountability. At the judgment seat of Christ there will be seven things for which we shall have to give an account :

1. An account of our LIFE, since we believed in Christ (1 Cor. iv. 5).

2. An account of our CONDUCT towards each other (Rom. xiv. 10).

3. An account of the MOTIVES which have swayed us (2 Cor. v. 9, 10).

4. An account of the QUALITY of the material we have put into the WORK of the Lord (1 Cor. iii. 12-15).

5. An account of how we have TRADED with the " pound " of the Gospel (Luke xix. 12-27, R.V.).

6. An account of how we have used the " TALENT " of opportunity (Matt. xxv. 14-30).

7. To receive from the Lord the REWARD for service rendered (1 Cor. iv. 5).

ALERTNESS

" Watch Thou in All Things."—2 Tim. iv. 5.

There is glory, beauty and attraction in a blameless and a stainless life. The incident is told of an Arabian princess who was once presented by her teacher with an ivory casket, not to be opened until a year had passed. The time, im-patiently waited for, came at last, and with trembling haste she unlocked the treasure ; and lo ! on the satin linings lay a shroud of rust ; the form of something beautiful, but the beauty gone. A slip of parchment contained these words : " Dear pupil, Learn a lesson in your life. This trinket, when enclosed, had upon it only a spot of rust ; by neglect it has become the useless thing you now behold, only a blot on its pure surroundings. So a little stain on your character will, by inattention and neglect, mar a bright and useful life, and in time leave only the dark shadow of what it might have been. Place herein a jewel of gold, and after many years you will find it still sparkling as ever. So with yourself, treasure up only the pure, the good, and you will be an ornament to society, and a source of true pleasure to yourself and your friends."

We need to avoid the rust that comes from neglect. In seven words, Paul showed Timothy, as a servant and a saint, how to do this (2 Tim. iv. 2-5) :

1. " PREACH THE WORD."—" The Word," not our own opinions, nor men's deductions, nor newspaper clippings, but the Word. Preach it faithfully, earnestly, wholly, practically, persistently, and personally.

2. " BE INSTANT IN SEASON," ETC.—The season to preach is every season. Men's palates are not to be pleased, but their need is to be profited.

3. " REPROVE."—Sin in others, and in ourselves, is not to be passed over, but called to the bar of truth and condemned.

4. " REBUKE."—As Nathan told David he was sinful, so sinners are not to be ignored when their conduct calls for censure.

5. " EXHORT."—The faithful tongue is to be followed by the helping ministry. This is to be done with " longsuffering," and according to the teaching of the Holy Spirit.

6. " DO."—The work of an evangelist is to be done ; that is, sinners are to be saved, and we are to tell them of the Christ of Calvary, who alone can do it.

7. " MAKE FULL PROOF."—A lop-sided ministry is not full, nor proven. Such a ministry means hard work, persistent prayer, loving counsel, consistent conduct, a Christ indwelt-heart, and a Holy Spirit's control.

ALL ISRAEL

" *All Israel shall be saved.*"—Rom. xi. 26.

Dr. Adolph Saphir says : " I have often thought of that triumphal arch of Titus, which was erected after the destruction of Jerusalem. There it still stands in Rome, and on that arch you can see represented the captive Jews, and the seven-branched candlestick of the temple, and the table of shewbread, and in front the great emperor and conqueror Titus. There is another triumphal arch which the apostle has also erected right among the Romans—the Epistle to the Romans, from the ninth chapter to the eleventh—and on this arch is written, ' All Israel shall be saved.' "

In the first book of Chronicles, " all Israel " is mentioned again and again, in connection with the reigns of David and Solomon, which we may take as foreshadowing the character of the reign of Christ over Israel in the future.

1. ALL ISRAEL NUMBERED.—" So all Israel were reckoned by genealogies " (1 Chron. ix. 1). Jehovah does not lose sight of one of His people, hence in the time of the end, we find He numbers a hundred and forty and four thousand of all the tribes of the children of Israel (Rev. vii. 4).

2. ALL ISRAEL GATHERED.—" Then all Israel gathered themselves to David unto Hebron, saying, Behold, we are thy bone and thy flesh " (1 Chron. xi. 1), which may be taken as typical of the time when those who are of the lineage of David will look upon the wounds of Christ, and He will say, " I was wounded in the house of My friends " (Zech. xiii. 6).

3. ALL ISRAEL CROWNING.—Of David's mighty men, it is said, " They strengthened themselves with him in his kingdom, and with all Israel, to make him king, according to the word of the Lord concerning Israel " (1 Chron. xi. 10). " David was anointed king over all Israel " (1 Chron. xiv. 8). " David reigned over all Israel " (1 Chron. xviii. 14 ; xxix. 26). This is prophetic of when David or his representative shall be king over the restored nation (Ezek. xxxvii. 24, 25).

4. ALL ISRAEL ACKNOWLEDGING.—" And David gathered all Israel together to Jerusalem " (1 Chron. xv. 3). As David was the central figure in Jerusalem, so in the days to come Christ will be the Ensign to whom the restored nation shall be gathered (Isa. xi. 10).

5. ALL ISRAEL OBEYING.—" Then Solomon sat on the throne of the Lord as king instead of David his father, and prospered ; and all Israel obeyed him " (1 Chron. xxix. 23).

This is a foregleam of the time when all nations shall serve Christ (Ps. lxxii. 8-11).

6. CONQUEST.—" David gathered all Israel . . . the Syrians fled before Israel . . . they were put to the worse . . . they made peace with David, and became his servants " (1 Chron. xix. 17-19). A greater victory will be achieved when Christ will have a kingdom in which all people, nations and languages will serve Him (Dan. vii. 14).

7. GLORY.—" And the Lord magnified Solomon exceedingly in the sight of all Israel, and bestowed upon him such royal majesty as had not been on any king before him in Israel " (1 Chron. xxix. 25). And yet a greater than Solomon will have a greater glory when He shall be King of kings and Lord of lords (Rev. xix. 16).

" ALL IS WELL, SINCE ALL GROWS BETTER "

" *Go on.*"—Heb. vi. 1.

" ' If ever I had a coat of arms,' said Mr. Carnegie, the millionaire, ' my motto would be : " All's well, since all grows better." ' That, we think, is the keynote of the true optimist. Ever alive to the shortcomings of the past, he looks to the present ; he lives from day to day : he

> Wails not for precious chances passed away,
> Weeps not for golden ages on the wane.

Rather does he turn from the archives of the past, and finds joy in the desire to live in the present. With him pleasure does not primarily arise from play ; it comes unconsciously when duty has been nobly done."

The Christian life does not allow for declension, nor relaxation. Paul recognises this. Take but seven references out of seven of his letters.

1. PRAYER.—" Continuing instant in prayer " (Rom. xii. 12). Never weary in coming to the Throne of Grace.

2. PRIZE.—" So run that ye may obtain " (1 Cor. ix. 24). Pressing on with increasing energy to gain the prize.

3. PERFECTION.—" Be perfect " (2 Cor. xiii. 9, 11). The figure is that of the limbs of the body, being in joint.

4. POWER.—" Walk in the Spirit " (Gal. v. 16). This is the realm where the Spiritual life thrives.

5. PROGRESS.—" Grow up into Him " (Eph. iv. 15). Grow upward into Christ ; downward into the truth ; and outward in usefulness.

6. PERSISTENCY.—" I press toward the mark " (Phil. iii. 14). Fired by love and power within, we are urged forward.

7. PRINCIPLE.—" As ye received Christ Jesus the Lord, so walk in Him " (Col. ii. 6). As we received Him by faith, by prayer, honestly, humbly, earnestly, gratefully, and wholly : so walk in Him.

ANGELIC MINISTRY

" *Ministering spirits.*"—Heb. i. 14.

The death of an English student in the Tyrol, who lost his footing while gathering edelweiss, recalls the legend which surrounds this beautiful Alpine flower. An angel, wearying of her celestial home, longs to taste once more the bitterness of earth. She receives permission to take her shape of flesh again, but, unprepared to mingle with humanity that even to her sympathetic eyes is enacting a tragedy of poverty, crime, oppression, misfortune, and discontent, she chooses a home among the highest and wildest of the Swiss mountains, where she may look out upon the world, yet not be of it. The angel soul of the visitant illumines her face, and, having been seen by a daring climber, the icy fastness where she hides her loveliness is soon invaded by men. She is kind but cold to all, and is taken back to heaven, leaving her human heart in the edelweiss as a memento of her earthly residence.

Angelic ministry occupies a large field of suggestion in the Scriptures. Taking the Book of Genesis alone we find :

1. The FINDING Angel (xvi. 7-11).
2. The ASSURING Angel (xxi. 17).
3. The CALLING Angel (xxii. 11).
4. The PROMISING Angel (xxii. 15-18).
5. The PROTECTING Angel (xxiv. 7, 40).
6. The DIRECTING Angel (xxxi. 11-13).
7. The REDEEMING Angel (xlviii. 16).

ANTICIPATING TROUBLE

" I shall now perish one day (David said) by the hands of Saul."
1 Sam. xxvii. 1.

A writer remarks :

" That is a true word of old ' Rabbi ' Duncan's : ' A prisoner of war is not a deserter.' Recognise that the Atonement has a forward as well as a backward look, and that your every fresh need, ere ever it arises, has been already met by the love of God in Christ Jesus our Lord. One wintry day during my early ministry I had occasion to pay a pastoral visit. There had been a thaw the day before, and during the night a keen frost had set in, and the road was sheeted with ice. I had difficulty in getting along, and, remembering that the house I was going to lay at the foot of a steep declivity, I wondered how I should ever get there, and was minded to turn back. But when I reached the place, I found that my friends, anticipating my coming, had strewn a pathway with sand ; and so, where I had expected difficulty, there was none at all. Is not this a parable ? The Lord ' prevents us with His goodness.' It is awaiting us at every difficult place. Have no fear for the unknown future. Though God forgives the guilt of sin so grandly, the fact of sin always abides—the fact and the memory of it in one's own heart. What has once been done, can never be undone. A lost opportunity is irretrievable ; and though the punishment be remitted, the loss is eternal."

1. DAVID anticipated he would lose his life at the hands of King Saul, but he did not, as he afterwards sang, "Who redeemeth thy life from destruction" (Ps. ciii. 4). Some of God's saints think they will be lost after all their faith, but how can they, when Christ says, His sheep shall " never perish," and none can pluck them out of His hand (John x. 28).

2. DARIUS anticipated that Daniel would be eaten when he was cast into the lion's den, hence, he had a sleepless night (Dan. vi. 18), but the man of faith knew God could shut the lions' mouths, and He did (Dan. vi. 22). We can picture Daniel reclining against one of the lions and having a good sleep. Faith rests when unbelief is restless.

12

3. THE WOMEN on the morning of the resurrection anticipated the difficulty of " rolling away the stone " from the mouth of the sepulchre, but when they got to it, the stone was " rolled away " (Mark xvi. 3, 4). Trouble surmised is more tormenting than when it is encountered. " Be anxious for nothing " is the Divine mandate (Phil. iv. 6).

4. ELIJAH ran away when Jezebel threatened to take his life, and he ran away from her, and then wanted the Lord to do her dirty work (1 Kings xix. 1-8), but the Lord sent His angel to encourage him by his ministry. The threats of the ungodly should drive us to our knees, and not make us run away (Acts iv. 21-31).

5. PETER thought something undesirable would come to him, when the damsel and others said he was identified with Christ (Luke xxii. 56-60), and his cowardice wounded the heart of his Lord. The world's hate and persecution will drive us from the Lord to backsliding from Him, or it will draw us nearer to Him in heart-fellowship with Him.

6. JOSEPH's brethren through their action towards Joseph anticipated their sin would find them out, as Reuben said (Gen. xlii. 22), but they found that there was the opportunity for Joseph to display his grace (Gen. xlv. 1-3), even as God commended His love towards us while we were yet sinners (Rom. v. 6).

ATONEMENT : WHAT IS IT ATONES ?

" It is the Blood that maketh an atonement for the soul."—
Lev. xvii. 11.

Talking with an eminent Harley Street physician, he emphasised how important it was to microscopically examine the blood to ascertain if any foreign elements were in it, when the writer answered, " The life of the flesh is in the blood." " Is that in the Bible ? " he enquired. " Yes, in Leviticus xvii. 11."

Many are telling us that it is the life of Christ and not His death which atones for sin, and that He did not atone for sin vicariously, but sympathetically. What does God say in the Book ? Lev. xvii. 11, is the central verse on the

question. He says, " The life of the flesh is in the blood :
and I have given it to you upon the altar to make an atonement for your souls ; for it is the blood that maketh an atonement for the soul." There are three things in this verse :

1. A DIVINE EXPLANATION.—" The life of the flesh is in
the blood." The Hebrew word for " life " is " soul "
(nephesh). The soul or life is identified with the blood.

2. A DIVINE GIFT.—" I have given it to you upon the
altar." The altar is identified with sacrifice and the life
taken for sin. The altar upon which Christ offered His
sacrifice was His Deity.

3. A DIVINE PROVISION.—" It is the blood that maketh
an atonement for the soul." The blood speaks of the life
given up to death. Our lives were forfeited on account of
sin. Christ gave His life for us—" He poured out His soul
unto death." Christ did not live to save us, but He died.
The emphasis of the Holy Spirit is on the death of Christ.
" He died for our sins." " He died, the Just for the unjust,
to bring us to God." " Christ died for us."

ATTRACTABILITY OF PERSONALITY

" I will draw all men unto Me."—John xii. 32.

Death recently ended the long vigil of Nero, a dog who
died on his master's grave in a lonely cemetery in Lancaster,
Pennsylvania.

His owner, Charles Farmer, was shot dead last July, in
a gun-fight with prohibition officers. Nero followed the
funeral procession to the cemetery, where he kept watch
daily, leaving the grave at short intervals for food. All efforts
to coax the dog away failed.

To-day a boulder marks the grave of Nero.

Many have referred to the love and devotion of Nero
for his master.

The personality of the master was everything to the dog.
When one person attracts another, the attractability causes
the attracted one to do the unusual.

1. REBEKAH was attracted to go with ELIEZER to Isaac
(Gen. xxiv. 58). So the Spirit attracts us to Christ.

2. RUTH was attracted to NAOMI (Ruth i. 16, 17). Believers are attracted to each other.

3. JACOB was attracted to RACHAEL (Gen. xxix. 20). So Christ loves the Church.

4. JONATHAN was attracted to DAVID (1 Sam. xviii. 1). So the friend loveth his friend.

5. MARY was attracted to her LORD (John xii. 3). So the consecrated one gives all to Him.

6. CALEB was attracted to his GOD (Num. xiv. 24). So love follows the Lord fully.

7. PAUL was attracted to CHRIST, and loved to serve Him (2 Cor. v. 14).

> When love within the spirit burns,
> The soul with real affection yearns ;
> It looks not to the cross it bears,
> But walks with Christ, whose yoke it shares.

ATTRACTIVE SPEAKER

" Very attentive to hear Him."—Luke xix. 48.

The Publishers' Circular says, " We wonder if second-hand booksellers are aware that many people construe the letters ' V.D.' after the price of a book to mean ' very dear ' as well as ' very dry.' There is often considerable excuse for the error."

We shall never find the Book of books " very dry " if we ponder it carefully and prayerfully, but we shall find as we listen to our Lord as He speaks to us therein, that

1. His " thoughts are VERY DEEP," for they are a deep which cannot be fathomed (Ps. xcii. 5).

2. His " testimonies are VERY SURE," for they are an impregnable rock (Ps. xciii. 5).

3. They are " VERY FAITHFUL," for they speak of the faithful God (Ps. cxix. 138).

4. His " Word is VERY PURE," even as refined gold (Ps. cxix. 140).

5. His " Word runneth VERY SWIFTLY," for the Lord is never behind in His messages (Ps. cxlvii. 15).

6. His Word is " VERY NIGH," therefore there is no need to seek for it (Deut. xxx. 14).

7. And we are responsible, because the Word is what it is, to write it in our testimony " VERY PLAINLY " (Deut. xxvii. 8).

AUTHORITY

" *I am a man under authority.*"—Matt. viii. 9.

In Ethel M. Dell's *A Man Under Authority*, she makes one of her characters say to the Vicar, known to his intimate friends as " Bill," " I know it is His will." " How do you know ? How can you be sure you are not making a mistake ? "

" He made answer very quietly, with a confidence there was no gainsaying, ' That is the blessed part of being under authority. . . . There is no chance of making any mistake when we know He will be our guide.' "

There can be no mistakes when we act under the authority of the Lord : we are sure we have the Lord in all His authority.

1. The authority of HIS MESSAGE of salvation in the Scriptures gives the assurance of salvation (John v. 24).

2. The authority of HIS LOVE gives us the knowledge that Christ died for us (Rom. v. 8).

3. The authority of HIS GRACE gives us the joy of His all-sufficient strength in trial (2 Cor. xii. 9).

4. The authority of HIS PEACE gives the authority of His protecting calm, as we are careful for nothing, prayerful in everything, and thankful for anything (Phil. iv. 6, 7).

5. The authority of HIS PRESENCE gives us the " I will " of His sustaining help (Isa. xli. 10).

6. The authority of HIS INTERCESSORY PRAYERS gives us the joy of His constant care (Rom. viii. 27).

7. The authority of HIS GUIDING SPIRIT gives us the gladdening hope He will see us safely through (1 Pet. i. 3-5).

A WHOLE BURNT-OFFERING

" *Present your bodies a living sacrifice.*"—Rom. xii 1.

Many have thought, and a careless reader of the Scriptures might so think, that Jephthah's daughter was slain in her father's keeping to his vow, which he vowed when he promised that if the Lord would give him the victory over the Ammonites, then " whatsoever " came forth out of his house, he would " offer it up for a burnt-offering " (Judges xi. 30, 31). This was not so, and for the following reasons :

1. The " whatsoever " is masculine, whereas what met him was feminine, therefore his rash vow was impossible of fulfilment and had to be repented of.

2. He could not offer his daughter as a burnt-offering, for this was distinctly forbidden by the Lord (Lev. xviii. 21 ; xx. 2-5).

3. If any one vowed " a singular vow " (Lev. xxvii. 2, etc.), the thing he vowed was irrevocably the Lord's, and could not be taken back.

This is what happened to the daughter of Jephthah. She was dedicated to the Lord as a virgin, and that to perpetuity ; hence, we read, she " bewailed her virginity," " she knew no man," and " the daughters of Israel went yearly to lament the daughter of Jephthah four days in a year " (Judges xi. 34-40)—that is, to rehearse with her the great event in her life, not her death.

What an illustration is this of thorough consecration—namely, having surrendered to the Lord, there is no going back from the Lord. That which was vowed to the Lord became the Lord's irretrievably.

BELIEVER'S CALLING

" *Ye see your calling, brethren.*"—1 Cor. i. 26.

Meditation upon God's Word has been defined as " Attention with intention." Dr. W. H. Griffith Thomas has summarised as follows : " What are the stages or elements of true meditation ? They are five in number :

1. The careful reading of the particular passage or subject, thinking over its real and original meaning.

2. A resolute application of it to my own life's needs, to conscience, heart, mind, imagination, will ; finding out what it has to say to me.

3. A hearty turning of it into prayer for mercy and grace, that its teaching may become part of my life.

17

4. A sincere transfusion of it into a resolution that my life shall reproduce it.

5. A whole-hearted surrender to, and trust in God for power to practice it forthwith, and constantly throughout the day."

Following up what is said above, we can see what the mind of the Spirit is in calling attention to the believer's calling.

The word " Calling " means a " vocation," and is so rendered in Eph. iv. 1.

The Calling is :

1. " HOLY " IN CHARACTER.—" Called us with a holy calling " (2 Tim. i. 9).

2. " HEAVENLY " IN SPHERE.—" Partakers of the heavenly calling " (Heb. iii. 1).

3. " HIGH " IN PLACE.—" High calling of God in Christ Jesus " (Phil. iii. 14).

4. DIVINE IN ITS SOURCE.—" His calling " (Eph. i. 18).

5. PARTICULAR IN ITS CHARACTER.—" Count you worthy of this calling " (2 Thess. i. 11).

6. EXCLUSIVE IN ITS FELLOWSHIP. — " Your calling brethren " (1 Cor. i. 26 ; Eph. iv. 4).

7. ATTRACTIVE IN ITS GOAL.—"One Hope of His calling " (Eph. i. 18 ; Titus ii. 13).

8. REMUNERATIVE IN ITS PRIZE.—" Prize of the high calling " (Phil. iii. 14).

BELIEVER'S RIGHTS

" *To them gave He the right,*" *etc.*—John i. 12, Marg.

In a New York police court, a little boy appeared one day, followed by a big policeman, who was looking much amused. The boy went straight up to the presiding magistrate, and said, " Please, sir, are you the judge ? "

" Yes, I am the judge in this place. What do you want ? "

" Please, sir, I am Johnny Moore, and I'm seven years old, and in the lot by our house there's only one smooth piece of ground where we can play marbles. But lately the butcher's gone and put his cart there, and this morning, when me and my brother were playing marbles, he drove us away and took six of my marbles and threw them over the fence. I went to the police about it, but they laughed and said I'd better go to the magistrate ; so I've come, and I want my marbles back, please sir."

Not only the policeman but all the people in the court laughed as he finished his eager story ; but the magistrate rapped on his desk for silence. Then he said, " Yes, my little man, you have just as much right to your six marbles as the richest merchant in New York to his money."

The magistrate directed a policeman to go to the butcher and tell him to pay for the marbles at once, or he would be arrested ; and addressing the boy, he remarked, " If every American citizen claimed his rights as you have done, we should not have so much crime in the land."

There are certain rights which the Lord gives to His children, and it is their privilege to see that they enjoy them. The following things God has given His own indicate some of the rights He has bestowed :

1. The Right to BECOME THE CHILDREN OF GOD.—" To them gave He the right to become His children " (John i. 12, marg.).

2. The right of ETERNAL LIFE.—" I give unto them eternal life " (John x. 28).

3. The right of PEACE.—" My peace I give unto you " (John xiv. 27).

4. The right of GOD'S WORD.—" I have given them Thy Word " (John xvii. 14).

5. The right of the HOLY SPIRIT.—" The Holy Ghost, which is given unto us " (Rom. v. 5).

6. The right of POWER.—" He giveth power to the faint " (Isa. xl. 29).

7. The right of GRACE.—" To me is this grace given " (Eph. iii. 8).

BE WHAT YOU ARE

" *Be followers of God as dear children.*"—Eph. v. 1.

A great anatomist has said : " One of the greatest reasons why so few people understand themselves is that most writers are always teaching men what they should be, and hardly ever trouble their heads with telling them what they are."

The same principle might be applied to believers. We are not told to become, in order that we may be, but we are exhorted to be, because we are.

1. Because we are children of God, we are TO BE HOLY and obedient (1 Peter i. 14).

2. Because we are saints, we are TO DO EVERYTHING " as becometh saints " (Eph. v. 3).

3. Because we are the salt of the earth, we are TO BE PUNGENT in godliness (Matt. v. 13).

4. Because we are the light of the world, we are TO SHINE in holiness (Matt. v. 14).

5. Because we are the epistle of Christ, we are TO BE LEGIBLE in Christian character (2 Cor. iii. 3).

6. Because we are sanctified, we are TO BE SEPARATE from all uncleanness (1 Cor. vi. 9-12).

7. Because we are members in the body of Christ, we are TO HOLD the Head, and love one another (Eph. iv. 12-16).

BIBLE : WHAT THE BOOK DOES

" Thy Word is a lamp unto my feet, and a light unto my path."
—Ps. cxix. 105.

Cardinal Wiseman once complained that all the cases he had known of a Roman Catholic becoming a Protestant were due to the same cause, the reading of the Bible. "The history in every single case is simply this : that the individual . . . became possessed . . . of the Bible. . . . He perhaps goes to the priest and tells him that he cannot find the doctrines (of Rome) in the Bible. His priest argues with him, and endeavours to convince him that he should shut up the book that is leading him astray ; he perseveres . . . and becomes a Protestant."

No honest reader of the Bible can for one moment subscribe to the assumptions of Romanism. The Book says, " There is one Mediator " (not many, nor Mary) " between God and man, the Man Christ Jesus, who gave Himself a ransom for all " ; and gave Himself " once for all," and not as Rome teaches in the Eucharist, He is still being offered.

What does the Book do ?

1. CRITICISES THE INNER BEING.—" The Word of God . . . is a discerner (critic) of the thoughts and intents of the heart " (Heb. iv. 12).

2. CONVINCES OF SIN.—" As it is written, there is none righteous, no not one . . . all have sinned " (Rom. iii. 10-23).

3. CLEANSES THE WALK.—" Wherewithal shall a young man cleanse his way ? by taking heed according to Thy Word " (Ps. cxix. 9).

4. COUNSELS THE LIFE.—" Thy testimonies are my delight, and my counsellors " (Ps. cxix. 24).

5. CONFIRMS OUR FAITH.—" Stablish Thy Word unto Thy servant, who is devoted to Thy fear " (Ps. cxix. 38).

6. COMFORTS OUR HEART.—" This is my comfort in my affliction : for Thy Word hath quickened me " (Ps. cxix. 50).

7. CONVERTS THE SOUL.—" The law of the Lord is perfect, converting the soul " (Ps. xix. 7).

BITER BIT

" *Man looketh on the outward appearance.*"—1 Sam. xvi. 7.

The following hypothetical story often finds an embodiment in life :

" Sister Henderson," said Deacon Hypers, " you should avoid even the appearance of evil."

" Why, deacon, what do you mean ? " asked Sister Henderson.

" I observe that on your sideboard you have several cut-glass decanters and that each of them is half filled with what appears to be ardent spirits."

" Well, now, deacon, it isn't anything of the kind. The bottles look so pretty on the sideboard that I just filled them halfway with some floor stain and furniture polish, just for appearances."

" That's why I'm cautioning you, sister," replied the deacon. " Feeling a trifle weak and faint, I helped myself to a dose from the big bottle in the middle."

Many an admonition finds its genesis in an experience like the above. The deacon would not have had an admonition to give, if he had not tasted the furniture polish. The best admonition is the admonition of a consistent life. Prating lips do not count, but practical godliness counts all the time.

How often we find the outer appearance does not correspond to the inward reality.

1. The SEEMING ESAU is the wily Jacob (Gen. xxvii. 22, 23.)

2. The AVOWED DISCIPLE is the betraying Judas (Mark iii. 19).

3. The SEEMING BEAUTIFUL SEPULCHRE is the embodiment of death (Matt. xxiii. 27).

4. The SEEMING CONSECRATION is a lying subterfuge (Acts v. 1-5).

5. The SEEMING CHURCH of affluence is devoid of Christ (Rev. iii. 17).

6. The SEEMING MESSENGER of God is a lying prophet (1 Kings xiii. 18-29).

7. The SEEMING OBEDIENCE is allied with sin, as in the case of King Saul (1 Sam. xv. 22).

" BLESSED " ONES

" Blessed is the man."—Ps. i. 1.

Outside the Westpark Cemetery in the City of Dundee, Scotland, there are panels on the entrance iron gates, and on each of the panels is one of the Beatitudes of Matthew v. On the last panel is one of the beatitudes of Revelation, namely, " Blessed are the dead which die in the Lord." What may have been the thought in the mind of the designer we do not know. Presumedly it was, those who live the beatitudes in their lives are blessed in their death, and certainly that is so ; but may there not be another thought, namely, that it is only as we die with Christ to sin and self, and He lives within us, that it is possible for us to know the beatitudes as a matter of experience ? There must be death with Christ before there can be living like Christ. The negative side of holiness is death to self in the death of Christ ; and the positive side of holiness is Christ living out the beatitudes in our lives.

What a bank of Blesseds we find in the Psalms. In our so-called " Authorised Version," we find no less than nineteen " Blesseds," and if we take the Blesseds of praise we have eighteen more. These generally are found in the " Blessed be the Lord." In connection with the former, we find the sentence " Blessed is the man." Note the kind of man who is happy or " blessed."

1. SEPARATION.—" Blessed is the man who walketh not," etc. (Ps. i. 1).

2. JUSTIFICATION.—" Blessed is the man unto whom the Lord," etc. (Ps. xxxii. 2).

3. DECISION.—" Blessed is the man that maketh," etc. (Ps. xl. 4).

4. ELECTION.—" Blessed is the man, whom Thou choosest " (Ps. lxv. 4).

5. POWER.—" Blessed is the man whose strength is in Thee " (Ps. lxxxiv. 5).

6. CONFIDENCE.—" Blessed is the man that trusteth in Thee " (Ps. lxxxiv. 12 ; xxxiv. 8).

7. CHASTISEMENT.—" Blessed is the man whom Thou chasteneth " (Ps. xciv. 12)

See also Ps. cxii. 1.

BLESSING FOUND WHERE LEAST EXPECTED

" *In the Isle called Patmos.*"—Rev. i. 9.

The shadows lay thick beneath the tree, and where they were deepest a figure crouched.

Suddenly he heard a sound, a light footfall on the grass.

" That you, mate ? " he whispered hoarsely.

" Yes," came the answer.

" What are you doing with that dog ? " he muttered, as his burglar partner drew near.

" Why," answered his confederate, " there was nothing worth taking in the house, and it's bad luck to come away without anything. So I pinched the watchdog and these burglar alarms ! "

If the above is true, the burglar made the most of a bad situation. If we view things rightly, we can make the most of a bad situation.

1. PAUL'S THORN in the flesh was a means to the sufficient grace of the Lord (2 Cor. xii. 7-9).

2. JOB'S LOSSES and crosses were in the end the precursors of double gains and blessings (Job. xlii. 10-17).

3. JOSEPH'S PIT and prison were the channels to the palace and power (Gen. xlv. 1-8).

4. PAUL AND SILAS in the inner DUNGEON at Philippi gave them the opportunity to sing praises and save the jailer (Acts xvi. 25-34).

5. JOHN'S BANISHMENT to the Isle of Patmos was the forerunner to the vision of the glory (Rev. i. 9-18).

6. The APOSTLE being LET DOWN in a basket is associated with his being caught up into the third heaven (2 Cor. xi. 33 ; xii. 1-4).

7. GOLIATH'S TAUNT against David gave the latter the chance to triumph over him (1 Sam. xvii. 42-46).

BLOODLESS GOSPEL

" *Without shedding of blood is no remission.*"—Heb. ix. 22.

Possibly the plainest statement ever made by a high Mason on the subject of Masonic salvation is that of Rev. E. A. Coil, minister of the Unitarian church at Marietta, Ohio, and master of the Masonic lodge there. In 1915 Rev. Mr. Coil published a sermon which has been highly recommended in Masonic magazines. In this sermon Rev. Mr. Coil says that in the lodge there are Jews, and that hence no prayer must be spoken which refers to salvation by Christ. As, he says, that both Jews and Christians as well as Buddhists and Mahomedans will be granted " rich rewards " in heaven. Rev. Coil also says that such a hymn as " Rock of Ages " is out of place in the lodge, because it implies a " restricted condition of salvation out of harmony with Masonry." In other words, Mr. Coil admits that the way of salvation taught by the lodge is one that excludes Jesus Christ.

If Christ and His blood are excluded, then the persons who exclude Him, exclude themselves from the following seven things, among others :

1. PEACE IS EXCLUDED without Christ's blood, for He made peace by the blood of His Cross (Col. i. 20).

2. PROTECTION FROM WRATH is excluded without Christ's blood (Rom. v. 9).

3. PURIFICATION OF THE CONSCIENCE is excluded without Christ's blood (Heb. ix. 22 ; 1 John i. 7 ; Rev. i. 5).

4. POSITION is excluded without Christ's blood, for it is His blood which makes nigh (Eph. ii. 13).

5. PURCHASE RIGHTS are excluded without His blood, for by His blood He purchased us (Acts xx. 28).

6. PROPITIATION IS NOT POSSIBLE except through Christ's blood, for He has given satisfaction to God by it (Rom. iii. 25).

7. PARTICIPATION WITH CHRIST is only possible as we know the spiritual fact behind and in His shed blood (John vi. 54).

BLOOD OF CHRIST

" The precious blood of Christ."—1 Peter i. 18.

A man lay dying. His pastor called to see him. The man said : " I dreamed a remarkable dream last night. I dreamed that I was on my way to a city ; and I came to a mountain. The mountain was between me and the city. There was no way to get around it ; and so I started to climb it, intending to go up on this side and down on the other side. I climbed up a little way, and then I lost my hold and rolled down to the base of the mountain, and there I lay in utter despair. ' I shall never be able,' I said, ' to get over to the other side, and reach the city.' As, thoroughly discouraged, I lay there and looked at the mountain, I saw a little drop of blood fall upon it, and the mountain melted away as the mist melts away before the rising sun ; and there was the city in full view ; I was at its gates ; there was nothing between me and it." " That was certainly a very strange dream," said the minister. " What do you think it may have meant ? " The dying man seemed to be surprised that the minister should ask such a question as that. " That mountain," he said, " represented my sins, and the drop of blood that fell upon it was a single drop of the precious blood of Jesus Christ by which the mountain of my guilt has been melted away. There is nothing between me and the city now. The heavenly city is just yonder, and I am about to pass through its pearly gates."

Thank God for the precious blood, the life-blood of the Son of God, the blood of Him who " was made sin for us, although He knew no sin, that we might be made the righteousness of God in Him " !

What does the Blood of Christ do ? What are its characteristics ? Let us see what Paul says.

1. REDEMPTION-SECURING BLOOD.—" In whom we have redemption through His blood " (Eph. i. 7).

2. NEARNESS-OBTAINING BLOOD.—" Made nigh by the blood of Christ " (Eph. ii. 13).

3. PEACE-MAKING BLOOD.—" Made peace by the blood of His Cross " (Col. i. 20).

4. JUSTIFYING-COVERING BLOOD.—" Justified by His blood " (Rom. v. 9).

5. CHURCH-BUYING BLOOD.—" Purchased with His own blood " (Acts xx. 28).

6. SIN-PROPITIATING BLOOD.—" Propitiation, through faith in His blood " (Rom. iii. 25).

7. FELLOWSHIP-UNITING BLOOD.—" Communion of the blood of Christ " (1 Cor. x. 16).

BLOOD OF CHRIST

" *The cup of blessing which we bless, is it not the communion of the blood of Christ.*"—1 Cor. x. 16.

A converted Jewess, in a prayer-meeting in the Church of the Open Door, prayed : " We thank Thee for Thy Servant, and the way He spoke about the blood of Christ. We never heard it like that before. We thank Thee for the blood of Christ."

The way in which the Holy Spirit speaks about the blood is unique and significant.

1. " THE BLOOD OF THE NEW COVENANT " (Luke xxii. 20, R.V.) tells us of the passing of the old covenant.

2. " THE BLOOD OF JESUS " proclaims the Perfect Human, and the Perfectly Human in His death (Heb. x. 19).

3. THE BLOOD OF GOD (Acts xx. 28). God cannot die, but He who died for us is God.

4. " THE BLOOD OF JESUS CHRIST " (1 Peter i. 2). He is the " Christ " as well as " Jesus." Jesus leads to the Throne.

5. THE BLOOD OF CHRIST JESUS (Rom. iii. 24, 25). When the names occur in this order, the Throne is the starting-point and Bethlehem the goal.

6. " THE BLOOD OF JESUS CHRIST HIS SON " (1 John i. 7). The emphasis here is on " His Son."

7. " THE BLOOD OF CHRIST " (Heb. ix. 14). The Anointed One, as the sent of God, is the thought here.

8. " THE BLOOD OF THE LORD " (1 Cor. xi. 27). The Lord's death is associated with the Lord's table, as the Lord bids us think of the Lord who died.

BLOOD OF CHRIST : A NECESSITY

" *Without shedding of blood there is no remission,*" *or forgive-ness.—*Heb. ix. 22.

In a recent book on Atonement we are told : " Forgive-ness, according to Jesus, follows immediately upon repen-tance. There is not the slightest suggestion that anything else but repentance is necessary—the actual death of a Saviour, belief in the atoning efficacy of that death, or in any other article of faith, etc.—not a hint of any of these. The truly penitent man who confesses his sin to God receives instant forgiveness."

This is nothing short of salvation by the sinner's works instead of the Saviour's work.

" According to Jesus," this writer says, " repentance is the ground of forgiveness." Let us see what Christ says.

1. ATONEMENT.—He makes the publican say : " God make an atonement " (the word " merciful " is rendered " make reconciliation for " in Heb. ii. 17) " for me, the sinner " ; and atonement, we are told, is " by means of the blood " (Lev. xvii. 11 ; Luke xviii. 13).

2. " MUST BE LIFTED UP."—Christ declared His death was necessary that we might have eternal life ; hence, " The Son of Man must be lifted up " (John iii. 14, 15).

3. RANSOM.—Christ said He came to give His life a ransom for many. The word " for " (" anti ") means " in-stead of the many " (Matt. xx. 28).

4. AFFIRMATION.—The Lord affirmed His flesh and blood were " true meat " and drink (R.V.M., John vi. 55) ; that is, they were essential to satisfy the need of man.

5. LIFE GIVEN.—We are told, too, the Good Shepherd would " give His life " for the sheep (John x. 11, 15, 17, 18).

6. FINISHED.—His sixth cry on the cross was the cry of the Satisfied Worker, hence He said, " It is finished " (John xix. 30).

7. OUTCOME.—And He said the outcome of His sacrifice would be He would reap " much fruit " (John xii. 24, 26).

In the light of these words of Christ, to say " Forgiveness according to Jesus " is acquired by repentance is to give the lie direct to Him.

BLOOD OF THE LAMB

" *The Blood of the Lamb.*"—Rev. vii. 14.

There is a little piece of silk in the museum of Springfield, Illinois, that could not be bought for any amount of money. Why the value attached to it ? Because of its significance. That little bit of silk is all covered with blood. It was once a part of a dress worn by a beautiful girl, who sat by Abraham Lincoln when he was shot ; and it was that beautiful girl who took his head in her lap, as a mother would receive the head of a baby, and it was that girl who held him while he bled his life out. The State of Illinois purchased that dress, and cut out this piece of silk covered with the blood of the great statesman, emancipator of an enslaved race, and the man who in the programme of God became a cohesive force in the salvation of this great nation.

If a state would do that for the blood of a man, what should the world do for the Blood of Jesus with all its emancipating power, and all its cohesiveness for a scattered race ? For, if the race of man, without regard to nationality or colour or condition of life, is ever to be united and held, it will be by the cohesiveness of that Blood.

O for a new value to be placed on that Blood ! O for a new appreciation of that infinite gift of God—the Blood which has loosed us from our sins and saved us from our judgment ! O the Blood, the precious Blood ! Let your ministry, O preacher, be a Calvary one ! Preach Christ and preach His Cross.

In the Book of Revelation we find four references to Christ's Blood.

    1. LIBERTY.—" Loosed from our sins in His own blood " (Rev. i. 5, R.V.).

    2. PURCHASE.—" Purchased us to God by Thy blood " (Rev. v. 9, R.V.).

    3. " MADE WHITE."—" Washed their robes, and made them white in the blood of the Lamb " (Rev. vii. 14).

    4. VICTORY.—" Overcome by the blood of the Lamb " (Rev. xii. 11).

BOOK TO PUT US RIGHT

" Order my steps in Thy Word."—Ps. cxix. 133.

Once a brother came to me with a manuscript on some subject which he wanted printed. He said, " Brother, the Lord has given me such light on this subject that my book will put everybody right." I have only known one book that will put everybody right and that is the book I have right here, the Bible. The Lord help us to have a teachable spirit.

If we carefully read the 119th Psalm we shall find it will right us in many ways.

    1. It will give us A CLEAN WAY (9).

    2. It will PREVENT US FROM SINNING (11).

    3. It will COMFORT us in AFFLICTION (50).

    4. It will GUIDE our FEET (105).

    5. It will ENLIGHTEN the MIND (130).

    6. It will ASSURE the SOUL (160).

    7. It will REVERENCE the SPIRIT (161).

    8. It will ENRICH the UNDERSTANDING (162).

    9. It will QUIETEN the HEART (165).

  10. It will BEGET PRAISE (171).

BUSINESS : THE KING'S BUSINESS

" I rose, and did the King's business."—Dan. viii. 27.

Dr. Carey, the pioneer missionary in India, before he left this country, was a shoemaker, rather, as he himself put it, a cobbler, but he used to go about from village to village preaching, for his soul was filled with the love of God. One day a friend came to him and said, " Mr. Carey, I want to speak to you very seriously." " Well," said Carey, " what is it ? " The friend replied, " By your going about preaching as you do, you are neglecting your business. If you only attended to your business more, you would be all right, and would soon get on and prosper, but as it is, you are simply neglecting your business." " Neglecting my business ! " said Carey, looking at him steadily. " My business is to extend the kingdom of God. I only cobble shoes to pay expenses meanwhile."

1. REQUIRED BUSINESS.—" The King's business required haste " (1 Sam. xxi. 8). Diligence and alacrity are required by the Lord.

2. ORDERED BUSINESS.—" The Levites wait on their business " (2 Chron. xiii. 10). The Levites had to act according to the Lord's direction.

3. INDIVIDUAL BUSINESS.—" Appointed every man in his business " (Neh. xiii. 30). Each and all have their several spheres to fill.

4. FULFILLED BUSINESS.—Daniel did not discuss the King's business, he " rose " and " did it " (Dan. viii. 27).

5. DILIGENT BUSINESS.—" Not slothful in business " (Rom. xii. 11). Slothfulness is born of laziness.

6. STUDIED BUSINESS.—" Study to do your own business " (1 Thess. iv. 11). Mix thought with the task, then the task will be done well.

7. ASSISTED BUSINESS.—" Assist her in what business she hath need of you " (Rom. xvi. 2). A helping hand is a happiness producer.

CAUSE OF THE TROUBLE

" For this cause."—1 Cor. xi. 30.

" I have been troubled about the criticism of the Bible during the past six years," said a young man at the close of a Bible reading in Edinburgh. I sought to remove his difficulties, but suddenly turned around and said, " When did you begin to be troubled ? "

" Well," he replied, " I was filled with the Holy Spirit

and moved by His love, but after a little I began to be careless and critical."

" In other words, you got out of touch with the Lord, and then you began to doubt His Word. Don't you see there is a moral and spiritual reason for your trouble ? Get back to where you were and you will not be troubled as you are."

1. Cause of weakness, sickliness, and death.—The cause of loss of power, loss of health, and loss of life in the case of the believers in the Church in Corinth was because of their carnal condition (1 Cor. xi. 30 ; cf. iii. 1).

2. Cause of loss of power.—When Samson consorted with Delilah he lost the locks of his Nazarite separation (Judges xvi. 17-23), and was the spoil of the Philistines. Mr. Spurgeon speaks of him as a " shaven saint." When the world shaves us, the devil laughs at us.

3. Cause of defeat.—After the victory of Israel over Jericho's walls and warriors, they were defeated before Ai, and the reason was because of the Achan in the camp (Joshua vii. 10-26). One wicked way will spoil many things.

4. Cause of cowardice.—The quenching influence of unholy associations will put out the flame of consecrated courage for the Lord. We see how Peter was made a coward by being mixed up with the ungodly (Luke xxii. 55-61).

5. Cause of compromise.—Jehosaphat joined affinity with Ahab, instead of keeping to the place of separation to the Lord, hence, he nearly lost his life (2 Chron. xviii. 1).

6. Cause of damage.—Peter let down a " net " when the Lord told him to let down the " nets." The consequence was the net broke (Luke v. 5-8). Partial obedience always brings damage.

7. Cause of backsliding.—Quitting the companionship with the Lord. When Abram went to Egypt, he left God at Bethel ; but when he left Egypt and came back to Bethel he found the Lord was waiting for him (Gen. xiii. 4). We pick up the lost threads where we let them fall.

CERTAINTIES

" *Certainty of those things.*"—Luke i. 4.

Sir Robertson Nicoll, once Editor of the *British Weekly*, in referring to the proposition that the " certainties " of the

Higher Criticism should be taught in the Sunday school, pertinently said, " What these ' certainties ' are we do not know ; it seems to us as if many of these ' certainties ' were ready to vanish away." The statement reminds us of what the late John Gregory (the Wesleyan minister) is recorded to have found, namely, that he had kept tally of 700 theories of the Higher Critics and found they themselves had abandoned 500 of the 700 theories ! While the critics are floundering in the bogs of speculation, we shall be wise to keep to the Rock of Revelation. The Sure Word of Prophecy is better than the speculative word of pretension. We have had so many bad eggs from the H.C. that we prefer to get our eggs from a more reliable source. We have not cultivated the taste of the Scotchman who was so elated in being asked to stay to breakfast by his landlord, when he had gone to pay the rent of his farm, but found one of the eggs served to be rotten, " I am afraid that egg is rather high, John," the laird said. To be very polite and being somewhat flurried, the farmer replied, " Na, na, me laird, I prefer them sae ! "

1. " A CERTAIN RATE " of manna was to be gathered every day by the children of Israel (Exod. xvi. 4). Regulations are essential for health of body and of soul.

2. " A CERTAIN CONTRIBUTION " for the poor was to be made (Rom. xv. 26). Our obligation to help the Lord's poor is a privilege and a responsibility.

3. " CERTAINLY I WILL BE WITH THEE," is the Lord's promise (Exod. iii. 12). He knows we need His presence to keep us, to guide us, to feed us, to guard us, to sustain us, to cheer us, and to strengthen us.

4. " CERTAINLY THIS WAS A RIGHTEOUS MAN " (Luke xxiii. 47) was the centurion's confession. There is no uncertainty about Christ. He is beyond all question.

5. " CERTAINLY I HAVE ADMONISHED YOU," was the Lord's word through the prophet (Jer. xlii. 19). The admonitions of the Lord are for our attention.

6. " KNOW FOR CERTAINTY " (Josh. xxiii. 13) was the warning word of Joshua, what the Lord would not do, if obedience was not given to Him.

7. " KNOW THE CERTAINTY OF THOSE THINGS " (Luke i. 4) were the words that Luke wrote.

CERTAINTIES OF THE FAITH

" The certainty of those things."—Luke i. 4.

One, in writing on the trend of the times, says : " In the intellectual sphere, Christianity in its dogmatic position has been badly shaken by destructive and disruptive criticism from all sides ; the result is that, save in the Roman Catholic Church (which at least knows where it stands, and therefore keeps going as a vital religious institution), there is something of a theological panic in all the Churches. There is a chaos of conflicting opinions on all doctrinal points, and some modern divines are out to ' save ' Christianity by explaining it away."

The same journalist remarks :

" Small wonder that the layman, who can obtain no clear teaching on the things that puzzle him, abandons institutional religion altogether, and carries on as best he can."

May we not remind the writer, that if he will but follow the teaching of Christ, he will find His teaching is clear and satisfying. He will find it in the following seven great and glorious facts.

1. THE FACT OF GOD'S LOVE, in Christ's assurance, " For God so loved the world, that He gave His only-begotten Son " (John iii. 16).

2. THE FACT OF PROMISED REST, in Christ's loving invitation, " Come unto Me, all ye that labour and are heavy laden, and I will give you rest " (Matt. xi. 28).

3. THE FACT OF ATONEMENT FOR SIN, in Christ's emphatic Word, " The Son of Man came not to be ministered unto, but to minister, and to give His life a ransom for many " (Matt. xx. 28).

4. THE FACT OF GOD'S PATERNAL CARE, in Christ's hallowed words, " Your Father knoweth what things ye have need of " (Matt. vi. 32).

5. THE FACT OF THE TRUE SECRET OF LIFE, in His Example of serving others, finding the true life in losing the soulish one (John xii. 24-26).

6. THE FACT OF TRUE RELATIONSHIP IN LIFE, to the Divine and the human, in doing the will of God (Matt. xii. 50).

33

7. THE FACT OF CHRIST'S SOUL-HEARTENING PROMISE for the future, that He will come again, and receive us to Himself (John xiv. 3).

CHEERFULNESS

"*Be of good cheer.*"—Acts xxvii. 22, 25.

R. L. Stevenson says of cheerfulness : " Gentleness and cheerfulness . . . they are the perfect duties . . . if your morals make you dreary, depend upon it they are wrong. I do not say ' give them up,' for they may be all you have, but conceal them like a vice, lest they spoil the lives of better and simpler people."

From the above it will be apprehended that cheerfulness is the outcome of a right condition of mind and life. Christ was continually bidding those with whom He came in contact to " be of good cheer," and in each case he had a reason for the " cheer " He enjoined. " Tharseo " comes from " Tharsos." The latter is rendered " courage " (Acts xxviii. 15), hence the former means to have courage. The following instances where " Tharseo " is found suggest that,

1. Christ Himself is the SOUL of cheerfulness (Acts xxiii. 11).

2. Forgiveness of sins is the CAUSE of cheerfulness (Matt. ix. 2).

3. Christ's Word is the BASIS of cheerfulness (Mark vi. 50).

4. WHOLENESS or salvation from sin and disease is the life of cheerfulness (Matt. ix. 22).

5. The calling of Christ is the FEEDER of cheerfulness (Mark x. 49).

6. Christ's victory is the PRICE of cheerfulness (John xvi. 33).

" Tharseo " in each of the above verses is rendered " Be of good cheer " and " Be of good comfort." Christ's cheer is the joy of grace, the comfort of love, the product of holiness, the stimulus of hope, the companion of faith, the contentment of humility, and the courage of confidence.

CHRIST'S COMMANDS ARE HIS ENABLINGS

" Then Jesus saith to the man, Stretch forth thy hand. And he stretched it forth."—Matt. xii. 13.

The man with the withered hand did as he was told without wavering or questioning. It was an act of decision, faith, and obedience. When God tells us to " believe," He means us to do just that. A minister sat in his study when his little boy knocked at the door. The father said, " Come in." " I can't, papa," replied the little one. " Open the door and come in," repeated the father. The boy put his hand to the knob, and the minister, recognising the spirit of obedience, and the physical inability of the child, laid his own hand on the knob and opened the door. The little one entered the room joyfully. Our Father never gives His children a command without adding His strength. " All God's biddings are His enablings." Trust Him.

Think of the blessings which came to those who obeyed Christ.

1. LIFE.—" Come forth," Christ said to Lazarus, " and he that was dead came forth " (John xi. 43, 44).

2. POWER.—" Rise and walk," Christ commanded the impotent man, and he arose and walked (John v. 8, 9).

3. PROGRESS.—" Go forward," God said to Israel ; and the Red Sea receded (Exod. xiv. 15).

4. SERVICE.—" Go," said Jehovah to Gideon ; and he got the victory over the Midianites (Judges vi. 14 ; vii. 22).

5. HEALING.—Look, said Moses to the bitten Israelites, and they were healed and lived (Num. xxi. 9).

6. SIGHT.—" Wash," said the Lord to the blind man, and he got his sight (John ix. 7).

7. WHOLENESS.—" Stretch forth," Christ commanded the man, and his withered hand was made " whole " (Matt. xii. 13).

CHRIST'S CROSS : ITS SUBJECTIVE POWER

" He died that they should live to Him."—2 Cor. v. 15.

Dr. Orchard, in the course of a sermon on the heroism of Christ, delivered at King's Weigh House, said that he had lately been speaking to a mother who had lost five sons in the War. " You talk of the sufferings of Jesus on the Cross," she said to him fiercely, " but did He know a mother's agony in the death of her sons ? What is His suffering compared with mine ? " When she had calmed a little, Dr. Orchard put to her the searching question, " If any of your five sons had not fallen in war, but had fallen in sin, would you not have suffered more ? " " Oh," she said, " infinitely more." " And that," said Dr. Orchard, " is what He suffered." And then she understood.

How many things there are we learn at the Cross ! For that Cross is not only an objective reality of a completed work bringing salvation (Heb. ix. 26-28), but it is also a subjective power ministering untold blessing to us.

1. Christ in His Death and Passion is the DEATH of sin (Rom. vi. 10, 11).

2. The END of self (Gal. ii. 20).

3. The INCENTIVE to consider others (Rom. xiv. 7-9).

4. The POWER to live to the Lord (2 Cor. v. 14, 15).

5. The MINISTER to comfort in sorrow because of loved ones fallen asleep (1 Thess. iv. 14-17).

6. The INSPIRATION to sacrifice (Phil. ii. 17).

7. The EXAMPLE in giving (2 Cor. viii. 9).

8. The DELIVERANCE from the world (Gal. i. 4).

9. The POWER to cause us to love one another (1 John iii. 16).

10. The LIBERATOR to loose us from lawlessness (Titus ii. 14, R.V.).

11. The ATTRACTION to sanctify us to Himself (Eph. v. 25).

12. The INSPIRATION to lead us to be imitators of God in forgiving injuries (Eph. v. 1, 2).

13. The MAGNET to cause us to yield ourselves without reserve to God (Rom. xii. 1).

CHRIST'S DEATH

" *Through His blood.*"—Eph. i. 7.

We do not like the system with which he was associated, but we love to hear Faber's clear testimony to the Saviour's worth and work. No one could be more emphatic nor clear in his declaration of Christ's vicarious death, and that salvation is found alone in Christ's atonement. In speaking of the horror and calamity of sin, he says : " Whither shall we look for deliverance ? Not to ourselves, for we know the practical infirmity of our weakness, and the incorrigible vitality of our corruption. Not to any earthly power, for it has no jurisdiction here. Not to philosophy, literature, or science, for in this case they are but sorry and unhelpful matters. Not to any saint, however holy, not to any angel, however mighty, for the least sin is a bigger mountain than they have faculties to move... Neither may he look for deliverance direct from the patience and compassion of God Himself for in the abysses of His wisdom it has been decreed that without shedding of blood is no remission of sin. It is from the precious blood of Jesus Christ alone that our salvation comes. Out of the immensity of His merits, out of the inexhaustible treasures of its satisfactions, because of the resistless power of its beauty over the justice and the wrath of God, because of that dear combination of its priceless worth and its benignant prodigality, we miserable sinners are raised out of the depths of our wretchedness, and restored to the peace and favour of our Heavenly Father."

Everything comes to us through Christ, and by means of His death. See how this is brought out in the use of the preposition " Dia," in Romans v, rendered " By " and " Through."

1. PEACE.—" Through our Lord Jesus Christ " (1).

2. ACCESS.—" By whom we have access " (2).

3. SALVATION.—" Saved from wrath through Him " (9).

4. RECONCILIATION.—" Reconciled to God by the death of His Son " (10, 11).

5. RIGHTEOUSNESS.—" By the obedience of One shall many be made righteous " (19).

CHRIST'S INDWELLING

" I in you."—John xv. 4.

A certain popular novelist says that Christ is in every man. What we have to do is to recognise Him. Here are some of his sentences.

" Christ is a common principle in every human being."
An " Element which is common to us all." " Resident in
every man."

When we read the writings of the apostle Paul, as inspired by the Holy Spirit, he does not recognise Christ is in
every man.

1. CRISIS.—Paul in his personal experience declares there
was a time when Christ did not live in him—" I live, yet no
longer I, but Christ liveth in me " (Gal. ii. 20, R.V.).

2. FORMATION.—In his soul travail for the believers in
Galatia, who were not right in relation to the Grace of God,
he prays, " I travail in birth till Christ be formed in you "
(Gal. iv. 19).

3. EMPOWERMENT.—In his letter to the Ephesian saints
he prays that they might be strengthened, that Christ might
dwell in them (Eph. iii. 16, 17).

4. EVIDENCE.—In writing to the carnal Christians in
Corinth, he states the fact that Jesus Christ might not be in
them.—" Jesus Christ is in you except ye be reprobates "
(2 Cor. xiii. 5).

5. POSSESSION.—In penning his epistle to the believers in
Rome, he says, " If any man have not the Spirit of Christ,
he is none of His " (Rom. viii. 9), which implies that those
who are not His have not His Spirit.

Exhorting the Philippian Christians, he pleads with them
to have the mind of Christ, which certainly implies not
having His mind (Phil. ii. 5).

6. CORRESPONDENCE.—Looking out into the future, Paul
distinctly states to the exclusion of all others except those who
" are saints and brethren in Christ Jesus," " Christ in you "
(mark, " In you," not " all men ") " the Hope of Glory "
(Col. i. 27).

7. ADMISSION.—Lastly, but not least, what does Christ's
message to the Church in Laodicea unfold ? It is the
possibility of a Church being without the indwelling Christ ;
hence He says, " Behold, I stand at the door and knock. If
any man hear My voice, I will come in to him, and sup with
him, and he with Me " (Rev. iii. 20).

These Scripture statements prove the unscripturalness
and delusiveness of the modern novelist.

Illustrated Bible Study Outlines

CHRIST'S MESSAGE

" These things I say unto you."—John v. 34.

The saintly Samuel Rutherford understood Christ better than many. He would not allow anything to be put in the place of Christ Himself. He said : " I renounce all that He ever made me will or do as defiled or imperfect as coming from myself. I betake myself to Christ for sanctification as well as justification." " Holiness is not Christ ; nor are the blossoms and flowers of the Tree of Life the tree itself." " My Lord and Master is Chief of ten thousands of thousands. None is comparable to Him, in heaven or in earth. Dear brethren, do all for Him. Pray for Christ. Preach for Christ. Do all for Christ ; beware of men-pleasing." " Oh, how sweet to be wholly Christ's and wholly in Christ ! " Rutherford could only speak thus of Christ by having his mind and heart steeped in Scripture, which the Holy Spirit used to form Christ in him.

When Christ is the Joy of our hearts, and the Expectation of our Hope, what a difference He makes ! To know this we need to know Christ's living messages.

Some of the Lord's living messages are found in relation to the words, " In Me." Let us ponder a few in John's Gospel.

1. SPIRITUAL INCORPORATION.—" He that eateth My flesh and drinketh My blood, dwelleth in ME, and I in him " (John vi. 56). As the food becomes part of the body and nourishes it, so Christ becomes part of us, as we feed upon Him by means of the Word.

2. SPIRITUAL IDENTIFICATION.—" He that believeth in ME, though he were dead " (" Though he die "), " yet shall he live ; and whosoever liveth " (Is living when I come) " and believeth in ME, shall never die " (John xi. 25, 26). Christ is the Resurrection to raise the dead in Him, and the Life to make alive the living one, when He comes.

3. SPIRITUAL INDUCTION.—" Believe also in ME " (John xiv. 1). Faith not only leads us to Christ, but into Christ. We may assent to all Christ says, and not be in Him. A graft needs to be in the stock if the life of the stock is to get into it.

4. SPIRITUAL INDWELLING.—" IN ME " occurs no less than six times in John xv. (verses 2, 4, 4, 5, 6, 7), and this

39

abiding is the secret of fruit-bearing, and is evidenced in obedience to the Lord (1 John iii. 24, R.V.).

5. SPIRITUAL INLET.—" These things I have spoken, that in ME ye might have peace " (John xvi. 33). The Word of the Lord leads to the peace of the Lord.

6. SPIRITUAL INCLUSION.—" That they all may be one, as Thou, Father art IN ME and I in Thee " (John xvii. 21). To be enclosed by His grace and love, is to be inclosed in the sphere of His glory (xvii. 23).

7. SPIRITUAL INDIVISIBILITY.—The Father and the Son are inseparable, they cannot be divided ; hence, Christ says of the Father, I am in the Father, and the Father IN ME.

CHRIST'S RESURRECTION IS THE GREATEST EVIDENCE OF CHRISTIANITY

" *Declared to be the Son of God with power, according to the Spirit of Holiness, by the resurrection from the dead.*"— Rom. i. 4.

The late W. E. Gladstone once said that " Christianity is Christ." Yes, but not Christ piece-meal, but Christ in His entirety. Unitarianism stops at the other side of the cross ; Romanism stops at the cross ; Christendom stops at Easter ; but we need to go on to Pentecost, and to wait for the trumpet sound of the Jubilee of the Lord's return.

He " showed Himself alive by many infallible proofs " (Acts i. 3). Generally speaking, the following seven proofs may be stated.

1. RECOGNITION.—He was seen by many brethren (1 Cor. xv. 5-8).

2. REPETITION.—In " many days " (Acts xiii. 31).

3. RECIPROCATION.—He ate with some at the sea of Tiberias (John xxi. 12-14 ; Acts x. 41).

4. REALISATION.—Thomas was invited to touch His body (John xx. 27).

5. REUNION.—His disciples walked and talked with Him (Luke xxiv. 32).

6. RECEPTION.—Received His blessing (Luke xxiv. 50).

7. RESPONSE.—And met Him by special appointment (Matt. xxviii. 7).

CHRIST'S RESURRECTION IS THE GREATEST EXHIBITION OF GOD'S POWER

'' *What is the exceeding greatness of His power to us-ward who believe, according to the working of His mighty power, which He wrought in Christ, when He raised Him from the dead, and set Him at His own right hand in the heavenly places."*—Eph. i. 19, 20.

One of the three wonderful " whats " to which the Apostle directs attention in his earnest prayer for the saints at Ephesus, is that which is associated with Christ's resurrection. When we look around at creation, we see the excellence of God's creative skill ; but when we look at Christ in His risen power we have the display of " the exceeding greatness of His power."

1. That power is the might that quickens us from the death of sin (Eph. ii. 1).

2. The power to make us one with Christ (1 Cor. xii. 12, 13).

3. The power to keep us from the servitude of sin (Rom. vi. 9).

4. The power to save to the uttermost of God's purpose (Heb. vii. 25).

5. The power to urge us to press on to the prize of the upward calling in Christ (Phil. iii. 14).

6. The power to make alive our present mortal body (Rom. viii. 11).

7. The power to bring us through to the inheritance reserved for us (1 Peter i. 3-5).

The spiritual forces of principalities and powers of evil can only be met and overcome as we are equipped in the power of His might (Eph. vi. 10). It is not without meaning that the " might of His power," or " the power of His might," only occurs in two places, and both of them in the Epistle to the Ephesians (compare margin of i. 19, and vi. 10). The great want of our times is the recognition of the supernatural, for it is only when believers get on their knees in earnest and consecrated prayer that they find themselves in touch with the effective dynamite of God's power.

CHRIST'S RETURN

" He that shall come will come."—Heb. x. 37.

Dr. Thomas Chalmers, the great Scotch scholar and preacher, rightly called " the great Chalmers," was a strong believer in our Lord's Second Coming. We do not know of any clearer testimony as to the return of Christ than the following :

" Of this I am satisfied, that the next coming of Christ will be a coming, not final judgment, but a coming to usher in the Millennium. I utterly despair of the universal prevalence of Christianity as the result of a missionary process. I look for its conclusive establishment through a widening passage of desolations and judgments, with the demolition of our civil and ecclesiastical structures. ' Overturn, Overturn, Overturn,' is the watchword of our coming Lord." In his *Sabbath Readings*, Chalmers says : " I desire to cherish a more habitual and practical faith than heretofore in that coming which even the first Christians were called to hope for with all earnestness, even though many centuries were to elapse ere the hope could be realised ; and how much more we who are so much nearer this great fulfilment than at the time when we believed ! " We believe He will come again,

1. Because He HAS COME once (Heb. ix. 26-28).
2. Because He has said HE WILL " come again " (John xiv. 3).
3. Because He is NEEDED (Rom. viii. 23).
4. Because He WANTS TO COME (Rev. xxii. 7).
5. Because the Father has so PURPOSED (Heb. i. 6).
6. Because the SCRIPTURES AFFIRM He will (2 Peter i. 19).
7. Because CREATION IS GROANING for Him and the sons of God (Rom. viii. 19-22).

CHRIST'S SAYINGS

" Verily, verily, I say unto you."—John v. 24.

WHAT HE SAID

Hurrying to board a train and out of breath, an inspector saw my puff-ability, and took compassion upon me by saying,

" There's plenty of time, sir." As I knew he was the man who would give the signal for the train to start, I immediately slowed down. The man in authority could speak the word of assurance. It would have been folly for me to have heeded what a passenger had said, or a passer-by, but when the man in power spoke, there was power to stop my hurry and flurry. When the Lord speaks, too, His word is arresting and assuring. How often He said, " Verily I say unto you." In the Gospel of John we have a series of double " Verilys." Note a few of them.

1. MEDIATORSHIP (John i. 51).—An opened heaven and an opportune blessing for earth are possible because of the Son of Man. He has by His death met the claim of heaven to God's satisfaction, and meets the need of man to his salvation.

2. " MUST " OF THE NEW BIRTH (John iii. 3-7).—To be begotten from " above " (margin) is essential to enter the life above. Mark the emphatic words " cannot," " except," " must," and the repeated double " Verily, verily, I say unto thee."

3. MESSAGE (John iii. 11).—Many speak to-day, not because they have something to say, but because they must say something. Every true speaker, relative to the Word of God, is one who is first a witness and then a messenger.

4. MUSIC OF GRACE (John v. 24).—How many notes from the harmony of grace are sounded in these words ! " My word," the assurance of grace ; " Believeth on Him," the terms of grace ; " Him that sent Me," the Giver of grace ; " Everlasting life," the blessing of grace ; " Shall not come into condemnation," the salvation of grace ; " Is passed from death unto life," the translation of grace ; and, lastly, " Verily, verily, I say unto you," the emphatic promise of grace.

5. MANNA (John vi. 32, 53).—Christ not only saves, He satisfies. To be in a house, and thus be saved from a storm, is good ; to be in a furnished house, and thus have a bed to rest upon, is better ; but a house and its furniture will not feed us ; hence, the best thing is to have a full larder. Christ saves from the storm of wrath, and He furnishes the inner being by His grace ; but He also feeds and satisfies our hunger.

43

6. MIGHT (John xiv. 12). To quicken a dead body is great, but a " greater " work is to make alive a person dead in sins. To open the eyes of a darkened understanding is a greater work than to open the eyes of the blind.

There are other double " verilys." Look them up, and remember " verily " means " amen." When Christ says " Amen," " so let it be."

CHRIST, THE CENTRE

" *Things concerning Himself.*"—Luke xxiv. 27.

Tradition says that when Thomas Aquinas was bowing before his crucifix, that the voice said, " Thou hast written well of Me, what recompense dost thou desire ? "

" None other than Thyself, O Lord," was the saint's reply.

Christ is the Answer to every question ; the Centre of everything.

1. The Central FIGURE of Truth is Christ (John xiv. 6 ; xviii. 18).

2. The Central POINT of the Gospel is the Death of Christ (1 Cor. xv. 3).

3. The Central FACT of Power is the Resurrection of Christ (Eph. i. 19, 20).

4. The Central ADMINISTRATOR in the Church is the Spirit of Christ (1 Cor. xii. 1-13).

5. The Central BUSINESS of the Church is to make Christ known (1 Cor. ii. 2).

6. The Central PURPOSE of God is to sum up all things in Christ (Eph. i. 10).

7. The Central GRACE which moves is the love of Christ (2 Cor. v. 14).

CLEANSING

" *If we confess our sins, He is faithful and just to forgive us our sins, and to cleanse us from all unrighteousness.*"— 1 John i. 9.

" Your sin must be cleaned out of your heart and life," a Christian worker recently said to one who had sinned, and who had been a prominent Christian worker. " Confession is not enough, there must be cleansing. The sin which led to the fall must be dealt with and put away."

Cringing like Agag will not do, Agag must be slain and done with. We must not be taken in with plausibilities as Joshua was by the wily Gibeonites (Josh. ix. 3-27). Compromise will bring condemnation. True confession does not mean owning up because we are found out, it means judging the sin and hating it because it is sin. Repentance is a change of mind which shows itself by a change of action. He ill repents who repeats his sins.

Is there not a lost note in modern preaching ? We are not saved for repentance's sake, but we are not saved without it. We do well to recall the fact that the broken heart on account of sin, and the broken life from sin, are truly blessed.

This leads one to say, confession is not sufficient, there must be cleansing. Mark the conjunction that follows the confession, " *and* to cleanse us from all unrighteousness." The grace, which cleanses the conscience from the penalty of sin, waits to cleanse from its pollution also.

How often cleansing is specially enjoined upon us. Let the following speak for itself.

1. CLEANSING IS ESSENTIAL TO SERVICE.—David in his confession, and prayer that he might have a clean heart, coupled with restoration and the equipment of the Holy Spirit, says as a subsequent to his cleansing, " Then will I teach transgressors Thy ways, and sinners shall be converted unto Thee " (Ps. li. 10-13).

2. CLEANSING IS THE ESSENTIAL TO SPIRITUAL SIGHT.— One of the beatitudes of Christ's teaching is, " Blessed are the pure," or clean, " in heart, for they shall see God " (Matt. v. 8). Sin and impurity blurs the vision, and stultifies love.

3. CLEANSING IS THE ESSENTIAL FOR SANCTIFICATION IN ITS ENTIRETY.—Our Father gives us the promises of ability and indwelling, but because of these, He says, " Cleansing yourselves from ALL filthiness of the flesh, and spirit, perfecting holiness in the fear of God " (2 Cor. vii. 1).

4. CLEANSING IS THE ESSENTIAL TO PRAYER.—The apostolic injunction on prayer is, " I will therefore that men pray

everywhere, lifting up holy hands, without wrath and doubting " (1 Tim. ii. 8). " Call on the Lord out of a pure (clean) heart " (2 Tim. ii. 22). Holy hands and a pure heart, the inner and outward, are to be clean.

5. PURITY IS THE FINALITY OF THE CHRISTIAN LIFE.— " Now the end of the commandment is love out of a pure heart and of a good conscience, and of faith unfeigned " (1 Tim. i. 5). Could a trinity be more comprehensive ? Pure flame of love burning on the altar of the heart. Conscience like a clean slate, nothing accusing on it, and faith which rests on God with an unbiased reliance.

6. PURITY IS AN ESSENTIAL QUALIFICATION FOR THE LORD'S SERVANT.—" Keep thyself pure " is the command of the Lord, to all privileged in the Lord's service, and this privilege is our responsibility (1 Tim. v. 22).

7. PURITY IS ESSENTIAL TO HAVE FELLOWSHIP WITH OTHERS.—Even in the house of Christendom, vessels of " dishonour " may be found, but the man of God has to " purge " himself from " these," and be a " vessel unto honour, sanctified and meet for the Master's use " (2 Tim. ii. 20-22).

COCOON CHRISTIANS

" *Live unto the Lord.*"—Rom. xiv. 8.

A novelist describes one of her characters as belonging to " the order of women who resemble silkworms, in being wrapped entirely round by the cocoon of their own atmospheres." This reminds us of what Lady Henry Somerset once said :

" I do not think it is unfair to say that the fault of American conversation is that it is often wearyingly personal."

Not only is it the fault of Americans, but the fault of many, who find in themselves, and what they are doing, the theme of interesting talk. If we talk about Jehovah and Jesus, we shall find our conversation to be edifying to others, and a joy to Jehovah (Mal. iii. 16, 17).

If we are personally right with the Lord, we shall be active towards Him. See how this is illustrated in Ps. cxliii. 4-9.

Note the personal pronoun " I," in the following sentences :

1. LOOKING BACK.—" I remember the days of old " (5). It is good to recall the days of the Lord's deliverances and grace, for this leads us to praise Him.

2. LOOKING OUT.—" I meditate on all Thy works " (5). To study the grasses of the field, the flowers in the garden, and creation all around, is to see the minutiæ of His care.

3. LOOKING UP.—" I muse on the works of Thy hands " (5). The heavens are specially said to be His handiwork. The sun declares His skill, the moon His faithfulness, and the stars His constant service.

4. LOOKING TO.—" I stretch forth my hands unto Thee " (6). The outstretched hand speaks of need in its appeal.

5. LEANING ON.—" In Thee do I trust " (8). Dependence upon Another, means He alone can do what we cannot do for ourselves.

6. LIFTING UP.—" I lift up my soul unto Thee " (8). We are lifted out of danger when we count upon Him to lift us.

7. FLEEING INTO.—" I flee unto Thee to hide me " (9). We hide in His atonement for safety, in His love for comfort, and in Himself for victory.

" COMFORTED WITH NAILS "

" *The comfort wherewith we ourselves are comforted of God.*"
2 Cor. i. 4.

An old English version of the Bible translates the sentence, " Fastened it with nails " in Isaiah xli. 7, " Comforted it with nails," in referring to the idols that were made strong by nails. The word rendered " fastened " is a primary one, and means to fasten, to seize upon, and in a figurative sense to encourage, to strengthen. The Hebrew word is translated " encouraged " in Isaiah xli. 7 ; " strengthened " in 1 Sam. xxiii. 16 ; " repair " in 2 Kings xii. 5 ; " fortified " in 2 Chron. xi. 11 ; and " help " in 2 Chron. xxix. 34. As the idol-maker comforted his idol with nails, so the Holy Spirit makes us strong with the fastenings of His grace.

1. He ENCOURAGES us with His promises, as the Lord did Joshua (Josh. i. 2-9).

2. He STRENGTHENS us by His power, as Christ said the Holy Spirit would the disciples (Acts i. 8).

3. He REPAIRS us by His grace, as the Lord did the Apostle in his weakness (2 Cor. xii. 8, 9).

4. He FORTIFIES us by His Word, as He did Jeremiah for his service (Jer. i. 6-12 ; xv. 16).

5. He HELPS us by His presence, as He pledged He would Moses, as the leader of Israel (Exod. xxxiii. 12-17).

COMING OF CHRIST

" *The coming of the Lord draweth nigh.*"—Jas. v. 8.

An unsympathetic writer in referring to the return of Christ says : " Critics of both schools of thought—Fundamentalist and Modernist—are nearly all agreed that Jesus Himself foretold His own return. Modern knowledge of physical science may impel us to reject the whole idea of a Second Coming as transcending the limits of human mental credibility ; but that does not in any sense justify us in concluding that Jesus Himself did not firmly accept the view and its possibility."

The issue raised by these words is, Are we to accept what Christ said, or to give up what He said by listening to and believing " Modern knowledge of physical science " ? If we are swayed by the latter, then He was not what He claimed to be, or He was mistaken ; then, in either case, we cannot believe Him, nor rely upon Him.

What did Christ foretell ?

1. He would go away and RETURN (John xiv. 1-3).

2. He went away to RECEIVE A KINGDOM, and to come back again to inaugurate it (Luke xix. 12).

3. He commissioned His servants to " occupy till " HE CAME BACK (Luke xix. 13).

4. He would reckon with His disciples when He came back TO REWARD THEM for talents used (Matt. xxv. 19).

5. He would gather the JEWS back to their OWN LAND (Matt. xxiv. 31-35).

6. He would JUDGE THE NATIONS for their conduct towards His brethren (Matt. xxv. 31, 32).

7. He enjoined His own to WATCH AND WAIT for His coming back (Luke xii. 35-40).

COMING OF CHRIST: WHAT DOES IT MEAN?

" A little while and ye shall see Me."—John xvi. 17.

The well-known writer Jane T. Stoddart, in reviewing a volume in which it said " the Christ in all men " is taught, says, " Mr. Hutchinson has tried to minister to souls beset. A disclosure has been made to his hero, but it is not the full disclosure of the Christian Gospel. When Paul spoke of ' the mystery hid from ages and from generations . . . which is Christ in you, the hope of glory,' he meant something infinitely more transcendant than the recognition of Christ-like qualities in himself or his converts. The teaching of Simon Paris might easily lead to a dangerous form of pantheism. Samuel Rutherford has this comment on the verse in Colossians, ' It is not for nothing that it is said " Christ in you the hope of glory." I will be content with no pawn of heaven but Christ Himself, for Christ, possessed by faith here, is young heaven and glory in the bud.' "

Those who deny the facts of the past generally drift into the ignoring of the glory of the future, or substitute something which blots out or dims the hope of the future. We agree and rejoice with Rutherford, when he says, " Christ, possessed by faith here, is young heaven and glory in the bud."

What does the coming of Christ mean for those who are looking for Him?

1. RECEPTION BY CHRIST.—His promise is, " I will come again and receive you to Myself " (John xiv. 3). What a reception!

2. LIKENESS TO CHRIST.—" We shall be like Him, for we shall see Him as He is " (1 John iii. 2).

3. TRANSLATION TO BE WITH CHRIST.—We shall be caught up to meet Him, and ever to be with Him (1 Thess. iv. 13-18).

4. REWARDED BY CHRIST (Luke xix. 13), for the Lord will come to reckon with His servants, and give to His faithful ones compensation.

5. PLACED BY CHRIST.—We shall not all occupy the same place, for there will be those who will have " a full reward " and an " abundant entrance " and there are those who will not (2 John 8 ; 2 Peter i. 11).

6. TESTED BY THE LORD.—Our lives will be scrutinised, and our work will be sifted, and for what comes through the fire we shall be rewarded (1 Cor. iv. 4, 5, R.V.).

7. MOTIVES WILL BE EXAMINED BEFORE CHRIST.—For it is at His judgment seat we shall be " well-pleasing " to Him or not (2 Cor. v. 9, 10, R.V.).

COMING OF THE HOLY SPIRIT

" *But wait for the promise of the Father, which, saith He, ye have heard of Me.*"—Acts i. 4.

When Nansen started on his Arctic expedition he took with him a carrier dove, strong and fleet of wing ; and after two years—two years in the desolation of the Arctic regions —he one day wrote a tiny little message, and tied it under the dove's wing, and let it loose, to travel two thousand miles to Norway ; and, oh, what miles ! what desolation ! not a living creature ! ice, ice, ice, snow and death. But he took the trembling little dove and flung her up from the ship, up into the icy cold. Three circles she made, and then, straight as an arrow, she shot south ; one thousand miles over ice, one thousand miles over the frozen wastes of ocean, and at last dropped into the lap of the explorer's wife. She knew by the arrival of the dove that it was all right in the dark night of the North. So, to the apostles and the rest of the disciples, when Jesus had finished the covenant, He said, " Wait till I send from heaven the promise of the Father. Go not home till He has arrived. The Dove that descended on Me at the inception of the New Covenant in the baptism of Jordan, He will come. I shall send Him. Wait till you hear from Me." They saw Him go ; they saw Him disappear into the blue of heaven. As they were all waiting with one accord, in one place, suddenly a noise as of a rushing mighty wind filled the house, and the Spirit descended, and there appeared cloven tongues like as of fire, and sat upon each of them. The Dove had arrived ! It is all right with the Mediator of the New Covenant.

At Pentecost the Holy Spirit came as—

1. The ENDUEMENT of power for service (Acts i. 8).

2. As the ENABLER to witness (Acts ii. 4).

3. As the ENFLATER, to fill for testimony (Acts iv. 31).

4. As the ENLIGHTENER to discern hypocrisy (Acts viii. 23).

5. As the EQUIPPER for missionary work (Acts xiii. 1-4).

6. As the ANOINTING, to reveal the glorified Christ (Acts vii. 56).

7. As the GUIDE to lead and preach in Christian work (Acts xvi. 7-10).

COMING OF THE LORD

" *This same Jesus shall so come in like manner as ye have seen Him go into heaven."*—Acts i. 11.

Three questions are raised by this statement. Who went away ? Who saw Him go away ? How did He go away ?

WHO WENT AWAY ? " This same Jesus." The Jesus of Bethlehem's incarnation ; the Jesus of Nazareth's business ; the Jesus of the Synagogue's revelation ; the Jesus of Sychar's Well, and all the other places He visited ; the Jesus of wonder-working benedictions ; the Jesus of prayerful supplication ; the Jesus of reliant dependence on the Holy Spirit ; the Jesus of Divine revelation ; the Jesus of Gethsemane's agony ; the Jesus of Gabbatha's suffering ; the Jesus of Golgotha's atoning death ; the Jesus of Satan's conquest ; the Jesus of resurrection power ; the Jesus of Old Testament prophecy ; the Jesus of glorious resurrection ; the Jesus of Pentecostal blessing ; and the Jesus of the coming glory.

WHO SAW HIM GO AWAY ?—The last sight the world got of Christ was on the Cross, when man was seen at his worst in crucifying Christ, and God at His best, in His redeeming love. Peter distinctly and definitely stated, that only disciples saw Him go away. His statement is as follows, " Him God raised up from the dead, and showed Him openly ; not to all the people, but unto witnesses chosen of God, even to us " (Acts x. 40, 41). As only believers saw Him as He ascended into the air, so only believers will see Him when He comes to the air for His own (1 Thess. iv. 13-18).

How DID HE GO AWAY ?—Luke tells us in his gospel, Christ " led " His disciples " out as far as Bethany, and He lifted His hands and blessed them " (Luke xxiv. 50). Can we not picture that scene ? Those pierced hands of Calvary's Cross and His atoning death, lifted up to heaven, and upon them descended the Father's benediction through those open wounds. He shall so come, and, oh, what blessings He will bring. The blessing of meeting Him (1 Thess. iv. 17), of seeing Him face to face (1 John iii. 2), of being like Him in glorified bodies (Phil. iii. 20, 21), of being rewarded by Him (1 Cor. iv. 5), of hearing Him say, " Well done ! " for all we have done well (Matt. xxv. 23), and of being for ever with Him (1 Thess. iv. 17).

George Macdonald, in his *Sir Gibbie*, represents two of his characters talking about the Coming of the Lord. One is made conscious of it by a thunder storm, and she starts to clean up her cottage. The novelist pens the following :

The same afternoon, a neighbour, on her way over the shoulder of the hill to the next village, had called upon her and found her brushing the rafters of her cottage with a broom at the end of a long stick.

" Save's a', Janet ! what are ye after ? I never saw sic a thing ! " she exclaimed.

" I kenna hoo I never thoucht o' sic a thing afore," answered Janet, leaning her broom against the wall, and dusting a chair for her visitor ; " but this mornin', whan my man an' me was sittin' at oor breakfast, there cam' sic a clap o' thunder 'at it jist garred the bit hoosie trim'le ; an' doon fell a snot o' soot intil the very spune 'at my man was cairryin' till's honest moo. That cudna be as things war inten'it, ye ken ; sae what was to be said, but sat them richt ? "

" Ow, weel ! But ye micht hae waitit till Donal cam' hame ; he wad hae dune 't in half the time, an' no raxed his jints."

" I cudna put it aff," answered Janet. " Wha kenned whan the Lord micht come ? He canna come at cock-crawin' the day, but He may be here afore nicht."

" Well, I's awa," said her visitor, rising. " I'm gaunin' ower to the toon to buy a feow hanks o' worset to weyve a pair o' stockins to my man. Guid day to ye Janet. What neist, I won'er," she added to herself as she left the house. " The wunan's clean dementit ! "

The moment she was gone, Janet caught up her broom again, and went spying about over the roof—ceiling there was none—after long tangles of agglomerated cobweb and smoke.

" Ay ! " she said to herself, " Wha kens whan He may be at the door ? an' I wadna like to hear Him say, ' Janet, ye micht hae had yer hoosie a bit cleaner, whan ye kenned I micht be at han ' ! "

" COMING OF THE SON OF MAN "

" *The Coming of the Son of Man.*"—Matt. xxiv. 27, 30.

A claim that Christ would " reappear " coming through the Heads of Sydney Harbour, which was made some time ago, by a fanatical woman, and that He would appear in the " Temple " on the shores of Sydney Harbour, is in contra-distinction to what our Lord declared. In two places He said the deceivers might come " in the desert," and in the " secret chambers." One outside place, and one inside one. These corresponded to the " Harbour " of the " desert," and the " secret chambers " of the temple. What did our Lord say as to the PLACE in which He would be seen ? Here are His words :

" For as the lightning cometh out of the east, and shineth even unto the west ; so shall also the coming of the Son of Man be. For wheresoever the carcase is, there will the eagles be gathered together. Immediately after the tribulation of those days shall the sun be darkened, and the moon shall not give her light, and the stars shall fall from heaven, and the powers of the heavens shall be shaken : and then shall appear the sign of the Son of Man in heaven : and then shall all the tribes of the earth mourn, and they shall see the Son of Man coming in the clouds of heaven with power and great glory " (Matt. xxiv. 27-30).

There are seven things in the above prophecy.

1. How He will come. Suddenly and universally. Like the lightning flashing across the sky, and as it is seen from the east to the west, so His coming will be in manifest and startling splendour.

2. What will precede His coming. Following the time of the Great Tribulation, wonderful phenomena will precede His coming, in the obscuration of the heavenly bodies, and the powers of the heaven being shaken.

3. When will Christ come. " Then shall appear the sign of the Son of Man." Mark the adverb of time—" Then." Not till " Then," but right " then " and there He will be seen.

4. Where He will come. " The Son of Man coming in the clouds of heaven." " Clouds of heaven " is explicit as denoting the place to which He will come, and where He will be seen.

5. What will be the effect of His coming ? " Then shall the tribes of the earth mourn." We have the scene graphically described in Revelation vi. 12-17. The word " mourn " describes the intensity of the grief and bewailment which will characterise men. The word " mourn " means to cut or beat one's self, and is rendered " cut down," in referring to the cutting of branches off a tree (Mark xi. 8), and to those who " bewailed " the death of the ruler's daughter (Luke viii. 52).

6. In what character will Christ appear ?—" As the Son of Man." This title is associated with His coming in judgment (John v. 22). Believers are looking for Him as the Saviour, and not as the Judge.

7. What will be prominent in His coming ?—The sign will be, He will come " in power and great glory." When He first came, it was in humility and great abasement, but then He will be the Man of Splendour and Might.

COMPROMISE

" *Kept back part of the price.*"—Acts v. 2.

" The Saxons, a warring tribe of Europe, were practically compelled to become Christians. They consented on one condition. That condition would only be known at the time of their baptism. When these warriors were put under the water, as a symbol that their old life was dead, they went under—all except their right arms. They held them out, above their heads. These were their fighting arms." There was a limitation in their confession, which marred the whole of it. The same holds good when believers compromise, or only yield partial obedience.

1. COMPROMISE IN WORK.—Peter was guilty of partial obedience when he let down a " net," instead of the " nets," as directed by the Lord (Luke v. 4-8).

2. COMPROMISE IN RESPONSE.—The same apostle was wrong again when he would not allow the Lord to wash his feet (John xiii. 8-10).

3. COMPROMISE IN FOLLOWING.—Abram was wrong when he stopped at Haran, when he should have gone on to the indicated land (Gen. xii. 1).

4. COMPROMISE IN FAITH.—Israel came short when they wandered in the wilderness, instead of going into the promised land (Heb. iii. 13-18).

5. COMPROMISE IN OUTLOOK.—Lot was infatuated when he looked towards Sodom, instead of keeping in the place of separation as Abraham did (Gen. xiii. 1-11).

6. COMPROMISE IN WATCHING.—The disciples were wanting when they were found sleeping instead of watching (Matt. xxvi. 40).

7. COMPROMISE IN DEVOTION.—The man of God was failing in devotion to the Word of God when he listened to the old prophet of Bethel (1 Kings xiii. 1-29).

" CONSCIENCE "

" Their conscience also bearing witness."—Rom. ii. 15.

One of the witnesses before the grand jury appointed to inquire into a case of alleged bribery in a local election, stated that he had received 25 dols. to vote Republican, and on cross-examination it was elicited that also he had received 25 dols. to vote Democrat.

The jury foreman in amazement repeated : " You say you received 25 dols. to vote Republican ? "

" Yes, sir."

" And you also received 25 dols. to vote Democrat ? "

" Yes, sir."

" And for whom did you vote at the finish ? "

The witness, with injured dignity in every line of his face, answered with great earnestness : " I voted according to my conscience ! "

The moral question which is aroused by the above incident is, Had the man any conscience at all ? It rather reminds me of what I heard C. H. Spurgeon say once, " Some men are all things to all men to save a sum " ! What kind of a conscience have we ?

1. JACOB had an ELASTIC CONSCIENCE, and stole his brother's birthright and blessing (Gen. xxvii. 36).

2. PILATE had a WEAK CONSCIENCE, and gave Christ to His murderers (Matt. xxvii. 19-25).

3. JUDAS had a SEARED CONSCIENCE, and sold his Lord for thirty pieces of silver (Matt. xxvi. 14-16).

4. JONAH had a SLEEPY CONSCIENCE, and had to be awakened to his disobedience by the mariners (Jonah i. 6).

5. BALAAM had an ACCOMMODATING CONSCIENCE, and compromised with the commands of Jehovah (2 Peter ii. 15).

6. GEHAZI had a SCHEMING CONSCIENCE, and tried to please his master and get what he could out of Naaman as well (2 Kings v. 20-27).

7. SIMON MAGUS had a COVETOUS CONSCIENCE, and thought the power of God could be got for money for his own advantage (Acts viii. 18-24).

CONSISTENCY

" *In all things shewing thyself a pattern of good works.*"—
    Titus ii. 7.

Consistency may be defined as consecration in practice. One has said, " The most successful preachers against Christianity are inconsistent professors. The bad sermons of the life are an overmatch for the best words of the lips. To pray in the sanctuary and to cheat on the Exchange ; to kneel at the Communion Table and to oppress the poor ; to profess brotherly love and to slander our neighbour ; to sing of Calvary and Heaven and put wrong figures in the ledger, is to bring about the scorn, and not the salvation of the world, and to brand ourselves as hypocrites whose false label the Master will indignantly tear off with His own hand at the last day." Consistency is made up of the following characteristics.

1. PURENESS of heart is its inner shrine (1 Tim. i. 5).

2. REALITY is its open face (2 Cor. iii. 18).

3. RIGHTEOUSNESS is its outward acts (Titus ii. 12).

4. SINGLENESS of aim is its ardent desire (2 Cor. v. 9, R.V.).

5. HOLINESS is its lovely bloom (1 Thess. ii. 10).

6. CONSTANCY is its even walk (Rom. ii. 7).

7. HAPPINESS is its loving service (Rom. xvi. 3, 9).

CORRUPT COMMUNICATIONS

" *Let no corrupt communication proceed out of your mouth.*"—
Eph. iv. 29.

When Plato was told people spoke " ill " of him, he said, " It is no matter, I shall so live that no one will believe them."

It is the life that tells. When the life corresponds to Christ, that correspondence confounds the critics. Reading through the Acts of the Apostles, the Christianity of the early Christians speaks volumes. Think of some of the telling things which speak out Christ's worth and the influence of His grace.

1. The SPIRIT-FILLED BELIEVERS " pricked " the hearers " in their hearts," that the believers possessed something they did not have (ii. 37).

2. The COMMUNITY OF INTEREST, and the love evidenced in mutual care, demonstrated the faith of the early Christians (ii. 41-47).

3. The BOLDNESS and SINCERE CONFIDENCE of Peter and John, made those who listened to them to marvel, and to recognise that they had " been with Jesus " (iv. 13).

4. The JUDGMENT OF GOD which came upon Ananias and Sapphira, caused great fear to come upon all the church (v. 11).

5. Gamaliel was so CONVINCED of the REALITY of the servants of God that he urged the authorities to " Let them alone " (v. 38).

6. Stephen's SHINING FACE and his sanctified life cut others in their hearts to their confusion (vi. 15 ; vii. 55).

7. The conversion of Saul SO IMPRESSED itself upon Ananias of Damascus, that he ceased to call him " this man," and spoke of him and to him as " Brother Saul " (ix. 13, 17).

8. The " GOOD WORKS " of Dorcas and her help of the poor were arguments which were beyond all argument (ix. 39).

9. The CHANGE IN THE LIFE of the Philippian jailer and his household was evident in the change from cruelty to kindness, that he and they were tangible witnesses of the conquering grace of God (xvi. 23-34).

10. The BONFIRE of UNHOLY BOOKS in Ephesus showed the reality of those fired by the Spirit and those who professed faith in Christ (xix. 17-20).

CREATION DECLARES THE CREATOR

" God Created."—Gen. i. 1.

All creation declares the existence of a Creator. The firmament, the blue skies, the sun, moon, stars, day and night, the seasons of the year, man in his marvellous physical constitution and his moral make-up, and the entire creation in its existence and orderly arrangement, declare the eternal God the Creator.

" Some years ago," it is said, " a Frenchman, who, like many of his countrymen, had won a high rank among men of science, yet who denied the God of all science, was crossing the great Sahara in company with an Arab guide. He noticed, with a sneer, that at certain times, his guide, whatever obstacles might arise, put them all aside, and kneeling on the burning sands, called on his God.

" Day after day passed and still the Arab never failed, till at last one evening the philosopher, when he arose from his knees, asked him with a contemptuous smile, ' How do you know there is a God ? ' The guide fixed his eyes on the scoffer for a moment in wonder, and then said solemnly :

' How do I know there is a God ?   How did I know that a
man and not a camel passed by my hut last night in the
darkness ?   Was it not by the print of his foot in the sand ?
Even so,' and he pointed to the sun, whose last rays were
flashing over the lonely desert.   ' That footprint is not that
of a man.' "

There are many things which prove God.

1. The HEAVENS in their glory and artistic skill (Ps. viii.
3, 4).

2. MAN in the nobility of his being and make (Ps. viii.
5-9).

3. GOD'S CONSTANT CARE in His daily provision and love
(Acts xvii. 24-29).

4. THE JEW in his preservation among the nations (Isa.
xi. 10-11).

5. The Christ in HIS CONTROL over the elements (Luke
viii. 22-25).

6. THE HOLY SPIRIT in His IMPARTING GRACE and
energetic power (Acts iv. 8-12).

7. THE SAINT in his appeal for help from the Lord, and
his experience of it (Ps. cxxi. 2).

CRIES

" Crieth upon the highest places of the City."—Prov. ix. 3.

The cries which are heard in the streets of a large town
are full of interest and suggestion.   The cries are not so many
and varied as they used to be.   By-laws regulate or extinguish them.   " Fresh 'erring " used to be heard ;   and
" muffins and crumpets," besides " water-cresses."   News-
vendors, sellers of fish,   and rag-merchants still have their
calls.

1. A CRY FOR MERCY.—" She cried unto Him " (Matt.
xv. 22).   She cried to the right Person—" Unto Him " ;
she cried the right cry—" Mercy " ;   and she cried with a
given purpose, for it was for her daughter, " grievously
vexed with a devil."

2. A MALICIOUS CRY.—" They cried out, Crucify Him ;
away with Him " (John xix. 6, 15).   The cry of the voice

revealed the sin and hate in their hearts. What's in will out.

3. A SAVIOUR'S CRY.—" When He had cried again with a loud voice " (Matt. xxvii. 46, 50). His last cry of yielding up His spirit was preceded by the orphaned cry of His forsaking. The bitternesses of the Cross were the procurements of blessing.

4. A QUICKENING CRY.—" He cried with a loud voice, Lazarus, come forth " (John xi. 43). The life-giving Christ can give life to those whom He calls forth. None can retard His " Come forth."

5. A DECIDING CRY.— " Then cried they all again, Not this Man, but Barabbas " (John xviii. 40). Evil hearts ever make a bad choice. A robber preferred to the Redeemer is an illustration of what so many do, when they prefer others to Christ.

6. AN AROUSING CRY.—" At midnight there was a cry made, Behold, the Bridegroom cometh, go ye out to meet Him " (Matt. xxv. 6). Christ is coming. Are we ready for Him, or asleep in the sloth of inactivity ?

7. A REJECTING CRY.—They cried out, " Away with such a fellow " (Acts xxii. 22, 23). When men are touched on the raw of their sinful personality they express themselves in embittered language.

CROSS ENDURED : OR A CROSS, A HEART, AND A ROSE

" *Instead of the joy, He endured the Cross.*"—Heb. xii. 2.

" I took for the symbol of my theology a seal on which I had engraven a Cross, with a Heart in its centre. The Cross is black, to indicate the sorrows, even unto death, through which the Christian must pass. But the Heart preserves its natural colour, for the Cross does not extinguish nature— it does not kill, but gives life. The Heart is placed in the midst of a White Rose, which signifies the joy, peace, and consolation that faith brings. But the Rose is white and not red, because it is not the joy and peace of the world, but that of the Spirit." So writes one who saw beyond the symbols into the realities.

1. SUFFICIENT GRACE was found through the hurting thorn, as Paul experienced (2 Cor. xii. 9).

2. The PALACE WAS REACHED through the durance vile of the prison, as Joseph knew (Ps. cv. 18-22).

3. The POSITION OF LEADER was entrusted to Moses, because he had qualified in the wilderness of adversity (Exod. iii. 1-10).

4. The SKILL OF ACCURACY was learned by David when he overcame the lion and the bear ; hence, he triumphed over the giant (1 Sam. xvii. 35-37).

5. The UNFOLDING OF THE FUTURE was made known to John, when he was banished to the Isle of Patmos (Rev. i. 9-20).

6. The COMPANIONSHIP OF THE LORD was enjoyed by the three Hebrews when in the fiery furnace (Dan. iii. 24-30).

7. The LORD'S DELIVERING POWER was felt when Daniel was in the lions' den (Dan. vi. 16-28).

CROSS FORGOTTEN

" The Cross."—John xix. 19.

Rev. W. H. Armstrong, when speaking at a Wesleyan Conference in England of the influence of the early Methodist preachers and those of to-day, said, " He ventured to think the reason for this was, that in emphasising the social implications of the Christian Gospel they had forgotten the Cross, which was the only effective dynamic of social service." The dynamic of the Cross is seen if we, having recognised its objective work (1 Cor. xv. 3, 4), ponder its subjective influence.

1. The Cross is the DEATH of sin (Rom. vi. 10, 11).
2. The SLAYER of self (Gal. ii. 20).
3. The SEPARATOR from the world (Gal. vi. 14).
4. The BEGETTER of love to others (1 John iii. 16).
5. The SOUL of holiness (Heb. xiii. 12, 20, 21).
6. The INCENTIVE to sacrifice (Matt. xx. 26-28).
7. The MAIN-SPRING of service (2 Cor. v. 14).
8. The MUSIC of worship (Rev. v. 9, 10).
9. The HOPE of the future (1 Thess. iv. 13, 14).

CROSS OF CHRIST : GOLDEN AND BLACK

" *God is Light.*"   " *God is Love.*"—1 John i. 5 ; iv. 8.

God is Light and God is Love shine out from the Cross of Christ with unmistakable meaning and lustre. There sin's desert and sin's Deliverer are seen. One has said of that cross in using the sign of the cross on the dome of London's cathedral :

" There are voices which say that our civilisation is a failure. If it has been a failure, the reason is that men have not allowed our social system to feel sufficiently the effect of the Cross. I have sometimes thought, as I saw the great dome of St. Paul's, like a mighty hand holding its gilded cross over the City, that this cross is a cruel and bitter sarcasm. Down below, competition goes on as fiercely as if Christ had never lived or died. Does not that cross some-times wear a threatening look ? When Savonarola was in the midst of his work for Florence he saw, in a dream, a black cross, and upon it were the words, ' Crux iræ Dei ' (' the cross of the wrath of God '). Round it were thunders, lightnings, rain, and hail. In some moods that cross in the City seems to be there for judgment and for judgment alone. But in another vision we remember that Savonarola saw a golden cross with the words, ' Crux misericordiæ Dei ' (' the cross of the mercy of God '), and bright rays streamed down from it into the darkness. That is the vision we must not allow to fade."

Do we not see that the holiness, righteousness, and love of God mingle at the Cross of Christ's death. See how these are manifest in the Epistle to the Romans.

1. RIGHTEOUSNESS.—" Whom God hath set forth to be a propitiation " (satisfaction), " through faith, in His blood, to declare His righteousness " (iii. 25).

2. ABANDONMENT.—" Who was delivered " (up) " for our offences " (iv. 25).

3. LOVE.—" God commendeth His love . . . Christ died for us " (v. 8).

4. JUDGMENT.—" God . . . condemned sin in the flesh " (viii. 3).

5. GRACE.—" He that spared not His own Son . . . with Him also freely giveth us all things " (viii. 32).

CROSS'S POWER TO LIFT UP

" Christ crucified, the Power of God."—1 Cor. i. 18.

" Look up " and " Lift up " were the words above and beneath a cross in a glass stained window in a church in the Kentuckian town of Louisville. The cross of Christ's atoning death does indeed tell us to look up and find in Him who died for us, the cancelling of the sinful past, the bringing of untold blessing in the present, and the making known of unparalleled glory for the future. But the cross, as the expression of what Christ has done for us, lifts us, as Matheson expresses it,

" O Cross, that liftest up mine head."

The Cross of Christ's atoning death, as we look to Him who died thereon, lifts from :—

1. THE THRALDOM OF SELF.—" He died for all, that they which live should not live unto themselves " (2 Cor. v. 15).

2. THE TRAVERSITY OF THE WORLD.—" The Cross of our Lord Jesus Christ, by whom the world is crucified unto me, and I unto the world " (Gal. vi. 14).

3. THE TYRANNY OF SIN.—" He died unto sin once . . . Likewise reckon ye also yourselves to be dead unto sin " (Rom. vi. 10, 11).

4. THE OLD MAN OF HABIT.—" Knowing this our old man is crucified with Him " (Rom. vi. 6).

5. THE SELF OF SINFUL SELF.—" I am crucified with Christ " (Gal. ii. 20).

6. THE LUSTS AND AFFECTIONS OF THE FLESH.—" They that are Christ's have crucified the flesh with the affections and lusts " (Gal. v. 24).

7. THE WORKS OF THE DEVIL.—" The Son of God was manifested, that He might destroy the works of the devil " (1 John iii. 8).

" CUT IN "—IN HIS HANDS

Behold, I have graven thee upon the palms of My hands."— Isa. xlix. 16.

The late George Silwood, of Keswick, in speaking of his safety in Christ, to a minister of the Gospel, said, " My

name is graven in the palms of His hands—that is, *cut in*.
Why, His hands would have to be *cut off* before He could
forget me."

There is a seven-fold cord which binds believers to Christ.
They are :—

1. Given TO Christ (John xvii. 2).
2. Saved BY Him (Rom. v. 9).
3. Secure IN Him (Rom. viii. 38, 39).
4. Hid WITH Him (Col. iii. 3).
5. Kept THROUGH Him (1 Peter i. 5).
6. United AS Him (1 Cor. xii. 12, 13).
7. Supplied FROM Him (Phil. iv. 19).

DAILY

" *To-day*."—Heb. iii. 13.

An older Christian in speaking to a younger one, said,
" My dear, as each day, the body needs food, and brings
its privileges and responsibilities, so does the Christian life."

True religion is an every day affair, not something
limited to special occasions and set times, as on the Sabbath,
for instance, when one wends his way to church, apparently
very pious and devout in outward countenance and carriage.
Then back again on Monday in the whirl of business, politics,
pleasure ; where " the world, the flesh and the devil " crack
the slave-driver's whip over him all the week through, with
hardly a moment left for Bible reading, prayer, and serious
reflection. A religion that is the genuine article will be
capitalised seven days in the week, 365 days in the year.

And it may be worth while to notice the insistent emphasis
that the Bible puts on the term " daily," as it relates to the
duties and obligations of the professed servant of God.

1. DAILY PRAYER.—" Be merciful unto me, O Lord ; for
I cry unto Thee daily " (Ps. lxxxvi. 3). We cannot live the
Christian life aright, it is doubtful if we can live it at all,
without this daily habit of prayer. For " Prayer is the
Christian's vital breath, the Christian's native air." That
busy man of affairs, the prime-minister of the Medo-Persian
empire, Daniel, felt the imperative importance of it, as he
daily climbed the palace stairs to his chamber of prayer.

The neglect of daily prayer is the hidden secret of many a sad trip into sin and fatal fall from grace.

2. DAILY PARDON.—This fundamental truth stood at the very fore in the ceremonial teaching of the ancient Tabernacle and Temple service. " And thou shalt offer every day a bullock for a sin offering " (Exod. xxix. 36). Not simply once a year, upon the Great Day of Atonement, but day by day was the smoke of a burning sacrifice for sin to ascend unto God. Daily are our spiritual garments filled with the dust, the ashes and the grime of this sinful world, in our pilgrimage to Heaven. Daily, then, do we need the cleansing blood of " the Lamb of God which taketh away the sin of the world."

3. DAILY FOOD.—" Give us this day our daily bread " (Matt. vi. 11). And this needed bread is no less spiritual than material, for " Man shall not live by bread alone, but by every word that proceedeth out of the mouth of God." While we daily attend to the wants of the body, we must not be indifferent to the more important needs of the soul. Otherwise our spiritual nature will grow anæmic and dyspeptic." Blessed are they which do hunger and thirst after righteousness."

4. DAILY GRATITUDE.—" Blessed be the Lord who daily loaded us with benefits " (Ps. lxviii. 19). No need to wait for an annual Thanksgiving Day to lump the thought of God's goodness towards us in one formal expression of gratitude. Every day should be Thanksgiving Day ; and daily should the child of God be a walking doxology of praise, with the heart question daily upon his lips, " What shall I render unto the Lord for all His benefits toward me ? " Count your mercies, and let the spirit of gratitude fragrance your daily life.

5. DAILY VIGILANCE.—" Take heed, lest there be in any of you an evil heart of unbelief, in departing from the living God. But exhort one another daily, lest any of you be hardened through the deceitfulness of sin " (Heb. iii. 12, 13). Daily watchfulness against our soul enemies is demanded. For not only does our adversary, the devil, walk about as a roaring lion, seeking whom he may devour : but he also assumes the disguise of " an angel of light " in order to deceive and destroy. Be vigilant. Off guard we are in danger.

6. DAILY CROSS-BEARING.—" And He said unto them, if any man will come after Me, let him deny himself, and take up his cross daily and follow Me " (Luke ix. 23). Not left to some notable day, when you are focused in the limelight for public applause for some heroic and self-denying act. But do it daily, in the thousand and one things, whether big or little, seen or unseen, that make up the sum total of your every day life. It is not the spectacular " stunt " before the grandstand, and the bleachers that brings the Divine acclaim, but the daily martyrdom, of which the world knows nothing and cares less. Christ knows ; that is enough.

7. DAILY SANCTIFICATION.—" I die daily " (1 Cor. xv. 31). Figuratively set forth in the sacrifice of " the whole burnt offering." " After this manner ye shall offer daily, throughout the seven days " (Num. xxviii. 24). In the whole burnt offering, as distinguished from the sin offering, the entire sacrifice was consumed. This typified the complete consecration of the person, body, mind, and soul to God. " A sacrifice well-pleasing to Him." Daily dying unto sin ; daily living unto holiness. Day by day made more fit for the Master's use. Day by day better prepared for heaven.

8. DAILY STRENGTH.—" As thy days, so shall thy strength be " (Deut. xxxiii. 25). You are not to be stocked up with strength in the bulk, to carry you through a long period of time, or a long stretch of journey. As the need, the supply. Strength day by day to plod the King's Highway to Zion ; to fight the good fight of faith ; to suffer loss and pain for Christ's sake ; to perform the work to which He has called you. " My God shall supply all your need, according to His riches in glory by Christ Jesus."

9. DAILY USE OF THE BIBLE.—" These were more noble than those in Thessalonica, in that they received the Word with all readiness of mind, and searched the Scriptures daily, whether those things were so " (Acts xvii. 11). A good example and a fine incentive are set for us by these Berean converts. " Search the Scriptures " should be a daily motto : and to search it like those that dig into it " as for hid treasure." That man gets more wealth out of his gold-mine who works it diligently every day, from Monday until Saturday night, than the one who merely stretches its surface

one day in the week. The rich treasure veins of promise and invitation, warning and instruction, stimulus and hope, are in profuse abundance in the mine of Inspired Truth. And all ours for the daily digging.

10. DAILY INGATHERING OF BELIEVERS.—" And the Lord added to the Church daily such as should be saved " (Acts ii. 47). " And so were the churches established in the faith, and increased in number daily " (Acts xvi. 5). These early Christians did not limit God's convicting and converting power in the salvation of sinners, as we moderns frequently do, to some special season or time of the year, and to stagnate in apathy and indifference for the rest of the twelve months, until the period arrives for starting another " Big Meeting."

That Apostolic Church was a veritable " Soul-Winners' Society," that believed in daily going out after lost sinners with the sweet invitation, " Come thou with us, and we will do thee good." " Back to the apostolic method ! " would not be a bad slogan for the churches.

As we face the day, knowing not what it holds in store for each of us, nor whether we shall see it close, we could not do a better thing than to incorporate this daily type of religion into our profession and practice. " For the sanctification of the daily life means sanctification of the whole life." And it is the only safeguard and guarantee against an unconscious drift into formalism of creed, with a glacier-like slide into worldliness of life, terminating in a final plunge into black apostasy.

He who lives his daily life for God will live forever above with God.

DEATH OF CHRIST

" *Signifying what death He should die.*"—John xi. 51 ; xii. 24, 33 ; xviii. 14.

In the gallery at Dusseldorf there is a painting with a history. It is the Crucifixion of Christ, by the German artist Sternberg. While he was painting it he called to his studio a very pretty gipsy girl who sat for a character sketch from day to day, and whose attention was attracted to this beautiful painting of Christ. One day she asked the painter who that Man was that they were treating so cruelly, and if He was a very bad Man. He told her He was a good Man, the best Man that had ever lived, and that He was dying for others that He might save them. She was very much touched, and she said to him, " I should think that you would love Him very much, for if anybody did that for me I should be willing to die for Him." Through this message the painter was led eventually to give his own heart to the Saviour. At length the painting was hung up in the great gallery, and among the thousands who came to admire it was a German Count of high rank and great worldly prospects. But the picture so impressed him that it changed his whole life. As he gazed upon it, the Master seemed to say to him :

" All this I did for thee.
What hast thou done for Me ? "

And he went back to his estates to consecrate his life, his means and his influence to the founding of the greatest missionary society of modern times. He was no other than Count Zinzendorf, the founder of the Moravian Society, which still leads modern Christendom in missionary zeal and unselfishness. Necessity was laid on him, and the law of love made him a missionary.

At the same time another form was kneeling before the painting. It was the little gipsy girl, and as she looked up at that heavenly face she gave a little cry, " Oh, I wish He had died for me ! " Then the painter was able to return the blessings he had brought to him, and he told the trembling little heart that He had died for her, and she went away rejoicing in salvation. A few months later that painter was called to her deathbed, and as she looked in his face, with tears of joy she could say, " Yes, He died for me, and I am going to die for Him and live with Him forever."

Seven facts about the death of Christ :

1. He PROPHESIED of His death (John xii. 24).

2. The PURPOSE of His death. " Christ died for our sins " (1 Cor. xv. 3).

68

3. The PEOPLE for whom He died—" ungodly," " us " (Rom. v. 6, 8).

4. The POWER of His death to deliver from the world and its evil (Gal. i. 4).

5. The PURIFYING effect of His blood, cleansing the conscience from penalty and pollution (Heb. ix. 14).

6. The POTENTIALITY of His death, causing us to die to sin and self (Romans vi. 1-13).

7. The PROPITIATION, or satisfaction of His death, meeting all the requirements of God (Rom. iii. 25).

DIVINE HEALING

" *The Lord that healeth thee.*"—Exod. xv. 26.

A Mrs. Jordan, who had always been a spiritually-minded woman had a long illness. She had a class in the Wesleyan Sunday school, and told a representative of a London Daily that she had received a divine message that she was about to be cured. She said she was " absolutely convinced that it was the Divine Healer who had cured her, and to Him must be given all the praise."

We have purposely refrained from making any comment upon the above interesting incident, as recorded in the Western edition of the London *Daily Chronicle*, rather letting it speak for itself. The newspaper says she believed in " faith-healing," but she herself said, " It was the Divine Healer who had cured her." This is a distinction with a difference, for in the one case emphasis is laid on faith and attention is drawn to the human who trusts, but in the other testimony is borne to the One who heals and the thought and attention is directed to Him.

There are four reasons, if in the line of the Lord's will, why we may expect healing of the body.

1. Because of the CHARACTER OF JEHOVAH. He is Jehovah Ropheca, the Lord that healeth (Exod. xv. 26).

2. Because CHRIST BARE OUR SICKNESSES, as well as carried our sins and sorrows (Isa. liii. 4, R.V.M.).

3. Because of what THE HOLY SPIRIT CAN DO. He can make alive our mortal bodies (Rom. viii. 11).

4. Because of what THE LORD PROMISES. He says " The prayer of faith shall save the sick " (James v. 15).

DIVINITY OF DRUDGERY

" *Eateth not the bread of idleness.*"—Prov. xxxi. 27.

One has said of the Spirit of Drudgery :

" ' A man may sit upon an office stool till all his bones are dried and full of chalk '—so sings Tennyson—or he may have to make one kind of rivet thousands of times over, and though the monotony may starve the tastes of the worker, it does not detract from the merit of his work. But that narrowed-down condition of mind will not do for a woman if she is tending an infant or nursing the sick, even though the same wants are repeated day by day.

" If the spirit of drudgery comes in, it is not only her own heart, but her work that suffers. Life must be met by life. The growing plant cannot be dealt with by the sledge-hammer of determined energy, nor even by the fine chisel of skill ; it is the human hand alone that must train and tie it, and pluck off the useless leaves."

To fill the common place, and to do the ordinary round, is to find the extraordinary in the ordinary.

1. It was while Gideon THRESHED THE WHEAT, he was called to be a victor for Israel (Judges vi. 11, 12).

2. It was while the shepherds KEPT THEIR FLOCKS, they heard the angels (Luke ii. 8, 18).

3. It was while the disciples were ABOUT THEIR BUSINESS they were called to be fishers of men (Matt. iv. 18, 19).

4. It was when Matthew was at the RECEIPT OF CUSTOM, he was bidden to follow Jesus (Mark ii. 14).

5. It was David's experience in CONQUERING the lion and the bear, that qualified him to conquer Goliath (1 Sam. xvii. 34-37).

6. It was while the early Christians PRAYED, the Holy Spirit came upon them in power (Acts i. 14 ; ii. 1-4 ; iv. 31)

7. It was after Elijah had REPAIRED the altar, laid the wood in order, and the sacrifice on the altar, that the fire fell (1 Kings xviii. 30-38).

DOLDRUMS : " IN THE DOLDRUMS ! "

" Come from the four winds, O breath and breathe on these slain, that they may live."—Ezek. xxxvii. 9.

Mr. Henry Varley once related : " I can remember, when a young man, going to Australia in a sailing vessel, and we got caught in the ' Doldrums,' that belt where at certain seasons of the year there is a great calm, and where sailing-ships may be delayed for days, or weeks, or even for months, vainly seeking a breeze to carry them on their voyage. Oh, it was hot as we lay helpless on the glassy sea ! Oh, the inertia, the unpleasantness of it, as the ship became heated with the tropical warmth of the sun ! One day I was looking over the taffrail at the unrippled sea, and there came just an incipient wind, just a moving of the air, a breath, and I could see the surface of the water broken in its glassiness as the wind with a feather touch caught it. This was the coming of the wind, and in two or three hours we had caught the trade wind, and the canvas of the vessel was gradually filling to the breeze, and within twelve hours she was speeding on her voyage like a thing of life. How many Christians are there who are in the ' Doldrums ' ! They are lying motionless ; they have no wind from heaven to fill their sails and waft them on the voyage heavenwards, and in many instances it is because they have not spread their sails to catch the heavenly, celestial breezes."

As the wind is the power to move the sailing vessel, so is the Spirit to move us.

1. THE BREATH OF LIFE TO INSPIRE.—As the breath of God made man a living soul (Gen. ii. 7), so the Spirit is the Life of grace to inspire us.

2. THE KINDLING BREATH —As the wind kindles the fire, so the Spirit fires us with His love (Job xli. 21).

3. THE SLAYING BREATH.—As the breath will put out the candle, so the Spirit can cause the flame of sin to cease (Isa. xi. 4).

4. SUSTAINING BREATH.—As the breath sustains the lungs, so the Spirit is the Power that sustains us in life (Dan. v. 23).

5. UNITING BREATH.—As the breath unites soul and body together, so the Spirit of God unites us to the Lord (James ii. 26).

" DON'T PASS THE CROSS ! "

" The Cross of our Lord Jesus Christ."—Gal. vi. 14.

When being motored from one place to another in Somerset, England, we were not sure of the road to take as we were approaching Cheddar, so we did the wise thing and asked a master builder on the roadside, " Would you kindly direct us to Wells ? "

Immediately came the response from the man who knew : " Keep right on ; don't pass the cross, but turn to the right when you come to it ! " The direction was explicit, direct, and suggestive. " Don't pass the Cross," for the

1. " BLOOD of the Cross " is the price of our redemption (Col. i. 20).

2. The LIGHT of the Cross is the light of Heaven's grace (2 Cor. iv. 6 ; Isa. lii. 14).

3. The DEATH of the Cross is the deliverer from sin's menace (1 Peter ii. 24).

4. The VICTORY of the Cross is the triumph of Christ's achievement (Col. ii. 14, 15).

5. The MESSAGE of the Cross is the unfolding of God's love (1 John iv. 9, 10).

6. The GLORY of the Cross is the fellowship it brings (Gal. vi. 14).

7. The WEALTH of the Cross is seen in the blessings which come by means of it (Acts iii. 14-19).

DOUBLES

" Just weight and balance are the Lord's."—Prov. xvi. 11.

One has said, " Hope is like the cork to the net, which keeps the soul from sinking in despair ; and fear is like the lead to the net, which keeps it from floating in presumption."

God's doubles always keep things evenly balanced, thus faith and works are the complement the one to the other, for works prove the root of faith, and faith declares itself in the fruit of works (James ii. 17-20). This same balance is declared in every truth of the Gospel. Let the following doubles speak for themselves :—

1. JUSTIFICATION.—The sinner who believes on the Lord Jesus is justified by grace without works before God (Rom. iv. 5, 6) ; but his faith is justified by works before men (James ii. 21-26).

2. ELECTION.—The assured election in Christ of those who are " chosen in Him " is clearly stated (Eph. i. 4) ; but the elect prove their election by making it " sure " in adding to their faith what the Spirit enjoins (2 Peter i. 5-10).

3. SANCTIFICATION.—There is positional sanctification, which is secured by the will of God through the means of Christ's perfect atonement for us (Heb. x. 10) ; and there is the practical sanctification which is the result of the former. Mark the " have been " and " perfected " of Heb. x. 10, 14, R.V., on the one hand, and the " being sanctified " on the other.

4. ETERNAL LIFE.—Eternal life is the gift of God in Christ which has laid hold of us to our blessing and betterment, and yet we are urged to " lay hold " of it to our uplifting and progress in the spirituality of its power (Rom. vi. 23 ; 1 Tim. vi. 12).

5. SALVATION.—Salvation from sin's guilt and government is of grace as to its source and substance ; but we manifest our knowledge of the grace of God by godliness, righteousness, and self-mastery, for the grace that saves teaches these things (Titus ii. 11-14).

If we would keep warm in the Christian life we must see that we are clothed with the double garments of the Spirit, and thus correspond to the wise and model woman of the Book of Proverbs, for of her we read, " All her household are clothed with double garments " (Prov. xxxi. 21, marg.).

DRINK : A TRAMP'S TESTIMONY

" Strong drink is raging."—Prov. xx. 1.

A tramp asked for a drink in a saloon. The request was granted, and when in the act of drinking the proffered beverage one of the young men present exclaimed :

" Stop ! Make us a speech. It is poor liquor that doesn't loosen a man's tongue."

The tramp swallowed down the drink, and as the liquor coursed through his blood, he straightened himself and stood before them with a grace and dignity which all his rags and dirt could not obscure.

" Gentlemen," he said, " I look to-night at you and myself, and it seems to me that I look upon the picture of my blighted manhood. This bloated face was once as handsome as yours ; this shambling figure once walked as proudly as yours, for I was a man of the world of men. I, too, once had a home and friends and position. I had a wife as beautiful as an artist's dream, but I dropped the priceless pearl of her honour and respect into a cup of wine, and, like Cleopatra, saw it dissolve, then quaffed it down in the brimming draught. I had children sweet and pure as the flowers of spring, and saw them fade and die under the blighting curse of a drunken father. I had a home where love lit its flame upon the altar and ministered before it, but I put out the holy fire, and darkness and desolation reigned in its stead. I had aspirations which soared as high as the morning star, but I broke and bruised those beautiful forms, and strangled them, that I might hear the cries no more. To-day I am a husband without a wife, a father without a child, a tramp without a home, and a man in whom every impulse is dead. All have been swallowed up in the maelstrom of drink."

The tramp ceased speaking. The glass fell from his nervous fingers, and shattered into a thousand fragments on the floor. The doors were pushed open and shut again, and when the group looked up the tramp was gone.

And this, gentle reader, is a true tale, the tramp at one time having been a prominent attorney at Tiffin.

1. FOLLOW the wisdom of the wise man, and be not deceived by drink (Prov. xx. 1).

2. IMITATE the action of the three Hebrews who would not touch the food and wine that was set before them because of its association (Dan. i. 12).

3. OBEY the Divine injunction and give not the bottle to your neighbour (Hab. ii. 15).

4. BE WARNED by the fall of Noah, who disgraced himself through drink (Gen. ix. 20-25).

5. REMEMBER the consecrated Nazarite, who would have broken his vow if he touched drink (Num. vi. 1-4).

6. CALL TO MIND the sin of Aaron's sons, who evidently offered strange fire to the Lord, through drink, for the priests were prohibited from using it directly afterwards (Lev. x. 1-11).

7. BE LIKE the Rechabites, who would not drink wine (Jer. xxxv. 14-19).

EARNESTNESS

" *Like the driving of Jehu, he driveth furiously.*"—2 Kings ix. 20.

No man ever yet carried out God's commission to His generation without fierce driving. No tower was ever yet taken in any war without the rush. No capture was ever yet made without an intense and rapid struggle. One said to a French soldier in the streets of Paris, who was showing his wounds, an old Crimean veteran, " What about the Alma ? what about Malakoff ? " He said, " We took it with a rush." So God's messengers everywhere take things with a rush. Jehu drives furiously because he has got a commission of God, he puts all his strength into it. His horses' feet seem barely to touch the ground ; more like with wings does that steed make his way across the plain. The King's business requireth haste. You will never do your life's work for God with your hands in your pocket, you will never do it with open mouth. You will have to do it with teeth firmly set, with a purpose resolved on, with a resolution that come what will you keep the ribbons in your own hands and drive where God would have you to be. This is an age of furious driving, and we would not have it otherwise.

1. WORK EARNESTLY, like Baruch in his work at repairing (Neh. iii. 20).

2. SPEAK EARNESTLY, like Nehemiah, who "earnestly requested" of the king what he desired (Neh. xiii. 6, marg.).

3. PRAY EARNESTLY, like Christ in His agonised prayer in Gethsemane (Luke xxii. 44).

4. COVET EARNESTLY, as we are enjoined to "covet earnestly the best gifts" (1 Cor. xii. 31).

5. CONTEND EARNESTLY, as Jude urges us to "contend earnestly for the faith once delivered to the saints" (Jude 3).

6. DESIRE EARNESTLY, as Paul expresses it, when he says, "Earnestly desiring" (2 Cor. v. 2).

7. HEED EARNESTLY, as we are told in Hebrew ii. 1, "To give the more earnest heed lest at any time we should be like leaky vessels" (marg.).

END OF LIFE

"Alive unto God."—Rom. vi. 11.

A recent writer in *Public Opinion* says : "Many years ago Emerson remarked that ' men are so prone to mistake the means for the end, that even natural history has its pedants who mistake classification for knowledge . . . .'

"That, in our opinion, is precisely what has happened to the sorely troubled world of to-day. It has fastened its attention upon the machinery of life, has ignored the one supreme human purpose for which all machinery exists, and now, in the resulting chaos, is amazed to find that the machinery fails to function. Let us be still more specific, and say that the supreme purpose in any rational life is the unfolding and perfecting of the human spirit."

The above suggests many questions.

1. WHAT IS " THE HUMAN SPIRIT " ?—Man as a spirit denotes man in his individuality and intelligence (1 Cor. ii. 11).

2. WHAT IS THE " PERFECTING OF THE HUMAN SPIRIT " ?—Man as man, means self-consciousness ; and the man who knows Christ has God-consciousness, and is " alive unto God," to do as He directs (Rom. vi. 11).

3. WHAT IS THE " MACHINERY OF LIFE " ?—Machinery has to do with the power of production ; therefore its life is to live only to produce material things (Eph. ii. 10).

4. WHAT IS MEANT WHEN THE " MACHINERY FAILS TO FUNCTION " ?—It means the end for which the machinery was made does not produce what was intended. Man's chief end is to glorify God, and when he does not " function," he is a failure (1 Cor. x. 31).

5. WHY IS THE WORLD " SORELY TROUBLED TO-DAY " ?—The reason why the world is " sorely troubled," is because men do not know Him who says, " Come unto Me, all ye that labour and are heavy laden, and I will give you rest " (Matt. xi. 28). Every one is restless and troubled who has not " come."

EPITAPH : JOHN WESLEY'S

" *Whose faith follow.*"—Heb. xiii. 7.

John Wesley wrote his own epitaph : " Here lieth the body of John Wesley, a brand plucked out of the burning, not leaving after his debts are paid ten pounds behind him ; praying God be merciful to me an unprofitable servant ! "

Three things are acknowledged by John Wesley in his epitaph :

1. SALVATION.—" Is not this a brand plucked out of the fire " ? (Zech. iii. 2). The " brand " signifies a " burning brand," that which is being consumed. What a picture of a sinner being consumed by sin. " Plucked " means to be snatched away, to be delivered from the consuming power. Salvation from sin by the blood of Christ means deliverance from sinning and hell.

2. SERVICE.—" Whose I am and whom I serve " (Acts

77

xxvii. 23) is another way of expressing John Wesley's penury. He was stingy to himself, and a supplying one to others.

3. SUPPLICATION.—John Wesley felt his unprofitableness ; hence his prayer for mercy. God's mercy is sovereign in its grace (Rom. ix. 15-18), helpful in its encouragement (2 Cor. iv. 1), considerate in its bestowment (1 Tim. i. 15), practical in its issue (1 Tim. i. 16), quickening in its life (Eph. ii. 4, 5), helpful in its ministry (Heb. iv. 16), and gladdening for the future (1 Peter i. 3).

ESSENTIAL

" Behold, to obey is better than sacrifice."—1 Sam. xv. 22.

Laura Richards has a parable of a child who so admired a new ruler that he hung it upon the wall to look at, but he never used it. His writing was therefore crooked. It is not enough to look at God, we must obey Him and use His power as it comes to us. And it is not enough to read, or even to defend the Bible. We need to direct our daily work and conduct according to its teaching.

The whole of the Christian life is summed up in the word " obey." If we read through the Book of Deuteronomy alone, we see how the Spirit of God emphasises the importance and influence of obedience.

1. Obedience is the PROOF OF REPENTANCE.—" If thou return unto the Lord, and shalt be obedient unto His voice " (iv. 30). The evidence of having returned to the Lord is response to Him in obedience.

2. Obedience is the PROCURER OF BLESSING.—" A blessing if ye obey the commandments of the Lord thy God " (xi. 27, 28). We command the Lord's blessings when we respond to the Lord's Word.

3. Obedience is the PREVENTOR OF CONTAMINATION.— " Ye shall . . . obey His voice. . . . So shalt thou put the evil away " (xiii. 1-5). Obedience is the circle which encloses us and separates from the evil around.

4. Obedience is the EVIDENCE OF RELATIONSHIP.—" Thou art become the people of the Lord thy God, thou shalt therefore obey the voice of the Lord thy God " (xxvii. 9, 10).

Because the Lord is " Thy God," we are under obligation to do His will.

5. Obedience is the SECRET OF VICTORY.—" Obey His voice . . . then the Lord thy God will turn thy captivity " (xxx. 2, 3). Obedience is the hand that knocks off the fetters of bondage, and the cause of freedom in the Lord's service.

6. Obedience is the SOUL OF PROSPERITY.—" Obey the voice of the Lord thy God . . . the Lord thy God will make thee plenteous in every work " (xxx. 8, 9). The prosperity of the soul, is the soul of all prosperity.

7. Obedience is the MEANS OF LONGEVITY.—" Obey His voice . . . for He is thy life, and the length of thy days " (xxx. 20). Length of days, and loyalty to the Lord, are bound together as cause and effect.

ETERNAL LIFE

" This is the true God and eternal Life."—1 John v. 20.

It is astonishing how little men know of what the Bible teaches about eternal life. Some would tell us, it is " the propagation of the race " ; others, it is " a perfect correspondence to our environment," and the following article, from the Detroit *Free Press*, summarises it, " continued physical existence." Let the article speak for itself : " Although he prudently refrains from making any sweeping, definite prophecy, Dr. Will Durant, formerly professor of philosophy at Columbia, remarks that ' eternal life ' (by which he means continuing physical existence without experience of death) is ' not an impossibility.' He insists that there ' is nothing either in science or in philosophy inconsistent with the idea of eventual immortality of the body.'

" The doctor certainly is optimistic, particularly in view of the fact that there is no reason to consider the earth which harbours man anything but finite and destined to dissolution, or at least to moonlike barrenness, sooner or later.

" While it is perhaps conceivable as a flight of fancy that a human being might continue in the flesh as long as the world lives (Dean Swift, Frank R. Stockton, H. Rider Haggard, and other romancers have imagined this more or less vividly), the imagination droops a little when called upon to invent a way in which the human animal or any other animal can persist after air, water, food, and even the earth itself have vanished. If Dr. Durant has a theory how this can be done, he certainly should inform an anxious world."

One essentiality is not recognised by the above—namely, eternal life and eternal existence are not one and the same. The Word of God distinctly says : " He that hath the Son hath life, but he that hath not the Son of God hath not life " (1 John v. 12).

Westcott says : " Eternal life is not a period of existence in time, but that which has to do with the Being of God." Eternal life is the specific message of the Gospel.

1. MEN are devoid of this life naturally—hence Christ came that they might have it (John x. 10), and till they come to Him they have not got it (John v. 40).

2. The ESSENCE of eternal life and its meaning, Christ declares, is union with the Father by means of Himself, who is the Life (John xiv. 6 ; xvii. 3).

3. FAITH in Christ is the only means by which this life can be obtained (John iii. 36).

4. This life is the GIFT OF GOD, and not an attainment of man's (Rom. vi. 23).

5. Eternal life finds its EMBODIMENT and expression IN CHRIST, who is called " The Eternal Life " (1 John v. 20).

6. PARTICIPATION WITH CHRIST by feeding upon Him by means of His Word, is the enjoyment of this life (John vi. 53, 63).

7. The FULNESS OF THIS LIFE will be experienced when Christ comes again, for " when Christ, who is our Life, shall appear, then we shall be manifested with Him in glory " (Col. iii. 4).

FACT OF CHRIST

" *This is He that came by water and blood.*"—1 John v. 6.

Mr. Belloc, the famous journalist, does not like the Modernist School. " Whence springs," he asks, " this lust for saying that the Gospel of St. John was not written by St. John, that Homer was not written by Homer, that the

Battle of Hastings was not called the Battle of Hastings ? "
He gives three reasons which, he declares, urge Dons to make
fools of themselves. First of all there is the vanity of learned
men ; second, the love of the marvellous ; and third, the
perpetual substitution of hypothesis for fact, which ends by
getting men into a state of mind where they can no longer
weigh the proportions of evidence.

Again and again we find the words, " This is " in the
Gospels, in relation to the fact of Christ.

1. " THIS IS MY BELOVED SON " (Matt. iii. 17).—The
One who went down into the Jordan of our death, is the
Object of Heaven's delight.

2. " THIS IS THE HEIR " (Matt. xxi. 38).—Everything
belongs to Christ, is in His hands, and for His glory. He,
who misses Him, misses everything.

3. " THIS IS MY BODY " (Matt. xxvi. 26), and " blood "
(Matt. xxvi. 28), proclaim worth and work for us on the
Cross.

4. " THIS IS HE " (John i. 30), the One " preferred," the
Lamb of God, whom John proclaimed. Behold Him, love
Him, and follow Him.

5. " THIS IS THE SON OF GOD " (John i. 34).—He proved
what He was by what He did, and the gift of the Holy Spirit.

6. " THIS IS INDEED THE CHRIST " (John iv. 42).—The
Messiah, the Sent One, and the Anointed Lord evidenced
His Christ-ship.

7. " THIS IS THE BREAD WHICH COMETH FROM HEAVEN "
(John vi. 50, 58).—He meets the need of men, and satisfies
all who receive Him.

FAITH, HOPE, AND LOVE

" *Now abideth faith, hope, and love.*"—1 Cor. xiii. 13.

A pastor sought to comfort a young dying doctor in the
North of England by telling him, " The past is all answered
for in the death of Christ's atonement ; the present is all
provided for in Christ's shepherd care ; and the future is
all secured in Christ's coming glory."

The three graces, faith, love, and hope, have their own
outlook and emphasis.

1. Faith's witness is, " He bore my sins in His own body on the tree " (1 Pet. ii. 24) ; Love's witness is, " I love Him because He first loved me " (1 John iv. 19). Hope's witness is, " I shall be satisfied when I awake in His likeness " (Ps. xvii. 15).

2. Faith sings, " He loved me and gave Himself for me " (Gal. ii. 20). Love sings, " Having loved His own, He loves them to the uttermost " (John xiii. 1) ; and hope sings, " Kept by the power of God, unto the salvation ready to be revealed " (1 Pet. i. 5).

3. Faith emphasises the death of Christ as the starting point of the Christian life, " I declared unto you first of all, Christ died " (1 Cor. xv. 3). Love emphasises the life of Christ in His resurrection power as the lifting power to the higher life, " That I may know Him and the power of His resurrection " (Phil. iii. 10) ; and hope emphasises the kinship of Christ and anticipates His Kingly glory by knowing His Kingly sway in the heart now. " Sanctify Christ as Lord in the heart " (1 Pet. iii. 15, R.V.).

FAITH'S LANGUAGE

" Whose faith follow."—Heb. xiii. 7.

It is a good thing to so work that we are willing to have the work of our hands established. Spurgeon once said : " My brother said to me the other day what Charles Wesley said to John Wesley, ' Brother, our people die well ! ' I answered, ' Assuredly they do ! ' I have never been to the sickbed of any of our people without feeling strengthened in faith. In the sight of their glorious confidence, I could sooner battle with the whole earth, and kick it before me like a football, than have a doubt in my mind about the Gospel of our Lord. They die gloriously. I saw, last week, a dear sister with cancer just under her eye. How did I find her ? Was she lamenting her hard fate ? By no means ; she was happy, calm, joyful, in bright expectation of seeing the face of the King in His beauty. I talked with a tradesman who fell asleep not long ago, and I said, ' You seem to have no fears ? ' ' No,' he said, ' how can I have any ? You have not taught us what will make us fear. How can I be afraid to die, since I have fed these thirty years on the strong meat of the kingdom of God ? I know whom I have believed.' I had a heavenly time with him. I cannot use a lower word. He exhibited a holy mirth in the expectation of a speedy removal to the better world. Now, dear brethren, thrice happy shall we be, if we can say, in the last hour, ' I have not shunned to declare the whole counsel of God.' "

The testimony of those who have passed on in the Faith of Christ is always inspiring and faith-begetting. The men of Faith have always been positive in their testimonies.

1. JOB COULD SAY, " I know that my Redeemer liveth " (Job xix. 25).

2. PAUL AFFIRMED, " I know whom I have believed " (2 Tim. i. 12).

3. JOHN PROCLAIMED, " We know we have passed from death to life " (1 John iii. 14).

4. ISAIAH WITNESSED, " Behold, God is my Salvation " (Isa. xii. 2).

5. PETER WROTE, " Who His own Self bare our sins on the tree " (1 Peter ii. 24).

6. DAVID SANG, " The Lord is my Rock and Fortress " (Ps. xviii. 2).

7. HABAKKUK JOYOUSLY EXCLAIMED, " The Lord God is my Strength " (Hab. iii. 19).

FAITH " SPREAD ABROAD "

" *In every place your faith to God-ward is spread abroad ; so that we need not to speak anything.*"—1 Thess. i. 8.

A learned Chinaman said to a missionary : " I like your doctrine, though I never heard you preach. I have seen it. My servant was a devil before he professed your religion, and now he is like an angel. I can trust him with everything, and he is in love with everybody."

Some of the most practical things are those about which no word is spoken.

1. Thus the WIDOW with her two mites spoke of GIVING (Luke xxi. 2).

2. MARY's broken box of ointment told out her LOVING (John xii. 3).

3. The WEEPING WOMAN by her tears manifested her BELIEVING (Luke vii. 38).

4. The WOMEN by their gifts declared the character of their MINISTRY (Luke viii. 3).

5. The WISE MEN by their offerings showed forth the heart of their LONGING (Matt. ii. 11).

6. The SHEPHERDS by their obedience evidenced their ALACRITY (Luke ii. 15).

7. The THESSALONIANS by their practical faith manifested its REALITY (1 Thess. i. 9).

" FIVE ALLS "

" All grace . . . always . . . all sufficiency . . . all things . . . every (all) good work."—2 Cor. ix. 8.

There are practically five " alls " in the above Scripture sentences.

Between Stratford-on-Avon and Bidford, in the county of Warwickshire, there is a country inn with the sign of " The Five Alls," and on the sign are painted the sun, a soldier, a ploughman, a lawyer, and the King. The meaning of which is, The sun shines upon all, the soldier fights for all, the ploughman ploughs for all, the lawyer pleads for all, and the King rules over all.

Among the many " alls " in the Scriptures are five which embody the message of the Gospel.

1. SIN.—" All have sinned, and come short of the glory of God " (Rom. iii. 23). To sin means not wrong-doing merely, but to miss the mark of God's requirements as expressed in the ten commandments, and to come short of God's holiness, righteousness, truth, love, and the Lord Jesus Christ. Christ is God's Perfect Ideal of what man ought to be.

2. SACRIFICE.—Of Christ in His death, it is written, " He gave Himself a Ransom for all " (1 Tim. ii. 6). Literally, it means " a procuring price." He laid down His life for all. The sacrifice He made was—" Himself." No one but Himself could pay the price, nothing less than giving His life could meet the need and the requirement. Nothing else

is needed, for He has given what was demanded. Those who receive Him know the loosing power of that ransom.

3. SUPPLY.—" Freely give us all things " (Rom. viii. 32). The greater includes the lesser. Since God has not spared His Son, He will not spare us anything. " All blessings " are ours (Eph. i. 3), " all grace " (2 Cor. ix. 8), " all might " (Col. i. 11), " all promises " (2 Cor. i. 20), and " all things " (1 Cor. iii. 21-23). With such a store we cannot starve, and with such a supply we shall have plenty to pass on to others.

4. SANCTIFICATION.—" To redeem us from all iniquity," was one of the purposes for which Christ died (Titus ii. 14). " Iniquity " means lawlessness, and lawlessness is man's self-will in opposition to God's will. Self-will is the essence of sin—any want of conformity to the will of God.

5. SERVICE.—" Whatsoever ye do, in word or deed, do all in the Name of the Lord Jesus " (Col. iii. 17, 23). If all we say and do, in all the relationships of life, are done in the Lord's name, all will be well done ; for to act in His name means to act as He would act, and with His authority and sanction.

FIVE : A SPEAKING NUMERAL

" Five porches."—John v. 2.

Very many superstitions have been, and are still, connected with numbers. In China, the " big five " is the most important and luckiest numeral, and they try to do everything by fives. For example, all reckoning must be by five and the multiples thereof. It is very fortunate to buy or sell on those dates in the calendar—weddings, birth ceremonies, journeys, and funerals must always be chosen with this in mind. An old Christian remarked that, " As we have five senses, five fingers on each hand, and five toes to equip our left and right foot, it must be ' the heavenly number.' " They strongly object to the teaching that seven is the perfect number in Bible arithmetic, and often refuse to accept it as such.

Five in Scripture is the number of grace, when it has to do with God, and weakness when it has to do with man.

1. THE NUMBER OF CHRIST'S NAME.—" His Name " (not

names) " shall be called Wonderful—Counsellor—The Mighty God—The Everlasting Father—The Prince of Peace " (Isa. ix. 6).

2. THE NUMBER OF GOD'S CHOICE OF WORKERS.—" Foolish things . . . weak things . . . base things . . . things despised . . . things which are not " (1 Cor. i. 27, 28).

3. THE NUMBER OF THE WARRIOR'S SUPPLIES.—David went against Goliath with " Five smooth stones " (1 Sam. xvii. 40). Here are five facts which will bring down any giant : God is—God has—God can—God will—God does.

4. THE NUMBER OF THE LORD'S MIRACULOUS SUPPLY.— " Five barley loaves " (John vi. 9). The smallness of the supply gave the Lord the opportunity to display the multiplicity of His supply.

5. THE NUMBER OF THE LORD'S CARE.—" Five sparrows sold for two farthings " (Luke xii. 6). " Two sparrows are sold for a farthing " (Matt. x. 29). When two farthings' worth of sparrows are sold an extra one is given—thrown in. This odd sparrow does not fall to the ground without His notice.

FOOD VERSUS BONES

" They keep not Thy law. . . . Thy servant loveth it."— Ps. cxix. 136, 140.

A shrewd, worldly agnostic and a Christian clergyman sat at the same table in the Pullman dining car. They were waiting for the first course at dinner, Hudson River fish. Eyeing his companion for a moment, the agnostic remarked. " I judge you are a clergyman, sir ? " " Yes, sir ; I am in my Master's service." " You look it. Preach out of the Bible, don't you ? " " Of course." " Find a good many things in the Old Book that you don't understand—don't you ? " " Some things." " Well, what do you do then ? " " Why, I simply do just as we do while eating this delicious fish. If I come to a bone, I quietly lay it on one side, and go on enjoying the fish, and let some fool insist on choking himself with the bones." The agnostic was silenced. " The **natural man receiveth not the things of the Spirit of God,** for they are foolishness unto him ; neither can he know them, because they are spiritually discerned " (1 Cor. ii. 14).

What did the Psalmist say the Word of God was to him ?

1. A CLEANSER to Purify his Way (Ps. cxix. 9).
2. A CONTROLLER in his Heart (Ps. cxix. 11).
3. A COMFORTER in Affliction (Ps. cxix. 50).
4. A CONDUCTOR in Life's Way (Ps. cxix. 105).
5. A COMMANDER to be Obeyed (Ps. cxix. 47).
6. A COUNSELLOR for Fellowship (Ps. cxix. 65).
7. A CONSECRATOR for Holiness (Ps. cxix. 101).

FORGIVING AS FORGIVEN

" *Forgive us our debts as we forgive our debtors.*"—Matt. vi. 12.

John Wesley was once travelling with a general who was angry with his servant. On the man's asking for forgiveness for his offence, the general replied, " I never forgive ! " " Then, sir," said Wesley quietly, " I hope you never sin ! "

1. The MANNER and METHOD of our actions towards others are to be based on the Lord's dealings with us (1 Pet. ii. 21).

2. We are to FORGIVE AS THE LORD has forgiven us (Eph. iv. 32).

3. We are TO BE PERFECT IN GRACIOUSNESS towards the unthankful, even as the Lord is (Matt. v. 44-48).

4. We are to be WILLING TO GIVE our lives for the Lord's people, even as the Lord has given Himself for us (1 John iii. 16).

5. We are to SERVE OTHERS AS the Lord Jesus serves us (John xiii. 14).

6. And believers in Christ are to LOVE EACH OTHER even AS CHRIST has loved them (John xiii. 34).

FULL CONSECRATION

" *Consecrate yourselves to-day to the Lord.*"—Exod. xxxii. 29.

Frances Ridley Havergal said of consecration, " Full consecration may in one sense be the act of a moment, and in another the work of a lifetime. It must be complete to be real, and yet, if real, it is always incomplete ; a point of rest, and yet a perpetual progression. Suppose you make

over a piece of ground to another person. From the moment
of giving the title-deed, it is no longer your possession ; it
is entirely his. But his practical occupation of it may not
appear all at once. There may be waste land which he will
take into cultivation only by degrees. Just so is it with our
lives. The transaction, so to speak, making them over to
God is definite and complete. But then begins the practical
development of consecration."

1. Consecrate like THE NAZARITE by keeping from things
that excite, and from dead things that defile (Num. vi. 12).

2. Be consecrated like THE PRIESTS, with the unction of
the Spirit's anointing (Exod. xxviii. 41).

3. Consecrate to the Lord's bidding, like THE LEVITES,
when they slew those who were idolators (Exod. xxx. 29).

4. Consecrate to the Lord's work, like the SONS OF
KORAH to the work of the tabernacle (Num. iii. 3).

5. Consecrate possessions like THOSE IN DAVID'S TIME,
who gave of their possessions for the temple (1 Chron. xxix. 5).

6. Consecrate the " holy things " LIKE ISRAEL AND
JUDAH when they brought the consecrated things and " laid
them by heaps " (2 Chron. xxxi. 6).

7. Consecrate LIKE CHRIST, who gave Himself for the
sake of others (John xvii. 19).

FUTURE LIFE

" *The life . . . that is to come.*"—1 Tim. iv. 8.

" A future life must always be a matter of faith and not
of absolute demonstration. (But it is well to remember,
in this connection, that if no man can positively prove that
there is a future life no man equally can prove that there is
not)," writes Canon Peter Green, in the *Evening News* of
London.

" But to the plain man I say, ' Are you sure that there is
such a thing as the difference between right and wrong ?
Do you, on the whole, believe that there is a God ? ' Then
you can rest sure that there is also a future life, for these
three things cannot be separated."

The Scriptures and Nature proclaim there is a life to
come.

1. NATURE ILLUSTRATES a life to come in the metamorphos of the grub to the beautiful dragonfly.

2. PROPHETS PROCLAIMED it, for Daniel said men should awake to a resurrection (Dan. xii. 2).

3. THE PSALMIST SANG of it, when he hymned the fact, he would not be left in Hades, nor see corruption (Ps. xvi. 10).

4. GOD EVIDENCES it, for He is not the God of the dead, but of the living (Matt. xxii. 32).

5. CHRIST STATED it, when He affirmed the fate of the unbeliever, and the bliss of the redeemed (John iii. 36).

6. THE HOLY SPIRIT REVEALS it, for He speaks of " the ages of the ages " (Rev. xxii. 5, R.V.M.).

7. CHRIST'S RESURRECTION PROVES it, for being raised from the dead, He lives in the power of an indissoluble life (Heb. vii. 16, R.V.M.).

FUTURE : WHAT IT HOLDS

" Things which are before."—Phil. iii. 13.

One of the most pathetic incidents occurred in Los Angeles, on Feb. 9th, 1925. An automobile accident was responsible for the death of a husband and wife and their son. The mother was taken to a hospital, and another life was born as she died.

A Los Angeles reporter writes of the child born under such tragic circumstances :

" Asleep—and happy. The fitful hours of the workaday world slip by in a phantasy of baby dreams.

"Asleep—and unafraid. But when he awakens, what then ?

" When he awakens from his babyhood to the realisation that he is alone—that his father, Sidney Kahn ; his mother, Minnie Kahn, and little brother were killed in the crash which gave him life ?

" Time holds a queer enigma for this Cæsarian baby. Born as his mother lay dying at the Receiving Hospital, through the skill of the surgeon's knife, there is no one to tell him what the future holds.

" Grief-stricken relatives, it is thought, will care for him when he is old enough to leave the crib. A name will be given him, and then his life will be what he makes it.

" But that is the future. Now he is happy."

Those who are Christ's should think of the things which are before, which they may miss or gain.

1. A " FULL REWARD " is before those who are faithful to the Lord (2 John 8).

2. An ABUNDANT ENTRANCE is before those who add to their faith the graces of the Spirit (2 Peter i. 5-11).

3. A CROWN OF GLORY is before those who faithfully shepherd the flock of God (1 Peter v. 4).

4. A REIGNING WITH CHRIST is before those who suffer with Him (2 Tim. ii. 12).

5. A CROWN OF RIGHTEOUSNESS is before those who keep the faith and fight the fight (2 Tim. iv. 8).

6. A " WELL DONE ! " is before those who faithfully improve the talents of opportunity (Matt. xxv. 21), and use the pound of the Gospel (Luke xix. 17).

7. A MULTIPLICITY OF REWARD is before those who are overcomers (Rev. ii. 7, 11, 17, 26 ; iii. 5, 12, 21 ; xxi. 7).

GETTING RIGHT WITH EACH OTHER

" Live in peace."—2 Cor. xiii. 11.

A minister says that for many years he had pleaded with God for a revival, but no revival had come. Finally, in despair, he gathered his church around him, and rolled the burden of his anxiety upon them, saying : " I have done all I can. It is now for you to consider your attitude toward God."

Then there rose up in the church a grey-haired elder, much respected. He said : " Pastor, I do not wonder that there is no revival in this church ; there never will be as long as Brother Jones and I do not speak to each other " ; and before all the people the old man went down the aisle to where his brother sat, and said : " Brother Jones, forgive me ; for ten years we have not spoken. Let us bury the hatchet." They made peace, and he came back to his seat, bowing his hoary head between his hands.

In the great silence that was on the people another officer of the church rose, and said, " Pastor, I think there will not be any revival in this church as long as I continue saying fair things to your face and mean things behind your back. Will you forgive me ? " The pastor forgave him. He says that for twenty minutes, in the awful stillness of the place, men and women rose and went to square up old accounts, with those with whom they were at feud ; and then the Spirit of God came down like the sound of a mighty rushing wind.

To get right with each other, is to get right with God.

1. RECONCILIATION PRECEDES CONSECRATION.—God's Word is, " First be reconciled to thy brother," before a gift is offered to Him (Matt. v. 23, 24).

2. AN OFFENDED BROTHER is not to wait to receive an apology, but to make one to the offender (Matt. xviii. 15).

3. THE ONE WHO HAS RIGHTS is not to stand up for them, but to allow others to adjudicate his cause (1 Cor. vi. 7, 8).

4. THE BLAMELESS WHEN BLAMED are to suffer wrongfully, and commit their cause to the righteous God (1 Peter ii. 20, 21).

5. Brethren are not to JUDGE OR DESPISE one another, but to remember that they are responsible to the Lord for their mutual conduct (Rom. xiv. 1-10).

6. INDIVIDUALLY brethren are to " purge out the leaven of wickedness from their hearts and lives " (1 Cor. v. 7).

7. All believers are to be FORGIVING ONE TO ANOTHER, as God has forgiven us (Eph. iv. 32).

GIVER OF VICTORY

" *Thanks be to God, which giveth us the victory.*"—

1 Cor. xv. 57.

One day while talking to a friend, Foch is reported to have said, " I know something about preparation for war, about formation and concentration, and I can follow up an advantage ; but victory does not depend on me."

Then drawing from his tunic a little crucifix hanging from a twist of twine, the Marshal continued, " There, nailed to the Cross, is the representation of the Giver of victory. Our triumph must come if we trust in Him."

After the victory of the Marne the Bishop thanked Foch.

" Monseigneur," replied the General, " thank not me, but Him who made use of me."

We might differ with Marshal Foch about wearing a crucifix, but we do agree with him that the Christ of the Cross is the Giver of victory.

1. By His death and resurrection He has " PUT AWAY sin " (Heb. ix. 26).

2. DESTROYED him that had the power of death (Heb. ii. 14).

3. ARRESTED from the custodian of hell the keys of Hades (Rev. i. 18).

4. BROKEN sin's mastery (Rom. vi. 6).

5. UNSTUNG the bitterness of death (1 Cor. xv. 57).

6. TRANSFIXED the malignant world (Gal. vi. 14).

7. SPOILED principalities and powers (Col. ii. 15).

GIVING : CHRISTIAN GIVING

" *Their deep poverty abounded unto the riches of their liberality.*"
—2 Cor. viii. 2.

A humble Scotch woman had lived for many years on porridge, that she might give to missions the cost of her comforts and luxuries. One day a friend gave her sixpence to " buy a chop," as he said. She looked at it a while, and then she said, " I have got on very well on porridge, so far, and I think I'll just stick to it." And so the sixpence went for missions. A minister was telling this at a missionary breakfast, and a comfortable woman who was sitting in the chair immediately got up and said, " Well, I declare, I never yet have done without a chop for Christ's sake, and so I shall begin to-day, to sacrifice by giving a thousand dollars to missions." Others followed suit, and before that breakfast was over twelve thousand dollars had been contributed for missions. That was the value of a consecrated sixpence. John Howard says, " We must learn to give up our luxuries to supply the comforts of others ; our comforts to supply their necessities ; and even our necessities to supply their extremities."

The following examples of giving are worthy of our imitation.

1. THE ORDER OF GIVING.—We should first give ourselves to the Lord, as the saints at Corinth did (2 Cor. viii. 5).

2. THE EXTENT OF GIVING.—The greatest giver in the Bible is the widow who gave her " all " (Luke xxi. 4).

3. THE SPIRIT OF GIVING.—We should give willingly, as those who offered willingly the things they brought for the Tabernacle (Exod. xxxv. 29).

4. THE MOTIVE IN GIVING.—When the love of Christ prompts and moves us to give, we are willing to spend and be spent, like Paul (2 Cor. xii. 15).

5. THE JOY OF GIVING.—" The Lord loveth a cheerful giver." If it hurts in our giving, we need to pray till it does not hurt (2 Cor. ix. 7).

6. THE WORSHIP OF GIVING.—We have this illustrated in the acts and attitude of Hezekiah and his people, when " all the congregation worshipped " and gave (2 Chron. xxix. 28-36).

7. THE CONSECRATION OF GIVING.—Like David, who " prepared with all his might," " set his affection," and urged all " to consecrate " his service unto the Lord (1 Chron. xxix. 1-6).

GLADSTONE'S SAYINGS ABOUT CHRIST

" *These Sayings.*"—Luke ix. 44.

William Gladstone, the great English statesman, believed :

" Every problem of life was a Gospel problem."

" The teachings of Christ when received and obeyed, will regulate all human life in the best possible manner."

" In Christ all the treasures of wisdom and knowledge are found."

He once wrote : " All I write, and all I think, and all I am, is based on my unfeigned faith in the Divinity of the Lord Jesus Christ, the One Central Hope of our poor wayward race."

One of the peculiar things about Christ, was, He could speak about Himself without the intrusion of Self. He reveals Himself for our benefit.

When our Lord speaks of Himself as " Myself," how we are attracted to Him, and what worth and wealth we find in Him.

93

1. A GREAT SACRIFICE.—Of His life given for us, He said, " I lay it down of *Myself* " (John x. 18).

2. A GREAT SANCTIFIER.—In His consecration of Himself to the work of redemption, He said, " I consecrate *Myself* " (John xvii. 19).

3. A GREAT PROMISER.—To those who love Him and keep His words, He says, " I will manifest *Myself* to him " (John xiv. 21).

4. A GREAT MESSENGER.—Of His mission and message He declared, " I have not spoken of *Myself* " (John xii. 49).

5. A GREAT REVEALER.—When He appeared as the Risen One, in the midst of His disciples, He assured them, " It is I *Myself* " (Luke xxiv. 39).

6. A GREAT MISSIONER.—In the authority that was at the back of Him, He avowed, " I came not of *Myself* " (John vii. 28 ; viii. 28, 42).

7. A GREAT RECEIVER.—He promised He will " come again," and receive His own to " Himself," for His word is " I will receive you to *Myself* " (John xiv. 3). Ponder and worship. Love and adore. Believe and rest. Receive and make known.

GLORIOUS THINGS

" *Glorious things are spoken of thee.*"—Ps. lxxxvii. 3.

A great violinist, in order to train, was sent as a girl to Professor Seveik, at Prague. One of the conditions laid down by those who sent her there, was that her father was not to see her, or to correspond with her, till her training was over. She went away a poor girl, she came back already famous, and her father and mother pressed their way on the first evening into the concert hall, with the eager crowd that had come to welcome her. When some one praised her amid the plaudits, the father simply said : " She is my daughter ; this is the first time we have seen her for two years." But the transformation was worth waiting for. It was cheaply bought by the price of exile. There are many things which have a future glory, or which are said to be, or will be, " glorious."

1. " THE GLORIOUS GOSPEL " (2 Cor. iv. 4 ; 1 Tim. i. 11).

—The Gospel of the glory (R.V.) proclaims what the Gospel declares as to the future.

2. " HIS GLORIOUS BODY " (Phil. iii. 21).—" His body of glory " (R.V.) is that to which believers will be " like."

3. " A GLORIOUS CHURCH " (Eph. v. 27).—He will not only set His Church in the glory, but will glorify the Church with glory.

4. " THE GLORIOUS APPEARING " (Titus ii. 13).—Christ's return will not only be a presence of reality, and an unveiling of Himself, but it will be a flashing forth of His august splendour.

5. " THE GLORIOUS LIBERTY " (Rom. viii. 21). or " The liberty of the glory " (R.V.), is what creation is waiting for.

6. A GLORIOUS PLACE (Isa. lx. 13).—Jerusalem is yet to be a praise and a glory in the earth.

7. A GLORIOUS DAUGHTER.—" The King's daughter is all-glorious within " (Ps. xlv. 13). Inner beauty is the glory of inward purity, and the Spirit of Christ.

" GOD OR NOTHING "

" We trust in the living God."—i Tim. iv. 10.

" The moment man is driven in upon himself, the moment the secular supports for his life have become unsettled, and he perceives that he must fall back either upon nothing or upon God, in that moment his heart and flesh cry out ; and, if he has access to the Bible, why, it is like the sight of land to voyagers on a wild sea," so said one, who saw the direct issue. How much we have when we trust in the Living God. How destitute we are if we do not know and possess Him.

To trust in the living God is to have something which can meet our need and satisfy our deepest longing, for He is

1. The GOD OF TRUTH to enlighten us (John xvii. 17).

2. The GOD OF GRACE to save us (Eph. ii. 8).

3. The GOD OF LOVE to provide for us (1 John iv. 10).

4. The GOD OF PEACE to sanctify us (Heb. xiii. 20 ; i Thess. v. 23).

5. The GOD OF POWER to keep us (1 Peter i. 5).

6. The GOD OF COMFORT to console us (2 Cor. i. 3).

95

7. The GOD OF PATIENCE to quieten us (Rom. xv. 5).
8. The GOD OF HOPE to cheer us (Rom. xv. 13).
9. The GOD OF GLORY to fascinate us (Acts vii. 2).

GOD'S CERTAIN ACTS

" God hath spoken unto us."—Heb. i. 2.

Three leading men of the United States (T. Roosevelt, Grover Cleveland, and John Hay) once made the following statement about God's Word : " No social fabric of modern States has a surer foundation than the Bible, especially in a Republic like ours, which rests upon the moral character and educated judgment of the individual. No thoughtful man can doubt that to decrease the circulation of the Bible, and its use, among the people would seriously menace the highest interests of civilised humanity."

" GOD HATH."—These two pregnant words crystalise again and again around the acts of God as revealed in the Bible. The following statements illustrate :

1. APPOINTMENT.—" Whom HE HATH appointed Heir of all things " (Heb. i. 2). Christ was willing to take the lowest place in death (Phil. ii. 8), and the consequence is, the Father has given to Him the highest place in government.

2. AUTHORITY.—" The times and seasons the FATHER HATH put in His own authority " (R.V., Acts i. 7). Faith does not seek with prying eyes, but is content to leave all in the hands of Him who doeth all things well.

3. ADMINISTRATION.—" THE HOLY GHOST HATH made you overseers," or bishops (Acts xx. 28). Those who are in the place of responsibility in Christ's redeemed Church are to be faithful to the Holy Spirit who appointed them.

4. ADJUSTMENT.—" GOD HATH set the members " . . . " GOD HATH tempered the body together " (1 Cor. xii. 18, 24, 28). He hath given to each member his place, and adjusts each to Christ and the members one to the other.

5. AMBASSAGE.—" GOD . . . HATH committed to us the word of reconciliation " (2 Cor. v. 19). This is the message we are responsible to pass on to others for Him who died for us, for that is God's provision for sinful men (2 Cor. v. 21).

6. ACKNOWLEDGMENT.—" Whom GOD HATH raised up "

(Acts ii. 24, 32). The greatest exhibition of God's power is seen in Christ's resurrection (Eph. i. 19, 20).

7. Acts of Grace.—" The Father hath made meet " ... " Delivered " ... " Translated us " (Col. i. 12, 13).

GOOD OUT OF THE SEEMING BAD

" Out of the eater cometh forth meat."—Judges xiv. 14.

Goethe in his " Faust," makes Mephistopheles say in answer to the question, " Who art thou ? "

" Part of that Power, not understood,
Which always wills the bad, and always works the good."

We are not prepared to agree that he who " wills the bad," " always works the good," but we do know that good comes out of the seeming bad, and that even Satan's ill-intent may be heaven sent.

1. Grace through the Thorn.—" There was given me a thorn in the flesh, the messenger of Satan to buffet me " (2 Cor. xii. 7), and yet the messenger of ill, led the apostle to the munificence of impotence. Grace would not have been so highly appreciated if the man of God had not been so hardly oppressed. Trials often irk us (as the old English word says), and hurt us too, but then they drive us to the Throne of Grace as well. Scouring paper is rough, but then it removes the rust and brightens also. The grindstone wears the knife, but the knife is sharper for the grinding. The ore is melted in the fire, but the fire separates the dross from the metal.

2. Pillow of Comfort found in the Pillar of Stone (Gen. xxviii. 11).—It was a hard pillow Jacob had when his head rested on a pillar, but it led to the Bethel of heaven's stairway.

3. Prison Fare led to the Feast in the Palace (Gen. xl. 20).—Prison fare was not palatable to Joseph's taste, but it gave him a keen appetite for the feast in the palace.

4. Bitterness Turned into Sweetness (Exod. xv. 23).—Marah's bitter waters made the water from the rock all the sweeter.

5. Husks Preceded the Fatted Calf (Luke xv. 16).—The calf of the father's home was the more appreciated because of the want of the husks in the far country.

97

GRACE, GRACES

" Contrary to sound doctrine."—1 Tim. i. 10.

Maclaren, of Manchester, tells that he once heard of a man of very shady character who was sound on the Atonement. " What," he asks, " is the use of being sound on the Atonement if the Atonement does not make you sound ? "

The above reminds us of what Spurgeon once said, " The grace of God is not a clean glove for a dirty hand."

We often read of things that are " sound " in Paul's epistles. The word " sound " in the following Scriptures signifies to be healthy, to be well, to be uncorrupt, to be whole.

1. " A Sound Mind " (2 Tim. i. 7), is the product of God's giving, and the result of thinking God's thoughts after Him. When our minds accept God's conclusions, we have conclusions which conclude.

2. " Sound Words " (2 Tim. i. 13).—The healthy words of God's Word are like the ozone of the sea breeze, they give life and vigour to the lungs of our spiritual being.

3. " Sound Doctrine " (2 Tim. iv. 3).—Unholy men do not like the healthy teaching of God's truth, for it is like fresh air to a dead body, it only procures added corruption ; but the contrary is to those who receive it.

4. " Sound Speech " (Titus ii. 8).—Healthy speech proves a healthy soul. A dirty tongue proves a dirty heart. When our speech is seasoned with God's grace, it will be seasonable on all occasions.

5. Sound Faith.—" Sound faith " means to be " sound in the faith " of God's truth (Titus i. 13 ; ii. 2, R.V.). Unbelief, doubt, and fear do not reside in the heart of a believer whose faith is born of God's truth.

6. Sound Love.—" Sound in love " (Titus ii. 2, R.V.). A clanging cymbal makes a noise, but it is only noise. A loveless life is the same, but a loving soul is like good fruit, luscious and refreshing.

7. Sound Patience.—" Sound in patience " (Titus ii. 2). A healthy athlete will endure in the race, so those who have a sound constitution will run and not be weary and receive the crown.

GRASPING THINGS

" Hold Him fast."—Matt. xxvi. 48.

Samuel Rutherford in writing to a friend about spiritual things, urged him to " Tighten your grips." We are frequently urged to " hold " and " lay hold " on the Lord and spiritual things.

The word " Krateo " is rendered " Lay hold " (Matt. xii. 11), " Hold fast " (Matt. xxvi. 48), " Retain " (John xx. 23), and " Kept " (Mark ix. 10).

1. " HOLD THE TRADITIONS " (2 Thess. ii. 15).—The " Traditions " were what the apostle had received directly or indirectly from the Lord (1 Cor. ix. 2, 23 ; xv. 3). The verb " hold " means to hold fast, and when, as here, with the accusative, it means keeping a firm hold of the whole.

2. " HOLD FAST OUR PROFESSION " (Heb. iv. 14).—" Profession," or confession, means to say the same thing with another—that other is the Lord. To " hold fast " signifies to hold in one's power ; hence, to be master of it.

3. " TO LAY HOLD UPON THE HOPE " (Heb. vi. 18).— " The Hope " always denotes the coming of Christ for His people (Titus ii. 13), when they will be " like Him " (1 John iii. 1-3). This Hope is sure in its objective, and steadfast in its subjective accomplishment.

4. " HOLD FAST THAT WHICH THOU HAST " (Rev. iii. 11).—We cannot lose our salvation, for that depends upon Christ's hold of us (John x. 28), but we may lose our crown (Rev. iii. 11), a " full reward " (2 John 8), and the work we have wrought (1 Cor. iii. 15).

5. " HOLD FAST TILL I COME " (Rev. ii. 25).—He is coming ; hence we are " to hold fast." An obedient heart, a prayerful spirit, an ardent love, a living faith, a holy walk, a steadfast hope, and the soul of grace, will enable us to " hold fast."

6. " HOLD HIM FAST " (Matt. xxvi. 48).—Judas told others to hold Christ fast with ill intent. If we hold fast in the grip of faith, and the glow of love, we shall be able to hold other things fast.

99

GREATEST WORK IN THE WORLD

" It is finished " (*accomplished*).—John xix. 30.

The greatest work in the world has been done—namely, Christ has died and risen again to make atonement for sin ; and now next to this is to make Christ known as the Saviour of men. Civilisation is not the greatest work, nor education, nor philanthropy, nor socialism, but to save men. Missionaries and ministers are missing their vocation if they are occupied with any secondary work. Their main business is to preach the Gospel. The Gospel as embodying the death and resurrection was what Paul preached and which " saved " the people (1 Cor. xv. 1-4). Nothing else will save the people from sin's curse and consequence, and save them to holiness, purity, love, and God.

The Gospel of God in Christ's death—

1. Is a LIGHT TO REVEAL the sin and sinfulness of man ; for, as Peter said on the Day of Pentecost, it was the wicked hands of men that nailed Him to the Cross (Acts ii. 23, 36).

2. Is a HAMMER TO BREAK the hard hearts of men, for it was the truth of Christ's death that pricked men to their hearts' conviction, and made them cry out, " What shall we do ? " (Acts ii. 37).

3. Is a LIFE BOAT TO SAVE men from the perdition of sin, for we " obtain salvation by " (by means of) " our Lord Jesus Christ, who died for us " (1 Thess. v. 9, 10).

4. Is a REFUGE TO PROTECT from Sin's Power ; for it reveals One, who died for us, who causes us to die to sin's sway and pollution (1 Peter iv. 1, 2).

5. Is a HARBOUR OF REST to shield us from the unrest of sin's turmoil and lashing, for the " chastisement of our peace was laid upon Him," upon whom the storm of wrath fell (Isa. liii. 5, 6).

6. Is the HAND OF LOVE to lift us from the pit of iniquity, for it is " through the blood " of Christ we are " made nigh " to God (Eph. ii. 13).

7. Is the KEY OF HOPE to unlock the Door of Promise, and we can thus look on the Delectable Mountains of the glorious coming of our Lord (1 Thess. iv. 13-18).

HANDS

" *A little folding of the hands.*" Prov. vi. 10 ; xxiv. 33.

One, in writing about John Wesley and Dr. Johnson, says : " Wesley's greatness is not solely or primarily ecclesiastical. In himself he was a man so remarkable as not even to fear comparison with his great contemporary Dr. Johnson, who said of him that he could talk well on any subject. He added, however, the criticism that he was never at leisure. ' He is always obliged to go at a certain hour. That is very disagreeable to a man who loves to fold his legs and have out his talk, as I do.' "

Dr. Johnson is not the only one who liked to fold his legs in ease, or his hands in laziness. There are many who fold the active member of the hand, who ought to work with all diligence.

The Hebrew word " *Yad* " is frequently rendered " hand," and is the member which is identified with work (Eccles. ix. 10). The word for " folding " means more than to cover one hand over the other, it signifies to clasp together in lazy determination. Our hands should be :

1. POWERFUL Hands to Help (Prov. iii. 27).
2. DILIGENT Hands to Enrich (Prov. x. 4).
3. EFFICIENT Hands to Rule (Prov. xii. 24).
4. HOLDING Hands to Grip (Prov. xxx. 28).
5. WORKING Hands to Benefit (Prov. xxxi. 19).
6. INVESTING Hands to Profit (Prov. xxxi. 16).
7. HELPING Hands to Supply (Prov. xxxi. 20).

See how the virtuous woman uses her whole being to better and bless (Prov. xxxi).

HARDNESS OF HEART

" *Harden not your hearts.*"—Heb. iii. 8.

A well-known writer says :

" It is astonishing what hardness of heart is often exhibited by Christian folk. It breaks out in unexpected places, and adds a good deal to the sadness of the world. If the human soul could be purged of its selfishness, then we should not need to get ready for the millennium."

It is a sorry thing that such a statement should have to be made, yet, many of us have had to say, " The most unchristian things we have received have come from Christian people." We are exhorted to be " imitators of God " in kindness to each other.

How many hard things we read of in Holy Scripture.

1. HARDENED HEART.—" Pharaoh hardened his heart in rebellion against the Lord " (Exod. viii. 15).

2. HARDENED FACE.—" A wicked man hardeneth his face " (Prov. xxi. 29). The face without tells of the mind within.

3. HARDENED NECKS.—" Hardened their necks " (Neh. ix. 16, 17, 29). They would not bow their wills to God.

4. HARDENED LIVES.—" Hard bondage " was the effect of the oppression of the Egyptians upon the children of Israel (Exod. i. 14). So with sin.

5. HARDENED TRANSGRESSORS.—" The way of transgressors is hard " (Prov. xiii. 15), yea, and they are hardened by them.

6. HARDENED MIND.—" His mind hardened in pride " (Dan. v. 20). Pride coats the heart with callousness, the soul with unbelief, and the mind with self-confidence.

7. HARDENED UNBELIEVERS.—" Hardened through the deceitfulness of sin " (Heb. iii. 13). Sin clothes the unbeliever with a coat of mail.

HE ALONE IS WORTHY

" *Thou art worthy, O Lord, to receive.*"—Rev. iv. 11.

The writer often called upon the Rev. Charles Stirling, when living in Weston-super-Mare, and in course of conversation the latter would nearly always quote the following lines of Cowper's ascription of praise to Christ :—

" Come, then, and, added to Thy many crowns,
Receive yet one, the crown of all the earth,
Thou who alone art worthy ! It was Thine
By ancient covenant ere nature's birth,
And Thou hast made it Thine by purchase since,
And overpaid its value by Thy Blood.
Thy saints proclaim Thee King ; and in their hearts
Thy title is engraven with a pen,
Dipt in the fountain of Eternal Love."

1. As LORD, He is worthy of all homage and praise (Rev. iv. 11).

2. As OVERCOMER, He is worthy to open the Book of Earth's Government (Rev. v. 1-9).

3. As the LAMB, He is worthy to be exalted by, and above, angelic hosts (Rev. v. 12).

4. As the " GOOD " SHEPHERD, He is worthy of our faith and love, because He gave His life for us (John x. 11).

5. As THE ONE who bears the " worthy " Name, He is greatest of all (James ii. 7).

HEART IN THE RIGHT PLACE

" Where your treasure is, there will your heart be."—
Matt. vi. 21.

An old Lancashire woman, dreadfully crippled with rheumatism, used to hobble to church on two sticks, with the utmost pain and toil. " Mrs. X, how do you manage it ? " asked a friend. " My heart gets there first, and my old legs follow on after," was the answer.

When the heart is in the right place, it will place everything in the place it should be. Have we the right kind of a heart ?

1. A PURE HEART.—A pure heart is a seeing heart. " Blessed are the pure in heart, for they shall see God " (Matt. v. 8).

2. A POSSESSED HEART.—" That Christ may dwell in your hearts by faith " (Eph. iii. 17). When Christ is in possession, we possess His sanctifying grace, and His satisfying love.

3. A PRAYERFUL HEART.—" Call on the Lord out of a pure heart " (2 Tim. ii. 22). When the incense of prayer burns on the altar of a consecrated heart, the answering flame is sure to come.

4. A PERMANENT HEART.—" It is a good thing that the heart be established with grace " (Heb. xiii. 9). When the heart is built into the concrete of grace, it will weather the storms of temptation.

5. A PASSIONATE HEART.—" Love one another with a pure heart fervently " (1 Peter i. 22). A heart of fervent love is the best kind of passion. It is easy to love when the fire of God's love burns in the heart.

6. A PURPOSED HEART.—" Doing the will of God from the heart " (Eph. vi. 6). When the will of God sways us we are guided by the principles of His Word, and our heart responds with its hearty " Amen " of obedience.

7. A PROTECTED HEART.—" If our heart condemn us not, then have we confidence before God " (1 John iii. 20, 21). An uncondemning heart will be a fence to protect us from the wild beasts of doubt, despair, and fear.

HEART OF GOLD

" *Martha, Martha.*"—Luke x. 38-42.

" We all know Martha, the elder one, the worker, the good housekeeper, capable, strenuous, bustling, a little brusque and impatient in manner, but with a heart of gold, with her reverence for the Master tempered by the woman's mothering instinct toward the persecuted young Prophet, who had not where to lay His head." So writes Paterson-Smyth, and writes on : " The Martha of our own day is of the salt of the earth, the good manager, the skilful nurse, the strenuous, capable woman on whom most of the work falls. She has her faults, and is often misunderstood. She does not talk much of that religion which is the ruling power of her life. She hides her feelings. She hates sentiment. She does not suffer fools gladly. But under a dry, caustic humour she hides a very loving heart. Young people jest at her, but come to her in their troubles, and laugh about her tenderly, affectionately, when she is gone. The Marthas are great helpers of the world."

1. Martha's KINDNESS—" She received Him."
2. Martha's POSTURE—" She . . . at Jesus' feet."
3. Martha's ATTENTION—" Heard His word."
4. Martha's SERVICE—" Much Serving."
5. Martha's BLUNDER—" Cumbered . . ."
6. Martha's COMPLAINT—" Mary hath left me."

7. Martha's REBUKE—" Thou art careful and troubled about many dishes." (Trapp.)

8. Martha INSTRUCTED—" One thing is needful."

" HEART ": THE ESSENTIAL THING

" With the heart man believed unto righteousness."—Rom. x. 10.

A well-known writer, in describing an acute and brilliant barrister, who, by his eloquence and able pleading, was able to convince a jury that a man (a guilty man) who was charged with a crime was not guilty, was ironically complimented by the wife of the guilty man. The lawyer replied, " You owe me nothing. I had a brief before me, and a cause to plead. It was a chapter out of daily work."

Whereupon the wife of the guilty man replied, " It is a great gift to be able to argue from the brain, and plead as though from the heart." The woman recognised the possibility of saying one thing and believing another. Where the heart is wanting, all is wanting.

1. There is the heart of DEFINITE PURPOSE. As the Psalmist expresses it, when he said, " My heart is fixed, trusting in the Lord " (Ps. cxii. 7). This heart is like the rudder of a vessel : it guides the vessel of being to the port of accomplished act over the ocean of life.

2. There is the heart of DEVOTED AFFECTION, as the Apostle suggests in his letter to the saints in Philippi, when he declared, " I have you in my heart " (Phil. i. 7). This heart is like Ruth in her love for Naomi, she would not be turned back in her devotion to her mother-in-law.

3. There is the heart of DETERMINED MIND, of which the Apostle speaks when he refers to the " eyes of your understanding " (R.V., " heart ") being enlightened (Eph. i. 18), which reaches its goal in its quest for knowledge.

4. There is the heart of DIVINE POSSESSION, which we know when Christ dwells in our heart by faith (Eph. iii. 17). When Christ takes up His permanent abode within us, He has complete control of our being.

5. There is a heart of DELIGHTFUL REST, which trusts Him with perfect confidence, who says, " Let not your heart

be troubled, ye believe in God, believe also in Me " (John xiv. i. 2).

6. There is the heart of DEDICATED LOVE, which keeps on its steady way in spite of the unbelief of others. Like Caleb and Joshua, it says, " We are able," because God is able (Num. xiii. 30).

7. There is the heart of DIVINE WILL, which, like Christ, says, " I delight to do Thy will, O my God ; yea, Thy law is within my heart " (Ps. xl. 8 ; Heb. x. 7).

" HELPMEET "

" I will make him a helpmeet for him."—Gen. ii. 18.

The Rev. Philip Henry used to give two pieces of advice to his children and others, in reference to marriage. One was, " Keep within the bounds of profession." The other was, " Look at suitableness in age, quality, education, temper," etc. He used to observe, from Gen. ii. 18, " I will make him an helpmeet for him, that where there is not meetness there will not be much help." He commonly said to his children, with reference to their choice in marriage, " Please God, and please yourselves, and you shall never displease me " ; and greatly blamed those parents who conclude matches for their children without their consent. He sometimes mentioned the saying of a pious gentlewoman who had many daughters : " The care of most people is how to get good husbands for their daughters ; but my care is to fit my daughters to be good wives, and then let God provide for them."

The Hebrew word for " helpmeet " comes from a root which means to aid, succour, and protect. The root word is rendered " succour " (2 Sam. xviii. 3), and is the general one for " help." The word " helpmeet " is rendered " Help " in the following passages, and its use will illustrate its meaning.

1. To help others we need to HAVE THE LORD as our " Help " (Exod. xviii. 4).

2. We need to BE IN TOUCH with the God of the sanctuary, for it is from there " help " comes (Ps. xx. 2).

3. Help comes THROUGH HIM, upon whom " help " has been laid (Ps. lxxxix. 19).

4. We must LOOK PAST earthly aids, if we would find Divine Succour (Ps. cxxi. 1, 2).

5. And all the time to REMEMBER HIM, who says, " In Me is thine Help " (Hosea xiii. 9, marg.).

" HE WILL DO IT "

" He offered himself willingly unto the Lord."

2 Chron. xvii. 16.

Charles, King of Sweden, father of the great Gustavus Adolphus, was an ardent Protestant, and purposed for his country more good than he was able himself to accomplish. His son, who gave early promise of his brilliant qualities— speaking five languages, and understanding four others more or less, at twelve years old—was his father's great hope. Often, when a scheme of reformation, yet impracticable, was referred to, the king would lay his hand upon the boy's head and say to the bystanders, " He will do it."

Willingness is the soul's readiness to follow the Lord at all costs.

1. A " WILLING HEART " is the warmth of love (Exod. xxxv. 22).

2. A " WILLING MIND " is the heart of service (1 Chron. xxviii. 9).

3. A WILLING CONSECRATION is the soul of holiness (1 Chron. xxix. 5).

4. A WILLING OBEDIENCE is the securer of blessing (Isa. i. 19).

5. A WILLING WILL is the fellowship of Gethsemane (Luke xxii. 42).

6. A WILLING GIFT is the joy of giving (2 Cor. viii. 3, 12).

7. A WILLING RECEPTION of the Saviour is sure to bring a benediction (John vi. 21).

HOLY SPIRIT'S COUNTERACTING WORK

" The law of the Spirit of Life in Christ Jesus hath made me free from the law of sin and death."—Rom. viii. 2.

" Professor Lefroy, of the Imperial College of Science and Technology, has devised a solution expected to put an end to the ravages of the ' death watch ' beetle," says the London correspondent of the *Yorkshire Post*.

"This little creature, only a quarter of an inch long, spends its life burrowing about in old woodwork, until the infected wood becomes riddled and rotten. Its familiar ticking sound is produced by a small club-shaped extension of the antennæ, with which it knocks on any surrounding woodwork in order to call its mate.

"Many old buildings embodying wooden beams and rafters have been endangered by this beetle's tireless activities. Lincoln Cathedral, where the woodwork supporting the roof has been seriously attacked, is a notable example.

"Professor Lefroy's solution is built up from a white, sweet-smelling substance known as paradichlorobenzine. Certain oils are added to this, and the resulting mixture is sprayed on to affected surfaces. The mixture gradually sinks into the wood, poisoning the beetles inside, and so permeating the wood that fresh beetles are prevented from working their way in."

The solution is destructive and preventative. Killing the beetle, and preventing others from working their way into the wood. This is what the Holy Spirit does in the heart and life of the believer in Christ. If Romans viii is carefully and prayerfully pondered, it will be seen He destroys sin and prevents from sin. The Holy Spirit is :

1. The LIBERATOR from the law of sin and death (2).
2. The LEADER after things of Himself (4, 5).
3. The LIFE of the new nature (9-12).
4. The GUIDE who leads us in the ways of life (14).
5. The WITNESS to assure of our relationship (16).
6. The EARNEST of the glorified body (23).
7. The INTERCESSOR in the prayer life (26, 27).

INDIFFERENCE

" *Gallio cared for none of these things.*"—Acts xviii. 17.

One of the most oppressive facts of our times is the appalling and increasing indifference, especially in so-called "religious circles." Dr. Atkins, in preaching from the words "Gallio cared for none of these things," said : "Gallio has long been the type of man to whom religious truth was a matter of indifference. To call a man a ' careless Gallio ' was to our fathers, at least, to use a significant and familiar phrase. He did not care for the enforcements of the laws, for good morals, good training, and fine and well breeding. He did not care for the religious life. He was a brother of Seneca, the Roman philosopher and teacher. He belonged to his brother's school. They had practically divorced religion and morality.

" The world is full to-day of men of the type of Gallio, wholesome, lovable, correct, but spiritually sterile, and wholly indifferent to religion, either as comradeship in worship, communion with God, or eager search after truth," and we might add, they are indifferent to Christ and His claims.

We are not surprised at this indifference, for the Holy Spirit has distinctly told us that one of the signs of the Last Days is, " men shall be lovers of their own selves . . . having a form of godliness, but denying the power thereof " (2 Tim. iii. 2, 5). They are not indifferent to the " form " or outward show of religiosity, but they refuse the vitality of practical godliness, as the word " denying " implies. (The word is rendered " Refused " in Hebrews xi. 24, in referring to the indifference of Moses to be called the son of Pharaoh's daughter.)

The second Epistles all have something to say about the characteristics of the times of the end. Paul, in his second Epistle to Timothy, says to him, " This know also, that in the last days perilous times shall come " (2 Tim. iii. 1), and then he gives a number of detailed enormities which are manifest all around.

Peter in his second Epistle calls attention to many who are questioning the truth of the Lord's return, and are saying, " Where is the promise of His coming ? " (2 Peter iii. 4).

And John states that " many deceivers have entered the world, who deny the coming of Jesus in the flesh " (2 John 7).

If the setting of these Scriptures is pondered, it will be apprehended that the first deals with the immoral conditions which are revealing themselves in their fierceness ; in the second passage, a growing indifference is referred to, which practically says, " God is indifferent to the happenings on earth," therefore we have a right to be indifferent, too ; and John calls attention to the deceptive glamour of agnostic deceivers, who seek to fritter away the realities and facts regarding the personal reality of Christ, and the truth regarding His incarnation, life, death, resurrection, and His coming again.

INDIVIDUALITY

" I am."—1 Cor. xv. 10.

" The ceiling of the Sistine Chapel, at Rome, contains a fine painting by Michael Angelo, from the text, ' Man became a living soul.' It represents the Supreme Spirit floating in the ether and touching with His finger the body of Adam. As he touches it an electric spark flashes into the body, and Adam becomes a living soul."

Each individual knows he IS, and from the teaching of Holy Writ he is an indestructible spirit. God made man in His own image. That image refers not to character, but to man's NATURE. Man, like God, is lasting, since he is lighted. " The spirit of man is the lamp of Jehovah " (Prov. xx. 27). Not the " Candle of God," as the Authorised version, but the " lamp of Jehovah." Jehovah is the Unchanging, the Lasting One. Man is not the " candle," but the " Lamp of Jehovah." The undoubted reference is to the lampstand in the Tabernacle, of which we read, " It shall burn always " (Exod. xxvii. 20), " Cause the lamps to burn continually " (Lev. xxiv. 2-4). Man's being has been ignited, and as long as Jehovah has a being, his being must be. Hence, this makes the future of immense and paramount importance.

" I " expresses our individuality, hence our identity. Consciousness of being proves a personal entity. " COGITO, ERGO SUM " : " I think, therefore I exist." We can read this either way : because I am, I think ; and because I think, it proves I am. Man is more than a body, although he lives in it. " The brain is the SEAT of thought, it is not all to say it is the SOURCE of thought." The particles which form the brain are always changing, but memory insists we are more than brain. " I have a room wherein no one enters save I myself alone."

See how individuality is illustrated in seven " I am's " of Paul.

1. CRUCIFIXION.—" I am crucified with Christ " (Gal. ii. 20).

2. PERSUASION.—" I am persuaded " (Rom. viii. 38).

3. HUMILIATION.—" I am the least " (1 Cor. xv. 9).

4. AFFILIATION.—" By the grace of God, I am what I am " (1 Cor. xv. 10).

5. APPREHENSION.—" I am apprehended " (Phil. iii. 12).

6. INSTRUCTION.—" I am instructed " (Phil. iv. 12)

7. RESIGNATION.—" I am ready to be offered up " (2 Tim. iv. 6).

INTEGRITY AND UPRIGHTNESS

" *Let integrity and uprightness preserve me.*"—Ps. xxv. 21.

" In the Chartist times, before the introduction of factories, people often worked in little hovels for a mere pittance. There was a Christian man in Kettering who worked his stocking frames in a little lean-to behind a grocer's shop. He was clamant for food, not earning enough to buy enough for his wife and family. Each morning he came, a hungry man, and walked down between piles of the food his nature craved. They noticed he walked with clenched fists, muttering to himself, and they thought he was one of the dangerous Chartists. But as they listened and watched, by-and-by they heard what he was saying. Here he was with his ill-nourished body walking down between the things he might so easily have attempted to steal, and he kept saying the words that are at the end of the twenty-fifth Psalm. ' Let integrity and uprightness preserve me.' Why, that is the Old Testament form of holiness and righteousness. Integrity is holiness, uprightness is righteousness. Both phrases may be interpreted, ' To be whole and to be straight.' Integrity and uprightness preserved him. May they also preserve you and me ! "

The believer in Christ is expected to do differently than the worldling. Christ brings this out in the Sermon on the Mount.

1. He is to REJOICE when falsely accused (Matt. v. 12).

2. He is not to RESIST when assailed by evil (Matt. v. 39)

3. He is to RETURN BLESSING upon those who curse him (Matt. v. 44).

4. He is TO DO GOOD to those who hate him (Matt. v. 44).

5. He is NOT TO HOARD UP TREASURE on earth (Matt. vi. 19-21).

6. He is NOT TO JUDGE OTHERS by what seems to be (Matt. vii. 1-5).

7. He is NOT TO BE DECEIVED by empty profession, but to do the will of God (Matt. vi. 21-23).

INVISIBLE MADE VISIBLE

" Endured, as seeing Him who is invisible."—Heb. xi. 27.

Take a colourless solution of bisulphate of quinine, and write or draw with it on a sheet of white paper. When dry, the writing or design will be invisible, but a photograph made of it will show it very nearly black. This shows that there are lights in the world that our eyes see not. Our eyes are formed to be affected by certain colours of the spectrum, but there are others, perhaps equally powerful, that have no influence upon the human retina. Some recent experiments have brought the conclusion that ants, and perhaps other animals, see colours that we do not. This truth is worth pondering and applying to spiritual sight. There are aspects of God and His grace for which many have no power of vision. Our faith has at the best a limited spectrum. Let this teach charity to the views of others.

The sad part is that those who are not the Lord's " have eyes and see not " ; but what is even more sad, there are believers who are shortsighted and cannot " see afar off " (2 Peter i. 9). The eye of natural reason cannot see the things of God, but if we are willing to be taught by the inspired pages of God's Holy Writ, He will illuminate our minds to see the things He has prepared for them that love Him (1 Cor. ii. 9, 10).

There are seven prepared things which God will give to those who are prepared to answer to the conditions :

1. SALVATION for all people (Luke ii. 31).

2. COMPLETE salvation for His own (1 Peter i. 5 ; word " ready " same as " prepared ").

3. PLACE OF ABODE for the redeemed (John xiv. 2).

4. A KINGDOM (Matt. xxv. 34).

5. An EXALTED POSITION for those that stand the test (Matt. xx. 23).

6. A CITY (Heb. xi. 16).

7. The NEW JERUSALEM (Rev. xxi. 2).

ISOLATION

" I am a sparrow alone."—Ps. cii. 7.

How desolate, alone, abandoned, and isolated the lonely brick looked, as it lay by the roadside ! It was made for comradeship, to support and be supported by another. How did the brick come to its isolation ? It may have been jolted off the carrying cart through some defect in the road, or because it had not been properly placed. Many a life has been desolated because of its isolation. We cannot be independent of each other only at the expense of loss, and, most of all, we cannot be independent of God or Christ.

Think of the men who have been isolated, and what their isolation meant to themselves.

1. JACOB THE WANDERER.—" Jacob was left alone " (Gen. xxxii. 24). Alone he was left, when he in the long ago had to flee from Esau's ire, and now he is alone again, that he may know how dependent he is upon the Lord.

2. ELIJAH THE DESPONDENT.—" He came and sat down under a juniper tree, and he requested that he might die " (1 Kings xix. 4). Scared by a woman's threats, he throws up his hands and gives way to despair.

3. MOSES THE SHEPHERD.—" He led the flock to the backside of the desert. . . . The Lord appeared " (Exod. iii. 1, 2). When we tread the lonely path of duty, the Lord appears to bless us, and send us on larger service.

4. PETER THE BACKSLIDER.—" The Lord appeared to Simon " (Luke xxiv. 34). What the Lord said was evidently private, but Peter was questioned, forgiven, and restored, as he confessed his self-confidence.

5. DAVID THE PURSUED.—David said to Saul when he was

pursuing him, " he was like a partridge hunted in the mountains " (1 Sam. xxvi. 18-20).

6. PAUL THE AGED said with a note of sadness, as he felt his loneliness, " no man stood with me " (2 Tim. iv. 16).

7. JOHN THE SEER.—He says in his loneliness, " I was in the isle called Patmos " (Rev. i. 9).

ISRAEL'S FUTURE

" Behold the days come."—Jer. xxxi. 27-29.

That respected Christian Jew, Dr. Adolph Saphir, in speaking of Israel's future, has penned the following statement : " How many have wept over Israel ; for whose sorrow can be compared, as it says in the Book of Lamentations, with the sorrow of Jerusalem ? Your poet has said, ' The wild dove hath a nest, the fox its cave, mankind its country, Israel but a grave.' Oh, no ! a thousand times, no. Israel hath the Scripture, and this Scripture it is which has kept Israel alive up to this day. Different from all nations, Israel has the Scripture, and whenever the Holy Spirit breathes upon them, they shall behold Jesus, to whom Moses and the prophets have testified. For the future is still before them, and that future which is spoken of by all the holy prophets, even from the beginning."

Frequently, we find Israel's future is described, and found in many associations. Some of these references may be focussed around such sentences as " In those days," and " The days come." Seven new things await Israel in the future.

1. A NEW OCCUPANCY.—" Lo, the days come, saith Jehovah, that I will bring again the captivity of My people Israel and Judah, saith Jehovah, and I will cause them to return to the land which I gave to their fathers, and they shall possess it " (Jer. xxx. 3).

2. A NEW COMBINE.—" In those days the house of Judah shall walk with the house of Israel, and they shall come together out of the land of the North, to the land that I have given for an inheritance unto your fathers " (Jer. iii. 18).

3. A NEW COVENANT.—" Behold, the days come, saith

the Lord, that I will make a new covenant with the house of Israel, and with the house of Judah," etc. (Jer. xxxi. 31-34).

4. A NEW CITY.—" Behold, the days come, saith the Lord, that the city shall be built to the Lord, from the tower of Hananeel unto the gate of the corner " (Jer. xxxi. 38-40).

5. A NEW ADMINISTRATION.—" In those days, and at that time, will I cause the Branch of Righteousness to grow up unto David ; and He shall execute judgment and righteousness in the land " (Jer. xxxiii. 15).

6. A NEW BLESSING.—" I will pour out My Spirit . . . in those days " (Joel ii. 28, 29).

7. A NEW PROSPERITY.—" Behold, the days come, saith Jehovah, that the plowman shall overtake the reaper, and the treader of grapes him that soweth seed ; and the mountains shall drop sweet wine " (Amos ix. 13).

" Behold, the days come, saith the Lord, that I will perform that good thing which I have promised unto the house of Israel, and to the house of Judah " (Jer. xxxiii. 14).

" IS YOUR SOUL RIGHT ? "

" *Is it well with thee.*"—2 Kings iv. 26.

" Have you come to pay me a pastoral visit ? " one said to her pastor, and then, without waiting for an answer, as many another woman, she asked another question : " What would you say to me if you were paying me a pastoral visit ? "

The pastor replied, " I should ask you, ' Is your soul right ? ' "

" How am I to know if my soul is right ? " was the next question.

And the answer was, " If you are following the Lord fully, trusting Him entirely, yielding to Him continually, listening to Him constantly, obeying Him heartily, delighting in Him wholly, and seeking to please Him unreservedly, then your soul is right."

The answer was inspired by the Spirit through the Word, for He says, by precept and example,

1. We should FOLLOW HIM FULLY as Caleb and Joshua did (Num. xiv. 24).

2. YIELD to Him WHOLLY as Amasai did to David (1 Chron. xii. 18).

3. TRUST Him ENTIRELY as Paul declares (1 Tim. iv. 10).

4. LISTEN to Him REVERENTLY as Mary did (Luke x. 39).

5. OBEY Him UNHESITATINGLY as Christ says His sheep do (John x. 27).

6. DELIGHT in Him LOVINGLY as the Psalmist says when he exclaims, " My soul followeth hard after Thee " (Ps. lxiii. 8).

7. SEEK to PLEASE Him only as the Apostle says, " We make it our aim to be well-pleasing unto Him " (2 Cor. v. 9, R.V.).

JESUS A PROBLEM APART FROM DIVINE REVELATION

" Who is this ? "—Matt. xxi. 10.

The claims of Christ are either awful blasphemies, or Divine revelations. Browning hits off the probable attitude in the shrinking, apologetic " Epistle of an Arab Physician," who had spoken with Lazarus of Bethany :
" This man so cured, regards the Curer then,
　As—God forgive me ! who but God Himself,
　Creator and Sustainer of the world,
　That came and dwelt in flesh on it a while,—
　Sayeth that such a One was born and lived,
　Taught, healed the sick, broke bread at his own house,
　Then died with Lazarus by for aught I know,
　And yet was—what I said or choose repeat,
*　*　*　*　*
The very God ! Think, Abib, dost thou think ? "
Repeatedly the question was asked about Christ, as to who He was. See how the word " This " is used in all the following Scriptures :

1. Said to be " THE CARPENTER'S SON." " Is *this* not the carpenter's Son ? " (Matt. xiii. 55). He was more than He seemed to be. What seems is not always what is.

2. " Truly *this* is THE SON OF GOD " ; so affirmed the Centurion, when he saw all the happenings at the Cross (Matt. xxvii. 54). He saw in the rejected King the rulingMonarch.

3. THE RETURNING LORD.—" For *this* same Jesus shall so come " (Acts i. 11).   The ascended Saviour will be the returning One.

4. THE MAN OF MEN.—" What manner of man is *this* ? " (Matt. viii. 27).   Christ's power over the elements proved He was their Creator.

5. FORGIVER OF SINS.—" Who is *this* that forgiveth sins also ? " (Luke vii. 49).   God Himself, for He alone can forgive sins.

6. SON OF DAVID.—The people were right when they said, " *This* is the Son of David " (Matt. xii. 23).

7. THE JUDGE.—" Who is *this* that cometh from Edom ? " (Isa. lxiii. 1).   The Trodden One of Calvary is the Treader in judgment.

JEW AND THE GULF STREAM

" Thou art My people."—Isa. li. 16.

1. As the Stream RISES in the Gulf of Mexico, so the Jewish race had its rise in the PERSONALITY of him who was called out of Ur of the Chaldees, even Abram the Hebrew (Gen. xii. 1-3).

2. As the Gulf Stream can be TRACED in its COURSE to the Arctic seas, so amid all the vicissitudes of time the Jewish race flows on, and that in spite of Egyptian bondage, Assyrian conquest, Babylonish captivity, European hate, and Jewish sin (Jer. xxx. 1-3 ; Isa. xi. 10-12).

3. As the Gulf Stream is DISTINCT in its colour as it flows on, so the Jewish nation cannot, and will not, mingle with the nations of the world, for the Divine fiat is, " They shall not be reckoned among the nations " (Num. xxiii. 9).

4. As the Stream is BENEFICENT in its warm flow, so we recognise we owe our Bible and our Saviour to the Jewish race (Rom. ix. 4, 5).

5. As the Gulf Stream TOUCHES many countries, so the Jewish race is found everywhere—" scattered among the nations " (Isa. xviii. 2, 7).

6. As the Gulf Stream is often LASHED with the STORMS which sweep across the Atlantic Ocean, so the Jewish race has been lashed with the predicted " seven times " of punish-

ment, and broken because of its sin (Lev. xxvi. 18, 21, 24, 28 ; Rom. xi. 21).

7. As the Stream is rapid and POWERFUL in its FLOW, so the Jew is indomitable in his perseverance, acute in his sense of adaptation, and unquestioned in his financial success (Gen. xviii. 18).

8. And as the Gulf Stream is a wonderful PROVISION in God's PROVIDENCE—for instance, in making the British Isles possible to live upon—so the Jewish race is a triumphant testimony to the love and goodness of God, for, in spite of all their sin, He has purposed to restore them to their land and Himself (Rom. xi. 26-29).

JEWISH PROPHECIES
" Things written aforetime."—Rom. xv. 4.

Israel Zangwill, the great Jewish leader, was called by his people the Voice of Israel. Among his many writings is a poem entitled " Blind Children," which is indeed prophetic of his own race. In it he describes the contentment of blind boys and girls, happy at their play, with no knowledge in their blindness of the world's true beauty. As if, in a spirit of understanding and comradeship, he asks :

" How would they know or feel
They are in darkness ? "

and then, as he visualises the wonder of possible sight coming to them, he exclaims :

" But—O the miracle !
If a Redeemer came,
Laid finger on their eyes—
One touch, and what a world
Newborn in loveliness !

" Spaces of green and sky,
Hulls of white cloud adrift,
Ivy-grown cottage walls,
Shining loved faces.

" What a dark world—who knows ?
Ours to inhabit is !
One touch, and what a strange
Glory might burst on us.
What a hid universe ! "

It is clear from a comparison of Scriptures that the return of the Jews to their land is to be in two stages. The first stage is in unbelief, without any acceptance by the mass of Jesus as Messiah and Saviour. The vision of the valley of dry bones in Ezekiel xxxvii, points distinctly to a return apart from the guidance and help of the Holy Spirit in their individual lives : " There was no breath (Spirit) in them " (verse 8). Ezekiel xxxvi. 24-27, confirms the idea of a return of many before conversion.

1. PROPHECY ABOUT PALESTINE.—But other prophecies speak as clearly of a repentant people being led back to their land, as in Jeremiah xxxi. 8, 9. Thus the mass of the Jews, who remain in all the world until after the return of the Lord, will turn to Him in holy faith and repentance, and follow His leading back to their land.

2. PROPHECY OF SALVATION.—This return after judgment and conversion is seen in Isaiah lxvi. 15-20, a very instructive passage. We see there the awful fires that purify the Jews in the land (verse 15), which connect directly with the furnace passage of Ezekiel xxii. 17-22, and the fierce tribulation described in Zech. xiii. 8, 9 ; xiv. 1-7.

3. PROPHECY ABOUT THE WHOLE NATION.—The present Zionist Jews are wholly unaware of the terrible trials that await them in the land. The Word clearly foretells their return, and that later return of all Israel when God will leave none of the Jews among the Gentiles (Ezekiel xxxix. 28).

JOHN'S TELLING, TENDER, AND TRENCHANT TOUCHES IN HIS THIRD EPISTLE
" The Well-beloved Gaius."—3 John 1.

The late Joseph Parker of the City Temple, London, once wrote on John's concern about the one whom he calls " The Well-beloved Gaius " : " Here we have brethren engaging in Christian intercourse, ascertaining each other's moral conditions, and taking a deep and living interest in all that pertains to the education of the soul in the faith of Christ. This is a fine test of moral manhood. When we find men disposed to give the fullest credit for the growth and sincerity of their brethren in the faith, we may accept such witness as a proof that they themselves are firmly rooted in great principles, and are more and more resembling Him whose name they bear, and whose perfections it is the business of their lives to illustrate."

John continually makes use of the personal pronoun " I," in his brief epistle.

1. " I LOVE " (1).—John's love was no empty sentiment, but a solidarity of truth, expressed in help and sympathy.

2. " I WISH " (2).—The Elder's desire was " that in all things " (marg.) his friend might have prosperity, even as his soul prospered.

3. " I REJOICED " (3), John says, and that " greatly," and the cause of his joy was that " Gaius " was walking " in the truth." When others see what Grace is doing in us, Grace is commended by us.

4. " I HAVE no greater joy " (4), John declares, than when I see " my children walk in the truth." Spiritual prosperity in others is a benediction and a possession to us.

5. " I WROTE " (9).—The apostle's pen was busy and pointed. The apostolic hand used it to send stimulating words of encouragement, and also to chide those who were not right with the Lord.

6. " I WILL REMEMBER HIS DEEDS " (10), John says of prating Diotrephes, and doubtless he would deal with him faithfully, even as he rebuked his " malicious words and conduct."

7. " I TRUST I shall shortly see thee " (14). He loved the fellowship of saints, and desired to have saintly fellowship with them. Meantime he sends his greeting of " Peace."

JOYS : COMING ONES

" For the joy that was set before him."—Heb. xii. 2.

A small boy sat quietly in a seat of the day coach on a train running between two of the western cities in the United States. It was a hot, dusty day, very uncomfortable for travelling, and that particular ride was perhaps the most uninteresting day's journey in the whole land. But the little fellow sat patiently watching the fields and fences hurrying by, until a motherly old lady, leaning forward, asked sympathetically, " Aren't you tired of the long ride, dear, and the dust and the heat ? " The lad looked up brightly, and replied, with a smile, " Yes, ma'am, a little. But I don't mind it much, because my father is going to meet me when I get to the end of it." What a beautiful thought it is that when life seems wearisome and monotonous, as it sometimes does, we can look forward hopefully and trustingly, and like the lonely little lad, " not mind it much," because our Father, too, will be waiting to meet us at our journey's end !

There are many joys which are before the child of God.

1. THE JOY OF SIGHT.—" We shall see Him as He is " (1 John iii. 2). Not as He was, but as He *is*.

2. THE JOY OF MEETING.—Believers will be caught up to " meet " the Lord (1 Thess. iv. 17).

3. THE JOY OF RECEPTION.—His promise is, " I will receive you unto Myself " (John xiv. 3).

4. THE JOY OF CORRESPONDENCE.—" We shall be like Him " (1 John iii. 2).

5. THE JOY OF PRESENCE.—We shall be " with Him " (1 Thess. iv. 17).

6. THE JOY OF REWARD.—Not only rewarded by Him, but we shall enter into the joy of the Lord (Matt. xxv. 23).

7. THE JOY OF GLORY.—Christ has willed that we shall behold and be with Him in the glory (John xvii. 24).

KEEP OFF SATAN'S TERRITORY

" *Resist the devil and he will flee from you.*"—James iv. 7.

" Mums," said a little fellow, " I don't want to be a saint."

" Why not, dear ? "

" I don't want Satan to nurse me."

" What is my boy thinking of ? "

" Well, mother, the hymn says, ' Satan trembles when he sees the weakest saint upon his knees.' "

The boy failed to apprehend the sense of the hymn-writer, namely, that it is the saint upon his knees which makes Satan tremble, and not the saint upon the knees of Satan.

The remark of the boy suggested the possibility of a saint being in the power of Satan.

1. We are not far from him when we warm ourselves at THE WORLD'S FIRE, as Peter (Luke xxii. 55).

2. Company not with the allies of HIS CONFEDERACY, as Jehoshaphat (2 Chron. xviii. 1).

3. Slumber not in the COUNTRY OF UNWATCHFULNESS, as the virgins (Matt. xxv. 5).

4. Be not ENSNARED in the SNARE OF SELF-WILL, as the Spirit says (2 Tim. ii. 26, R.V.).

5. BE ARMED against " the wiles of the devil," as the Word declares (Eph. vi. 11).

6. BE NOT SMEARED by the lusts of the flesh, as the brother at Corinth (1 Cor. v. 1-5).

7. Be not in a SICKLY STATE OF SOUL, as the Corinthian saints (1 Cor. xi. 30).

Keep off the territory of Satan if you would avoid the tears of remorse and the denial of Christ.

KNOCK AT THE DOOR

" *Knock.*"—Matt. vii. 7.

Dr. Parker preached the official sermon of the National Council of the Free Churches at Cardiff, in 1901. He reminded the preachers present that the Gospel was not merely a message for the " insiders," the saints ; but God's manifesto to the whole world, and there was in the heart of the outside crowd a deep, if inarticulate, hunger for the truth possessed by the Church. The doors of the Park Hall, where the service was held, had been locked, as the building was crowded ; but some late-comer had found his way round to the back of the hall, and, eager for entrance, began to pound the back door with his fist. " Hark ! " cried the preacher, with a dramatic lift of his hand, " do you hear that knock ? It is always sounding there, though our ears are deaf to it. The world is surging round the sanctuary, and beating with its knuckles on the panel of the door."

1. THE KNOCK OF LOVE.—" The voice of my Beloved that knocketh " (Cant. v. 2). Love is disappointed when there is no response to its calls.

2. THE KNOCK OF PRAYER.—" Knock, and it shall be opened unto you " (Luke xi. 9). Prayer is urgent when it

feels its need, it goes from the " ask " of request to the " seek " of diligence, and on to the " knock " of urgency.

3. THE KNOCK OF URGENCY.—" Peter continued knocking " (Acts xii. 16). Determination is not put off by unresponsiveness, but continues its poundings on the door.

4. THE KNOCK OF CHRIST.—" Behold, I stand at the door and knock " (Rev. iii. 20). To keep Christ outside of the heart and life, proves the one who does it is lukewarm and cold.

5. THE KNOCK OF RETURN.—" Wait for their Lord . . . that when He cometh and knocketh, they may open unto Him immediately " (Luke xii. 36).

6. THE KNOCK OF PROCRASTINATION.—" Stand without and knock at the door " (Luke xiii. 25), but these were not admitted because they came too late.

7. THE KNOCK OF APPEAL.—" Made enquiry for Simon " (Acts x. 17-33).

The need of the Christless crowd in its wandering quest for happiness is ever a knock at the heart that is in sympathy with Christ. Alas ! so many who are professedly Christ's are content with their own salvation, forgetting they have been saved to save. Pentecost means a passion for souls, not a patronising of our own experience till we are so inflated with our own self-righteous superiority that we have no concern for any one but our own little and self-holiness selves !

LAWLESSNESS IN THE PULPIT

" *Christ died for our sins according to the Scriptures, and was buried, and rose again according to the Scriptures.*"—
1 Cor. xv. 3, 4.

What do we find in many of the pulpits to-day, and in the theological halls ? Listen to what a Professor in a Methodist college says, and also to a leading Free Church layman. Professor Peake declared, " The penalties of sin were not endured by Christ, nor do we escape from them by virtue of His death." He does away with atonement altogether.

Sir Joseph Compton Rickett, an ex-Chairman of the

Congregational Union, also found no use for this fundamental doctrine : " The remission of penalty, or the consequence of sin, does not depend upon the fact of Christ's death."

These statements are an evolution from man's carnal reason, and not according to Divine revelation. One of the greatest Bible teachers of the last century was the late Dr. Dale, of Birmingham, who declared, " Christ came that there might be a Gospel to preach," and as to the relative importance of Christ's life and ministry culminating in the goal of His death, as taught by our Lord Himself, Dr. Dale said, " In an indirect way, it might be said that His teaching from first to last, all that He did, all that He endured, was intended to secure for us the remission of sins."

Equally great a theologian was the late Dr. James Denney, and he said of Christ's atoning death, " His death is a solitary phenomenon—the one thing of the kind in the universe—a sinless submitting to the doom of sin. It was His death, certainly, for He had COME to die ; but it was NOT His, for He knew no sin ; it was FOR US, and NOT FOR HIMSELF, that He made death His own."

There will be no lawlessness in the pulpit, nor the life, if we listen to Him, who speaks in Revelation ii and iii, and ponder the seven times we find His message in connection with the words " THESE THINGS."

When the Lord speaks, it is for us to bow and obey, but when He speaks in a specific character and in a special way, it is for us to listen attentively and intently.

1. THE HOLDER OF THE STARS.—" THESE THINGS saith He that holdeth the seven stars in His right hand " (Rev. ii. 1). The stars represent the ministers whom the Lord uses in His ministry to the churches. When they are held by Him, and used in His service, He serves and speaks through them to purpose.

2. THE FIRST AND THE LAST.—" THESE THINGS saith the First and the Last, which was dead and is alive " (ii. 8). Between Him who is First in creation, and Last in consummation, is His death and resurrection. He can be to us the Genesis and Revelation, because He died for us, and lives for us.

3. THE POSSESSOR OF THE TWO-EDGED SWORD.—" THESE

THINGS saith He which hath the sharp sword with two edges "
(Rev. ii. 12). His Word cuts both ways, as His message to
the church at Pergamos illustrates, it cuts into the inner life
as well as the outward. He lays bare the heart of purpose,
and discovers where the life is barren and wanting.

4. THE EYES OF FIRE.—" THESE THINGS saith the Son of
God, who hath His eyes like unto a flame of fire " (Rev. ii.
18). The flame will not burn unless it has fuel on which to
feed, but when there is the combustibility of sin, it will
scorch and burn to the hurt of the sinner.

5. THE POSSESSOR OF THE SPIRIT.—" THESE THINGS saith
He that hath the seven Spirits " (Rev. iii. 1). Isa. xi. 2, 3
reveals the Holy Spirit in His sevenfold character. The Lamb
and the Spirit are always associated. The Bible begins with
a Brooding Dove, and ends with the Bleeding Lamb.

6. THE HOLY ONE.—" THESE THINGS saith He that is
holy," etc. (Rev. iii. 7). He is Holy and Truth. Holiness
and Truth are not merely attributes with Him, they express
what He IS in the essence of His being.

7. THE FAITHFUL WITNESS.—" THESE THINGS saith the
Amen, the Faithful and True Witness, the Beginning of the
creation of God " (Rev. iii. 14). The " Amen " comes first,
and the " Beginning " last, and between the two He is revealed
as " The Faithful and True Witness." Does this not reveal
to us Christ in His life and ministry, as the Revelation of
God ? And as such He is the Amen, so let it be, and as the
" Beginning " He can make it to be, as He did in the beginning.

LAYING UP TREASURE

" *Lay up for yourselves treasures in heaven.*"—Matt. vi. 20.

One wrote, in calling attention to superfluities, which
Christians might dispose of for the Lord's work :

" Might not believers be searching amongst their
treasures, and be giving up ' jewellery ' or, it may be,
' pictures ' or ' china '—something that we might lay at His
feet which will *cost* us something ? Perhaps it is not fully
realised how many own treasures the value of which they
are entirely unaware. A personal friend related a story to
another once how a friend of his came to stay with him.

Seeing two pieces of china—one somewhat damaged—hanging on the wall in the drawing-room, and knowing something about china, he asked whether he might inspect them. They were taken down, and he suggested that they might be sent to Christie's, in London, for sale. The result was a cheque for some £800."

The spirit of Christ's sacrificial love should animate our spirits. How does it operate ?

1. The DENIAL of Self (Matt. xvi. 24).
2. The SPENDING of Ourselves (2 Cor. xii. 15).
3. The ENDURANCE of Wrongful Suffering (1 Pet. ii. 19).
4. The MINISTERING to the Need of Others (2 Cor. viii. 1-4).
5. Love EXPRESSED in Deeds (1 John iii. 17).
6. SYMPATHISING with Those who are Sick and Infirm (Rom. xv. 1).
7. BEARING the Burdens of Others in Helpful Service (Gal. vi. 2).

LAZARUS

" *Lazarus was one of them who sat at the table with Him.*"—John xii. 2.

An English poet once tried to imagine the life of Lazarus on earth after our Lord had called him back from the grave, bringing a recollection of what he had seen beyond it. For him the whole aspect of life was altered ; great and small assumed henceforth new meanings ; he caught prodigious import in trifles, and found strange rapture even amid pain. For he judged things temporal by his vision of things eternal. Herein lies an illustration of Plato's mystical sentence that it is the art of measurement which can save the soul.

The references to Lazarus, in John xi and xii, are full of interest and suggestion.

1. A SICK MAN.—" A certain man was sick—Lazarus."
2. A LOVED BROTHER.—" Mary . . . whose brother Lazarus."
3. A LOVED FRIEND.—" Jesus . . . loved Lazarus." " He loved him."
4. A RECOGNISING LORD.—" Our friend Lazarus sleepeth." " Lazarus is dead."

5. A CALLED MAN.—" Lazarus, come forth ! "
6. A LOOSED FRIEND.—" Loose him and let him go."
7. A LIVING WITNESS.—" Raised from the dead."
8. A PRIVILEGED GUEST.—" Sat at table with Him."

LIBERTY BY SLAVERY

" *Paul, a servant of Jesus Christ.*"—Rom. i. 1.

It is the Christian life which is the abundantly free life.
Yet, in the face of this fact, Paul speaks of himself as the
" slave of Christ." In the hills of Delphi, in Greece, are the
ruins of the ancient temple to Apollo. All around it has been
constructed a vast retaining wall. On this wall are engraved
hundreds of Greek names. At the top of the list is the statement that those whose names are beneath are slaves to Apollo.
Whenever a man desired to free his slave he carved the name
on this wall. Now, since the freed man was the slave to
Apollo, no one else could possibly claim him. Hence slavery
to Apollo meant absolute freedom. Thus when Paul boasted
of the fact that he was a slave to Jesus Christ, he actually
meant that his was the most complete liberty.

Paul was continually glorying he was the slave of Christ.
In each of the following passages, where he speaks of himself
as the servant, the word he uses is that which describes a
slave or bondman.

1. THE JOY OF SERVITUDE.—" He that is called in the
Lord, being a servant, is the Lord's freeman " (1 Cor. vii. 22).

2. THE UNIVERSALITY OF SERVITUDE.—" For though I be
free from all men, yet have I made myself servant unto all "
(1 Cor. ix. 19).

3. THE EXAMPLE OF SERVITUDE.—" He took upon Him
the form of a servant " (Phil. ii. 7).

4. THE FELLOWSHIP OF SERVITUDE.—" A servant of
Christ . . . for you " (Col. iv. 12).

5. THE SPIRIT OF SERVITUDE.—" The servant of the
Lord must not strive, but be gentle unto all, apt to teach,
patient " (2 Tim. ii. 24).

6. THE BLESSEDNESS OF SERVITUDE.—" Blessed is that
servant, who, when his Lord cometh, shall find watching "
(Matt. xxiv. 46).

7. THE REWARD OF SERVITUDE.—" Well done, good and faithful servant, enter thou into the joy of thy Lord " (Matt. xxv. 21 ; Luke xix. 17).

To take the lowest place in being the Lord's bondman, is to find ourselves following in the steps of our Lord (Matt. xx. 27). The Lord's awards and rewards come to those who faithfully serve Him (Rev. xxii. 3).

LIFE·BEYOND

" Things to come."—1 Cor. iii. 22.

It has often been said that Christ did not say much about after death. A well-known preacher has said :

" Christ said little about personal revival or reunion after death, but much about the life that is lived with God and in God, the life that is our spiritual goal, and in the full possession of which is all the good that mind can conceive or heart desire."

Did not Christ say a great deal about " survival " after this life, and the condition of those who have passed on ?

Let the following seven Scriptures speak for themselves :

1. CHRIST'S WARNING.—" Fear not them which kill the body, but are not able to kill the soul " (Matt. x. 28). Here the soul stands for the individual, which He says man cannot kill.

2. CHRIST'S STATEMENT regarding the unchanging condition of those who " die in their sins," who " cannot " come where He is (John viii. 21). He also says they may " seek " Him, but He will not be found. They are in existence or they could not seek Him.

3. CHRIST ON AN ETERNAL ISSUE of those who believe in Him, and those who will not. " He that believeth on the Son hath everlasting life : and he that believeth not the Son shall not see life ; but the wrath of God abideth on him " (John iii. 36). The unbeliever may " see " many things, as Dives did (Luke xvi. 23), but he will not see life. And, further, the eternal present of the " abideth " shows the unbeliever is in existence, and that eternally.

4. CHRIST DECLARED the reason why God, in His love, gave Him, was, that we should not " perish " (John iii. 16).

Not to receive the Son in His redemptive atonement and remedial grace, is to be marred for ever, for that is the meaning of " perish " and not annihilation.

5. CHRIST'S WORD about the possibility of committing an " eternal sin " in the sin of blasphemy against the Holy Spirit (Matt. xii. 31, 32, R.V.), is meaningless, if the person is not eternally present.

6. CHRIST'S PROMISE to His own, in speaking of the purpose of His return for them, is, " I will come again and receive you unto Myself." This stirring promise is the cheering hope amid the darkness and trials of life, and gilds them with the gold of recompense (John xiv. 3).

7. When CHRIST IN HIS LAST PRAYER for His disciples, pleaded for His own, He also willed to them His glory, for His word is, " Father, I will that they whom Thou hast given Me, be with Me where I am, that they may behold My glory " (John xvii. 24). In these words, He did more than express a wish, He willed His last will and Testament.

All the above plainly proves a life beyond the present one, both for the believer and the unbeliever.

LIFTING POWER

" The Gospel is the power of God."—Rom. i. 16.

It is said that once a skilled artisan in the employ of an Oriental king, had become almost useless at his daily tasks, his hand had lost its cunning, and the work was marred by constant failure. The king sent for him and asked him what had caused the surprising change.

" Ah ! " he said, " it is my heart that makes my hand unsteady. I am under an awful cloud of calamity and discouragement. I am hopelessly in debt, and my family are to be sold as slaves. I can think of nothing else from morning to night, and as I try to polish the jewels, and cut the facets in the diamonds, my hand trembles, and my fingers forget their wonted skill."

The king smiled, and said, " Is that all ? Your debt shall be paid, your family saved, and your cares dispelled. You may take the word of your king, and go to work again with a free and fearless heart." That was done, and never was work so skilfully done, never were such carvings and cunning devices in precious gems as the hand of this happy artisan devised when set at liberty from his fears and burdens.

The king's grace made a new man of the artisan.

1. The power of CHRIST'S LOVE will lift us above hate, and cause us to love Him (1 John iv. 19).

2. The power of CHRIST'S JOY will banish the bane of misery, and gladden us with its song (John xv. 11).

3. The power of CHRIST'S PEACE will turn out carking care, and fill us with its own tranquility (John xiv. 27).

4. The power of CHRIST'S GRACE will stiffen the muscles of our spiritual nature, and make us of sterling worth (2 Tim. ii. 1).

5. The power of CHRIST'S PRESENCE will keep away all fear, and sustain us in every emergency (Isa. xli. 10).

6. The power of CHRIST'S ARMOUR will shield us in every assault of the enemy, as we are strong in Him (Eph. vi. 10).

7. The power of CHRIST'S BEAUTY will entrance and satisfy that we shall not be attracted from Him (S. of Sol. v. 16).

LIGHT'S REFLECTION

" Ye are the light of the world."—Matt. v. 14.

Dr. Amos A. Wells says : " Recently a flashlight of a single candle-power, in the aldermanic chamber of New York City, was turned on a portrait of Thomas Jefferson. Instantly the flash travelled by wire to Charlottesville, Va., and put into operation the most powerful searchlight in the world, one of 1,380,000,000 candle-power, which enables a newspaper to be read fifty miles away, and which is visible for two hundred miles. The searchlight was trained on Monticello, the home of Jefferson, and instantly a return impulse, reaching an aldermanic chamber in New York, illuminated a painting of Monticello.

" What a wonderful illustration of Christ's words about the light of our lives ! That one-candle light started a light more than a billion times as bright, and it was all to glorify Jefferson. So our lights, feeble as they are, may kindle lights that are enormously greater than ours, and may kindle them all over the world, while the entire flood of illumination is not at all for us, but to give glory to God from whom the light originally came.

" What we are to do is only to let our light shine. God will take care of the results. He will see that our light reaches the billion-candle lights and starts them up. It is our task to see that in the chamber of our soul the portrait of Christ is hung up, and that our one-candle rays are thrown upon it."

1. The LIGHT OF FAITH, which illuminated the hearts of Timothy's mother and grandmother, enlightened him (2 Tim. i. 5).

2. The LIGHT OF SALVATION, which was in the heart of Paul and Silas, illuminated the Philippian jailor (Acts xvi. 31, 32).

3. The LIGHT OF TESTIMONY, which irradiated from John the Baptist, shone into the hearts of his disciples (John i. 29-36).

4. The LIGHT OF LIFE, which had quickened the life of Andrew, conveyed its life to Peter (John i. 40-42).

5. The LIGHT OF LIBERTY was made known by the liberated demoniac to those in his home (Mark v. 19).

6. The LIGHT OF LOVE shone out of the heart of John the Beloved, and assured his spiritual children of Divine forgiveness and grace (1 John ii. 12).

7. The LIGHT OF KINDLY HELP moved Paul to be solicitous on behalf of Onesimus, and urged Philemon to act as the apostle had done (Philemon).

LOOK AND PRAY

" *Look on the Fields.*"—John iv. 35.
" *Pray ye therefore the Lord of the harvest, that He will send forth labourers.*"—Matt. ix. 38.

The *Montreal Witness* gives the following facts and figures of the great human family living on earth to-day.

It consists of 1,450,000,000 souls—not fewer, probably more. They are distributed literally all over the earth's surface ; there is no considerable spot on the globe where man has not found a foothold. In Asia, the so-called " cradle " of the human race, there are now about 800,000,000 people, densely crowded, on an average of about 120 to every square mile. In Europe there are 320,000,000, averaging 100 to the square mile. In Africa there are, approximately, 210,000,000, and in the Americas—North, South, and Centre —110,000,000. On the islands, large and small, there are probably 10,000,000. The extremes of the blacks and the whites are as five to three, the remaining 700,000,000 intermediate, brown, yellow, and tawny in colour. Of the entire race, 500,000,000 are well clothed—that is, they wear garments of some kind to cover nakedness ; 250,000,000 habitually go naked, and 700,000,000 only cover the middle parts of their body ; 500,000,000 live in houses, and 700,000,000 live in huts and caves, the remaining 250,000,000 virtually having no place to lay their heads.

Are we praying to the Lord, that He will thrust forth labourers into this great harvest field ? Are we concerned about the salvation of those who are living without hope, without Christ, and without God ? Do those of us who believe in Christ's near return go out of our way to obey our Lord's command, " Occupy," or " Trade with the Gospel till I come " ?

Paul was the ideal character in every way as one who looked on the fields, and laboured in them. In himself he felt he was nothing, but yet how effective he was. A nought stands for nothing, but when we put one against a nought, we have ten.

See how Paul uses the word " nothing " in the following passages :

1. A PENNILESS APOSTLE.—" As having nothing " (2 Cor. vi. 10). He might have an empty pocket, but he also had an endowed and enriched ministry.

2. A PERTINENT ADMONITION.—" Let nothing be done through strife " (Phil. ii. 3). Strife shows a wrong state of soul within. Fumes are born of ferments.

3. A PRICELESS ASSET.—" I know nothing against myself " (1 Cor. iv. 4, R.V.). A clear conscience within gives us a calm confidence in God.

4. A PARTNER'S AMBITION.—" Without thy mind I would do nothing " (Philem. 14). Paul's aim was to fall in with Philemon's wish, that together they might act about Onesimus.

5. A Preacher's Avowal.—" I have kept back nothing " (Acts xx. 20). True to his trust, he kept his trust to the full.

6. A Principle Asserted.—" There is nothing unclean " (Rom. xiv. 14). Sin contaminates everything, grace consecrates all that is not sinful.

7. A Prospector's Aim.—" According to my earnest expectation and my hope, that in nothing I shall be ashamed " (Phil. i. 20). When our aim is true, the result is certain.

LORD'S REQUIREMENTS

" *What doth the Lord require of thee?* "—Deut. x. 12, 13 ; Micah vi. 8.

Some Christians have the same idea of God's commandments as a little boy who was playing with his sister. A most unpleasant woman who lived near had been finding fault with them, and the boy said, " I just hate her." His little sister, greatly shocked, said, " Oh, no ! The Bible says we must love every one." " Oh, well," he remarked, " old Mrs. Blake wasn't born when that was written." Isn't that the idea some of us seem to have about the requirements of God's Word ?

The Lord's requirements remind us of our responsibilities. In the above Scriptures there are eight requirements which we are responsible to observe.

1. " To Fear the Lord Thy God."—To fear the Lord in His Word with reverence, is to recognise His claims, and to be in awe of His holiness. He is our " God " who has created us, and our " Lord " who claims us.

2. " To Walk in All His Ways."—His ways are ways of love to provide for us, ways of power to shield us, ways of holiness to sanctify, ways of wisdom to guide, ways of peace to calm, and ways of grace to beautify us.

3. " To Love Him."—To love Him for what He is, what He does, what He gives, what He promises, what He teaches, and what He requires.

4. " To Serve the Lord Thy God."—To serve Him like those who brought the materials of the Tabernacle— they served wisely, willingly, and warmly (Exod. xxv. 2 ; xxxv. 10, 21, 22).

5. " To Keep the Commandments of the Lord."—
To keep them as a sacred trust, as a holy treasure, and as an
honoured privilege.

6. " To Do Justly."—To treat others as we would wish
to be treated. Not to take advantage of their ignorance, nor
give to them anything that is unjust.

7. " To Love Mercy."—To see the need of others and
meet it. To exercise forgiveness when injured, and to help
those who are in dire necessity.

8. " To Walk Humbly with Thy God."—A contrite
heart, a lowly spirit, and a soul devoid of pride, are conditions which meet with the Lord's appreciation.

LOVE'S ATTITUDE

" *Waiting for the coming (revelation) of our Lord Jesus Christ.*"
1 Cor. i. 7.

Fiction has painted the picture of a maiden whose lover
left her for a voyage to the Holy Land, promising on his
return to make her his beloved bride. Many told her that
she would never see him again. But she believed his word,
and evening by evening she went down to the lonely shore,
and kindled there a beacon light in sight of the roaring waves
to hail and welcome the returning ship which was to bring
again her betrothed. And by that watch fire she took her
stand each night, praying to the winds to hasten on the
sluggish sails, that he who was everything to her might come.
Even so that blessed Lord, who has loved us unto death, has
gone away to the mysterious holy land of heaven, promising
on His return to make us His happy and eternal Bride. Some
say that He has gone for ever, and that here we shall never
see Him more. But His last word was, " Yea, I come
quickly," and on the dark and misty beach sloping out into
the eternal sea, each true believer stands by the love-lit fire,
looking and waiting and praying, and hoping for the fulfilment of His Word, in nothing gladder than in His pledge and
promise, and calling ever from the soul of sacred love, " Even
so, come, Lord Jesus." And some of these nights, while the
world is busy with its gay frivolities, and laughing at the
maiden on the shore, a form shall rise over the surging waves,

as once on Galilee, to vindicate for ever all this watching and
devotion, and bring to the faithful and constant heart a joy
and glory and triumph which never more shall end.

The attitude of the believer o the Lord's return, evidences
our faithfulness to Him.

1. We should look for Him expectantly (Titus ii. 13).
2. Watch for Him faithfully (Luke xii. 35-48).
3. Wait for Him ardently (Phil. iii. 20, 21).
4. Love Him supremely (2 Tim. iv. 8).
5. Occupy for Him diligently (Luke xix. 13).
6. Remember Him thankfully (1 Cor. xi. 26).
7. Yield to Him wholly (1 Thess. v. 23).

LOVE'S MINISTRY

" *The Love of Christ constraineth us.*"—2 Cor. v. 14.

A well-known editor says, " The greatest, if not the most
beautiful thing I ever saw, was in the city of Edinburgh.
A boy saw that his little sister's stockingless feet were cold,
so he took off his cap and said to her, ' Maggie, your feet are
cauld, put them in my cap.' " A capless head meant covered
feet, and doubtless, a " cauld " head was the result of warmed
feet.

Surely the incident tells us what love loves to do. A heart
of love ever expresses itself in a hand of labour.

1. Love " COVERS a multitude of sins " (1 Pet. iv. 8, R.V.).
2. FEEDS the sheep and lambs (John xxi. 15-17).
3. FORBEARS with another's weakness (Eph. v. 2).
4. SACRIFICES what is its own (1 Sam. xviii. 1-31).
5. MINISTERS to another's need (1 John iii. 17).
6. GIVES UP its rights (Exod. xxi. 5).
7. OVERCOMES difficulties (S. of Sol. viii. 7).
8. Is LONGSUFFERING in its kindness (1 Cor. xiii. 4).

LOVE'S MINISTRY

" *He loved . . . He gave.*"—John iii. 16.

A well-known writer has described the ministry of true
love as follows, " To give ! To give without hope of recompense, without question, without fear ! That was the

message of life." Who is there that answers to the ideal in all its reality ? Certainly there was One who did, and that One was Christ. He gave " without hope of recompense." His recompense was in giving.

Love gives out of its own nature, and cannot do any other than it does. It is not occupied with its own beneficence, for it is absorbed in its service. Christ gave " without question," and " without fear." He did not reason why ? His was to do and die. The threats of men did not daunt Him, nor did the hate of hell deter Him. In the absorbing passion of His Father's will, and in the pursuit of reaching the Father's goal of glory, He kept steadily on. What a " message of life " He gives us, and what an Example for imitation He leaves us. Can we imitate Him ?

We make the attempt, and soon we find ourselves like Peter " following afar " ! If the ideal of His perfect love is to be an actuality in us in any way, He must make it actual ; He alone can. The Christ within in His life, must walk in the life He lived without.

Christ ever went about doing good, and virtue was going out of Him all the time. Luke xxiv is one of the many chapters where Christ's activities are recorded.

1. LOVE'S APPROACH.—" Jesus Himself drew near " (15). Christ is ever coming to us that He may make Himself known, and He always comes with some definite blessing.

2. LOVE'S ANNOUNCEMENTS.—" He said " (17, 19, 25, 36, 38, 44, 46). His messages are ever meanful and soul-making. He sometimes rebukes in His love, that He may bless in His grace.

3. LOVE'S ASSOCIATION.—" He expounded . . . the Scriptures . . . concerning Himself " (27). The Living and the Written Word go together. We need Him to reveal to us the association.

4. LOVE'S ASIDE.—" He made as though He would go further " (28). His seeming withdrawals are made to draw us out and on, and that we may pray " Abide with us."

5. LOVE'S ABIDING.—" He went in to tarry " (" Abide," R.V., 29). Prayer answered means His abiding, and that means all we need.

6. LOVE'S ATTENTION.—" He sat . . . took . . . blessed

... brake, and gave " (30). He feeds, and blesses, and gives ; and He does all that we may know Him (31). He loves to make Himself known, and knowing Him, our hearts are at rest.

7. LOVE'S ASSIMILATION.—" He vanished . . . ." " He talked . . ." " He opened " (31, 32). He left the aroma of His presence behind, and He fused the hearts of the disciples into one, for they felt He had assimilated their hearts into one—" our heart."

8. LOVE'S APPEARANCE.—" The Lord . . . appeared to Simon " (34). The Lord knew the anguish of heart Peter was in, so He made a special visit to him, and restored him from his backsliding state.

9. LOVE'S ATTRACTABILITY.—" Jesus Himself stood in the midst. . . ." " He saith, Peace. . . ." " It is I Myself. . . ." " He showed them His hands and His feet. . . ." " Joy " (36-41). He was the Centre around whom the disciples gathered, and He Himself was the Joy of their hearts.

10. LOVE'S AFFIRMATION.—" I spake." " Opened He " (44, 45). He not only reminded them of what He said, but He confirmed it by opening the Scriptures and by opening their understanding. His affirmations are always confirmations and benedictions.

11. LOVE'S AUTHORITY.—" I send " (49). He sends the Holy Spirit as He promised, that we may know His authority and ability to carry out His pledges.

12. LOVE'S ACTION.—" He led " (50). His leadings are for our good and His givings.

13. LOVE'S ATTITUDE.—" He blessed them " (50, 51). Those nailed-printed hands are uplifted for our blessing. Gaze on those hands and hear them speak.

14. LOVE'S ADORABLENESS (52).—" They worshipped Him." We must adore Him in worship, when we behold His adorableness.

LOVE'S TRAITS

" God is Love."—1 John iv. 8.

Dr. John G. Paton had a bad character to deal with in his New Hebrides mission in a Tanna man named Nasi. Mr. H. O. Cady tells of a serious illness which befell Nasi and during which Dr. Paton ministered to him regularly, but no kindness seemed to move him. After the doctor had sailed for home, a band of native Christians held a consultation over the case of Nasi. They said, " We know the burden and trouble that Nasi has been to our dear pastor ; we know that he has murdered several persons with his own hands, and has taken part in the murder of others. Let us unite in daily prayer that the Lord will open his heart and change his conduct, and teach him to love and follow what is good, and let us set ourselves to win him for Christ just as we were won." So they began to show him every possible kindness, one after another helping daily. At first he repelled them and sullenly held aloof, but prayer never ceased and love grew. At last Nasi broke down, and said, " I can oppose Jesus no longer. If He can make you treat me like that, I yield myself to Him and to you. I want Him to change me ; I want a heart like that of Jesus," and when Dr. Paton returned from his furlough he found this former murderer a devoted, loving follower of Jesus.

The Essence of God's Nature " is Love." Love with Him is not an attribute, it is what He " *is* "; but as there are seven colours to the rainbow, so there are seven traits of Love.

1. " Compassion " is the *Heart* of Love. When the father saw the prodigal, his heart was " moved with compassion " (Luke xv. 20). His inner being was stirred to its depths, and showed itself in the kiss of forgiveness, the clasp of affection, the robe of adornment, the shoes of protection, the ring of honour, the feast of provision, the words of appreciation, and the joy of gladness.

2. " Kindness " is the *Act* of Love. " The kindness," as well as " the love of God," appeared (Titus iii. 4). When David would express his regard to Mephibosheth, he did it for Jonathan's sake (2 Sam. ix. 3-7), and showed his beneficence in what he did for him. So God, for Christ's sake, blesses us.

3. " Grace " is the *Munificence* of Love. Grace does not look at the deserts of the object upon which it shows its favour, but gives everything for nothing, when the recipient does not deserve anything. The grace came through Christ (John i. 17), and enriches those who were poor (2 Cor. viii. 9).

4. " MERCY " is the *Disposition* of Love. " God, who is rich in mercy, for His great love wherewith He hath loved us " (Eph. ii. 4). We sometimes sing that " Love moved the mighty God " ; but that is not so—He moved because He loved. His hands of mercy are extended towards us, because His heart of love determined to save us (Titus iii. 5).

5. " SACRIFICE " is the *Service* of Love. When the saints are exhorted to " walk in love," they are pointed to Him who " loved us, and hath given Himself for us, an offering and a sacrifice to God for a sweet-smelling savour " (Eph. v. 2). Love will sacrifice much for the object of its affection, as Jonathan did for David (1 Sam. xviii. 1-4), but it thinks not of the sacrifice it makes.

6. " PITY " is the *Help* of Love. When Jehovah acted for His people, we read, " In His love and pity He redeemed them, and He bare them, and carried them all the days of old " (Isa. lxiii. 9). Humans pity one another, but do not always help. God's pity shows itself in help and sympathy. Pity frees from bondage, carries our load, and is not weary in helping.

7. SYMPATHY is the *Fellowship* of Love. " Bowels of mercies " is expressive of the feeling of tender regard which one has for another (Gen. xliii. 30 ; Phil. i. 8 ; Col. iii. 12 ; Philem. 7, 12, 20 ; 1 John iii. 17). The tears of Christ revealed His heart of sympathetic love. To weep with another is to express the feeling one has for the other.

" MADE RADIANT "

" *They looked unto Him and were radiant.*"—Ps. xxxiv. 5, R.V.

Dr. G. Campbell Morgan relates : " It is now five-and-twenty years ago and more since a very simple thing came to my own personal knowledge which profoundly affected me at the time, and from the influence of which I have never escaped. A Yorkshire factory lass had given herself to Jesus Christ ; the light and the joy of it was in her soul, and her face became transfigured. She was walking up and down the platform of York Station, waiting for a train. Sitting in a first-class railway carriage was a lady of title and culture. She saw the lassie pass her carriage two or three times, and at last called to her and said : ' Excuse me, but what makes you look so happy ? ' The girl replied : ' Was I looking happy ? I did not know, but I can tell you why.' And she told the woman the secret of her joy. She did not know that her face was shining, but the shining face of the factory lassie arrested the woman who was in agony. The end of the story is that this woman was led to the same Christ, and her face also became transfigured."

1. MADE RIGHTEOUS in His radiant righteousness (2 Cor. v. 21).

2. MADE ACCEPTABLE by His radiant grace (Eph. i. 6).

3. MADE WHITE in His radiant blood (Rev. vii. 14).

4. MADE HOLY in His radiant Christ (1 Cor. i. 30).

5. MADE STRONG in His radiant power (2 Cor. xii. 9).

6. MADE MEET in His radiant working (Col. i. 12).

7. MADE PRIESTS in His radiant love (Rev. i. 6).

MAKINGS OF THE LORD

" *He maketh*."—Ps. xviii. 33.

A fable says : A thousand voices had poured forth a glorious chorus, and the conductor of the choir laid down his baton with relief and satisfaction.

" I'm sure I did that well," said the baton to the music-stand on which it lay.

" Did what well ? "

" Conducted that chorus."

" Foolish thing ! " said the stand ; " you had about as much to do with it as I had."

" You ! " shouted the baton indignantly. " Did you not see that my movements regulated the speed at which the singers went, called in the bass, or tenor, or alto, or signalled to the treble to cease ; bade them increase their voices or diminish them ? "

" I saw that the master used you to signify his commands, but you were little more than nothing in the business."

" You are simply jealous of me, that's all," retorted the baton. " Without me this music would be all confusion."

The master rose, and without lifting the baton gave the signal for his singers to be ready. He had, absent-minded man that he was, forgotten where he had laid it, so seized a roll of music, and used that with which to conduct. When the piece ended, the stand shook with laughter.

" What did you do that time ? " it asked of the discomfited baton ; but there was no reply, the baton was bitterly disappointed and humbled.

How often we find the words, " He maketh," when speaking of the Lord's doing. We are well made when He makes us.

1. ATONEMENT.—" The priest that maketh atonement " (Lev. vii. 7). Christ alone could make atonement for our sins.

2. PERFECTION.—" He maketh my way perfect " (Ps. xviii. 32).

3. SECURITY.—" He maketh my feet like hinds' feet " (Ps. xviii. 33).

4. REST.—" He maketh me to lie down " (Ps. xxiii. 2).

5. PEACE.—" He maketh war to cease " (Ps. xlvi. 9).

6. WHOLENESS.—" Jesus Christ maketh thee whole " (Acts ix. 34).

7. INTERCESSION.—" He maketh intercession for the saints " (Rom. viii. 26, 27, 34).

MAN OR MONKEY ?

" *God created man in His own image.*"—Gen. i. 27.

Dr. Barnes, Bishop of Birmingham, in an address to men, stated : " The fundamental question was—if man descended from the monkey, how could he have an immortal soul if the monkey did not ? He did not profess to answer that question. He did not know the machinery of evolution, but man was man and not a monkey, whatever his origin might have been. God was not the God of the dead, but of the living. God would preserve what He valued.

" He had given to man knowledge, virtue, the sense of beauty, aspirations, and conscience. Those things were the expression of God's nature if Christ's teaching be true. He had used the whole process of evolution to bring them into existence among ourselves, and would not allow the human personality in whom they blossomed to be destroyed. Those qualities of God were life-giving.

" There was enough knowledge to guide our religious

lives. We could see, though through a glass darkly, what God intended us to become as He planned this long process of which we were the product."

We do not want to know the bishop's inflated opinions about evolution, but we do believe in the Divine inspiration of Revelation.

1. Man was CREATED in the image of God ; but not the monkey (Gen. i. 26).

2. Man is the OBJECT of God's love ; but not the monkey (John iii. 16).

3. Christ DIED FOR MAN ; but not for the monkey (Rom. v. 8).

4. Christ was MADE in the LIKENESS of man ; but not in the image of a monkey (Rom. viii. 3).

5. Man is CAPABLE of appreciating the beauty of God's works ; but not a monkey (Ps. xix. 1-6 ; Isa. xl. 21-26).

6. Man knows the MEANING of ACCOUNTABILITY ; but not so the monkey (Ps. xxvi. 1-12).

7. Man KNOWS there is a LIFE TO COME ; but not the monkey (Heb. ix. 27 ; Eccles. xi. 8-10 ; xii. 7, 13, 14.)

MAN WHO WILL SUCCEED

" *By that Man, whom He hath ordained.*"—Acts xvii. 31.

The following terse advice by Theodore N. Vail, the President of the American Telephone and Telegraph Co., is sane and sound :

" This is the age of the specialist. Money is no object.

" There are no men as scarce to-day as those who can fill the high-salaried positions.

" I have from twenty to thirty positions open right now that I would gladly pay from ten to twenty-five thousand dollars per year.

" The great hindrance to those who might to-day occupy the big places is the continued cry of ' Where do I come in ? '

" The man who creates big situations in business does not need to ask ' Where do I come in ? ' He lands with both feet."

The man who will succeed, in the highest sense of the word, is the Lord Jesus.

" In those days, and at that time, will I cause the Branch

of Righteousness to grow up unto David ; and He shall execute judgment and righteousness in the land. In those days shall Judah be saved ; and this is the name wherewith she shall be called, The LORD Our Righteousness. For thus saith the LORD, David shall never want a man to sit upon the throne of the house of Israel ; neither shall the priests and Levites want a man before Me to offer burnt-offerings, and to kindle meat offerings, and to do sacrifice continually " (Jer. xxxiii. 15-18).

1. A SPECIFIED TIME.—" In those days." The day of Israel's restoration to the Promised Land, and their reconciliation to Jehovah.

2. A SUPREME CAUSE.—" Will I cause." When Jehovah is the cause of anything, His acts of grace and government are sure to succeed.

3. A STRIKING TITLE.—" The Branch of Righteousness to grow." Life, Rightness, and Progress, are the germinating thoughts in this sentence.

4. A SIGNIFICANT ASSOCIATION.—" Unto David . . . in the land." The Person and the Place are always together.

5. A SOVEREIGN RULE.—" He shall execute judgment and righteousness." Decision of right will characterise all He does.

6. A SPECIAL PEOPLE.—" Judah shall be saved " : Nationally, spiritually, and to Jehovah.

7. A SPIRITUAL NAME.—" She shall be called the Lord our Righteousness." As her Lord, so shall she be.

8. A SEATED MAN.—" David shall never want a Man to sit on the throne of the house of Israel." Great David's greater Son is the Man.

9. A SACRED RITUAL.—" Before Me," Jehovah declares, shall the new ritual be carried out.

" MARANATHA "

" *If any man love not the Lord Jesus Christ, let him be anathema* " (accursed). " *Maranatha.*"—1 Cor. xvi. 22.

One has written of the Lord's Coming, in explaining the word maranatha, the Lord cometh :

" The apostle had just finished dictating to his amanuensis his letter to the Corinthians. Then he took the pen, and in his familiar and bold characters proceeded to sign his own name. But before doing so he paused and prayed, and in the space still left upon the unfinished page, he added the remaining verses of this chapter. They were a sort of post-script to his great letter of twelve thousand words, and they may be expected to contain concentrated truth of great moment. His first sentence is a solemn warning to the enemies of Christ of the anathema awaiting them. There should be a full stop after " Anathema," for the next word is a complete sentence. " Maranatha " means the Lord is coming, and he writes it in his bold and striking hand as a great milestone and note of time for his fellow-pilgrims. Its significance and solemnity are emphasised by the place it occupies in his letter. It is not too much to say that this striking word is a keynote and a key in connection with all the greatest things of sacred truth and life."

The Second Coming of our Lord Jesus Christ comes in at every point of the Christian life, is associated with every Christian doctrine, and is constantly brought to bear upon the motives and actions of the Lord's people, and is set forth as a warning to those who are not His by redemption.

1. Is it a question of HEART COMFORT, during the absence of our blessed Lord, and amidst the trials and sorrows of this world ? The Lord's Coming, and our being for ever with Him, is presented as the one consoling object of the heart (John xiv. 1-3 ; 1 Thess. iv. 13-18).

2. Is it a question of HOPE FILLING THE SOUL with deep longing and holy emulation ? The coming of Christ to receive us to glory is brought before us as the " blessed hope " (Titus ii. 13).

3. Is it a question of MOTIVE POWER in service ? The coming of the Lord is brought to bear for this end (1 Cor. xv. 58 ; 1 Thess. ii. 19).

4. Is it a question of a HOLY LIFE ? This is looked at in view of the coming of Christ, which is also given as the motive of it (1 Thess. iii. 13 ; 1 John iii. 3).

5. Is it a question of FREEDOM FROM THE STING OF DEATH, and victory over the gloom of the grave ? For God's believing people this victory will be manifested by the coming of Christ (1 Cor. xv. 54-57).

6. Is it a question of an INTRODUCTION OF A NEW AND
GLORIOUS ERA for this world ? The coming of Christ is
the great event that shall bring this about. See Rev. xix.
But Scripture everywhere shows this.

7. Is it a question of THE SERVANT'S REWARD for faithful
service while his Lord is away ? It is associated with the
coming of Christ. Matt. xxiv. 45-47, and other passages
which the reader may look up.

8. INDOLENCE.—Does the evil servant begin to smite his
fellow-servants, and to eat and drink with the drunken ? It
is because he has said in his heart, " My Lord delayeth His
coming " (Matt. xxiv. 48-51).

9. And, finally, the coming of Christ is used as a
WARNING to the sinner (Luke xvii. 26-30).

MEDIATOR

*" There is one God, and one Mediator between God and men,
the Man Christ Jesus ; who gave Himself a Ransom for
all."*—1 Tim. ii. 5, 6.

The word " mediator " is a compound one. It is made
up of a word which means middle, and another which
signifies to go, hence, a go-between, that is one who acts
between two parties who are at variance, and makes peace
between them. God did not need to be reconciled to us,
but we needed to be reconciled to Him.

Bishop Hall says of Christ, our Mediator, " The Godhead
of man, and the blood of God are two such miracles as the
angels of heaven can never look enough into, never admire
enough. How necessary to peace and holiness is the faith
which accepts both ; how precious are both to those who
feel their need of both in the one Saviour."

Strong says on the word " mediator," " a go-between, a
reconciler, an intercessor." Christ acts for us in many ways.
Generally speaking, He acts from God to us, and from us
to God.

1. BETTER MEDIATOR.—Better than angels in His mediation, and others (Gal. iii. 19, 20 ; Heb. viii. 6 ; ix. 15), for
He brings in a " new " and " better covenant."

2. GOD-MAN MEDIATOR.—" Between God and man "
might be rendered " Partaking of God and man " (Westcott).

3. SIN-MADE MEDIATOR.—" Sin for us He was made,"
and God makes us His righteousness in Him (2 Cor. v. 21).

4. RECONCILING MEDIATOR.—" God was in Christ reconciling the world to Himself " (2 Cor. v. 19).

5. LOVING MEDIATOR.—" He gave Himself for us "
(Gal. ii. 20). Love prompted Him to give, and had satisfaction in giving.

6. PROCURING MEDIATOR.—" A ransom " He gave, that
is, a procuring cause to obtain us.

7. TESTIFYING RANSOM.—" To be testified in due time "
(1 Tim. ii. 6). He came to tell, to do, to die, and rise.

MISTAKES

" By one man's disobedience, many were made sinners."
Rom. v. 19.

A wiseacre has said : " Nature blundered when it decided
to make frogs' legs a delicacy and elephants' legs a total loss."

The wiseacre's remark reminds us of another one, who, in
commenting on the fact that acorns grew on oak trees, and pumpkins on slender vines, said that if he had been the Creator,
he would have put the pumpkins on the oak, and the acorns
on the vine. One day he went to sleep under an oak tree, and
he was awakened by an acorn falling on his face, which caused
him to exclaim, " Thank God that was not a pumpkin ! "

Nature makes no mistakes, but man is making them all
the time.

1. DISOBEDIENCE.—ADAM made a mistake when he took
of the forbidden fruit (Rom. v. 19).

2. COVETOUSNESS.—ACHAN blundered when he reached
out for the Babylonish garment (Josh. vii. 18-26).

3. COMPROMISE.—MOSES made a mistake when he smote
the rock instead of speaking to it (Num. xx. 11, 12).

4. SELF-ACTION.—PETER was hot-headed when he smote
off the ear of the servant of the high priest (Luke xxii. 50).

5. PRIDE.—The SONS OF AARON were guilty of an unholy
breach of God's commands when they brought the strange
fire (Lev. x. 1, 2).

146

6. BACKSLIDING.—ABRAM was unwise when he went down to Egypt, instead of abiding in Bethel (Gen. xii. 10 ; xiii. 4).

7. CONTENTION.—The DISCIPLES were grievously wrong when they quarrelled to see who should be the greatest (Luke ix. 46).

" MORE," YEA, " MUCH MORE "

" The Lord shall increase you more and more."—Ps. cxv. 14.

One writes : " God always gives you a little bit more. When I was a boy, I used to take my penny or twopence to the shop for sweets, buying the smallest ones because I got more of them, and I used to watch very carefully the scales as they went down on the side of the sweets. And do you know what I used to value ? The few over. I used to love to see the scale go down on the side of the sweets."

Our Heavenly Father loves to give us " more " of His grace, yes, " much more."

1. THE " MUCH MORE " OF HIS CARE (Matt. vi. 30).—He feels the cold of His children, and supplies clothes to keep them warm.

2. THE " MUCH MORE " OF HIS GIVING (Matt. vii. 11 ; Luke xi. 13).—The Spirit " given," and the " good things " received, make wealthy and healthy in grace and godliness.

3. THE " MUCH MORE " OF SALVATION (Rom. v. 9).— Justification before God leads on to sanctification in Him, and reaches the goal of glorification with Him.

4. THE " MUCH MORE " OF LIFE (Rom. v. 10).—Reconciliation to God ushers us into the life which makes us alive in Him.

5. THE " MUCH MORE " OF GRACE (Rom. v. 20).—At the Cross sin abounded, but grace did " much more abound." Man is there seen at his worst, and God at His best.

6. THE " MUCH MORE " OF VALUE (Heb. ix. 14).—The blood of the sacrifice was only temporary in its value ; but the Blood of Christ is of eternal value.

7. THE " MUCH MORE " OF TRIAL (1 Pet. i. 7).—The ore is purified by the fire ; but how much more the believer is purified by trial.

Go in for the super-abundant life in Christ.

MYSTERIES

" To you is given to know the mysteries."—Matt. xiii. 11.

The word " mystery " means " a revealed secret." The same Greek word is translated " secret " in the Septuagint Version of the Old Testament. It signifies a truth clearly to be seen, but too profound to be fully fathomed, and the word itself implies that it is only revealed to the initiated. It need hardly be said that the original word has nothing of that sinister significance which modern usage has attached to it, from its invariable association with crime in our every-day speech ! The word occurs twenty-seven times in •the New Testament, and always (except in Col. ii. 2 and 1 Tim. iii. 16) of matters which are revealed fully in the present dispensation, though dimly foreshadowed under the old.

There are several mysteries made known in the New Testament. The place where each is mentioned must determine the application. To mix up these mysteries is to make confusion worse confounded. If we take each mystery in the light of its declaration, we shall find, like the light of the lampstand, it gives radiance over against itself, and makes all to stand out in the meaning of its revelation.

1. THE MYSTERY OF ISRAEL'S BLINDNESS is no mystery regarding the blindness of Israel : but its duration is made known in the fact that it is until the fulness, or the number, of the Gentiles be gathered in (Rom. xi. 25).

2. THE MYSTERY OF GODLINESS is that God was made manifest in the flesh, hence its greatness and glory (1 Tim. iii. 16).

3. THE MYSTERY OF THE CHURCH is that God, in His electing grace, is blessing those who receive Christ, and making them, whether Jew or Gentile, one in Him (Rom. xvi. 25 ; Eph. iii. 3, 4, 9 ; v. 32 ; vi. 19 ; Col. i. 26, 27 ; iv. 3 ; 1 Tim. iii. 9). Hence it is called the " mystery " of what was kept secret since the world began.

4. THE MYSTERY OF LAWLESSNESS is the end of hell's working in the self-will of man, which will develop the production of the lawless one (2 Thess. ii. 7).

5. THE MYSTERY OF GOD and of the Father and of Christ is the centralisation of everything, whether in grace or govern-

ment, in Christ, and that in Him dwells all the fulness of the Godhead bodily (Eph. i. 9 ; Col. ii. 2 ; Rev. x. 7).

6. THE MYSTERY OF THE SEVEN STARS is that Christ holds all those who are in places of responsibility, in God's assembly, by His almighty power (Rev. i. 20).

7. THE MYSTERY OF BABYLON is that behind all the abominable mixture of the world's religions, and its commercial spirit, there is the Satanic spirit that governs it (Rev. xvii. 5).

8. THE MYSTERY ABOUT THE GLORIFIED SAINTS is that we shall not all sleep, but that we shall all be changed, and be made like to our glorified Lord (1 Cor. xv. 51).

9. THE MYSTERIES OF THE KINGDOM OF HEAVEN, in a general sense, is that behind the body of the outward meaning of revealed truth there is a soul of secret explanation (Matt. xiii. 11).

NAME ABOVE EVERY NAME

" *They that know Thy Name will put their trust in Thee.*"— Ps. ix. 10.

The H.R.H. Infanta Eulalia of Spain, in Courts and countries after the War, related the following personal incident : " I chanced to be staying at Cornwall, and stopped at a wayside cottage to ask for a cup of tea. Just as I was about to take my leave, my hostess went to a cupboard, and, with immense solemnity, produced a china cup, in the bottom of which was deposited a little brown sediment.

" ' Do you see this cup, ma'am ? ' she asked in an awed whisper.

" ' Yes,' said I ; ' you seem to prize it greatly. What is its history ? '

" ' Well, ma'am ' (in impressive tones), ' Queen Victoria herself drank tea from this very cup when she passed this way in grandmother's time. So, naturally, we think a powerful deal of it ; 'twas never rinsed out, and it never will be.' "

The cup was sacred because it had been used by Queen Victoria, and henceforth no one else was to drink from it. There are some things, too, in the life of our Lord which are sacred and alone. His miraculous birth, His holy life, His wondrous ministry, His wondrous teaching, His agonised prayer, His atoning death, His mighty resurrection, ascension, glory, and His prophetic Word of coming events. These stand alone.

The great ones, who bear great names may be honoured and loved, but what shall we say of Him, who bears the hallowed name of Jehovah ?

Jehovah-Jireh ; Jehovah will see or provide (Gen. xxii. 14).

Jehovah-Ropheca ; The Lord that healeth thee (Exod. xv. 26).

Jehovah-Nissi ; The Lord my Banner (Exod. xvii. 15).

Jehovah-Eloheka ; The Lord thy God (Exod. xx. 2, 5, 7).

Jehovah-Mekaddeshkem ; The Lord that doth sanctify you (Exod. xxxi. 13 ; Lev. xx. 8 ; xxi. 8 ; xxii. 9 ; Ezek. xx. 12).

Jehovah-Shalom ; The Lord send peace (Judges vi. 24).

Jehovah-Tsebahoth ; The Lord of Hosts (1 Sam. i. 3, 11).

Jehovah-Heleyon ; The Lord Most High (Ps. vii. 17).

Jehovah-Rohi ; The Lord is my Shepherd (Ps. xxiii. 1).

Jehovah-Hoseenu ; The Lord our Maker (Ps. xcv. 6).

Jehovah-Eloheenu ; The Lord our God (Ps. xcix. 5, 8, 9).

Jehovah-Nakah ; The Lord will guide thee (Isa. lviii. 11).

Jehovah-Tsidkenu ; The Lord our Righteousness (Jer. xxiii. 6 ; xxxiii. 16 ; see 1 Cor. i. 30).

Jehovah-Gemulah ; The Lord our Recompense (Jer. li. 56).

Jehovah-Shammah ; The Lord is there (Ezek. xlviii. 35).

Jehovah-Elohay ; The Lord my God (Zech. xiv. 5).

Jehovah-Sabaoth ; The Lord of Hosts (Rom. ix. 29 ; Isa. i. 9).

> Ye—He was   Prophet.
> Ho—He is   Priest.
> Ah—He will be King.
> Yehoah.
> Jehovah—Covenant-keeping God.

NEEDS MET

" Sufficient for his need."—Deut. xv. 8.

A tramp went into a chemist's shop ; he was a very poor, untidy man, and he said, " If you please, have you got anything for a bad cold ? " And the chemist, who was an eminently respectable chemist, said, " Have you brought your prescription with you ? " The man answered, " No, I have not, but I have brought my cold with me."

The man knew he had a need to be supplied.

1. As John the Baptist we need the BAPTISM of the Spirit for power (Matt. iii. 14).

2. The sick of sin and the sick in sin need a PHYSICIAN to heal (Mark ii. 17 ; Luke ix. 11).

3. All the members of the Body of Christ and the Lord have need of EACH OTHER to help (1 Cor. xii. 21).

4. Babes in Christ have need to have INSTRUCTION to grow (Heb. v. 12).

5. Believers have need of PATIENCE under trial to endure (Heb. x. 36).

6. The saints need their feet WASHED while travelling along life's dusty road to be clean (John xiii. 10).

7. Busy workers, like Martha, need to have the MARY SPIRIT coupled with Martha service for all-round spiritual life (Luke x. 42).

Over against the need remember the Lord knows about it (Matt. vi. 8). He can " supply " it (Phil. iv. 19), and is sufficient without additions (Rev. xxi. 23 ; xxii. 5).

" NO DISTINCTION OF THAT SORT THERE "

" *All ye are Brethren.*"—Matt. xxiii. 8.

On one occasion Dean Inge was rung up on the telephone by a newspaper reporter, who enquired about a John Bunyan commemoration service, which had been held in Westminster Abbey.

The voice said, " Is that the Dean himself ? I understand you have a Bunyan Memorial Service."

He replied, " We call it commemoration."

The reporter said, " Yes, yes, the same thing." He (the Dean) did not think it was, but the reporter went on to ask, " Was there something remarkable about this man ' Bunyan ' ? "

He said, " Well, he wrote a book."

" Oh, an author. Thank you very much." He could feel through the telephone that the reporter was writing down

" John Bunyan, author." Then the reporter said, " Could you tell me, Dean, the name of any work of his ? "

He replied, " Yes, a work called ' Pilgrim's Progress,' which had a considerable vogue at one time." Then the reporter told him that he had always understood that the author of " Pilgrim's Progress " was a Nonconformist. He replied that Bunyan had that reputation, but he did not suppose there was any distinction of that sort where Bunyan was now.

It is of interest to note and ponder what heaven's inhabitants are called. We can see at least seven classes mentioned in the Book of the Revelation.

1. " REDEEMED," and by one means, namely, by the blood of the Lamb (Rev. v. 9).

2. " WASHED."—The white-robed multitude are such, because they have been washed in the blood of the Lamb (vii. 14).

3. " SAINTS."—They are God's sanctified or holy ones (xvi. 6).

4. " MARTYRS."—Those whose lives had been laid down for Christ (xvii. 6).

5. " SERVANTS," that is, God's bond-servants (vii. 3).

6. " KINGS AND PRIESTS," or, a " kingdom of priests " (i. 6), indicating their royalty and priestly service.

7. " OVERCOMERS."—The overcomers are promised a place with Christ on God's throne (iii. 21).

NOT ASHAMED OF HIS COUNTRY
" I am not ashamed."—Rom. i. 16.

In the Mowbary Park in Sunderland, there is a statue of Jack Crawford, the brave sailor, who is represented as nailing the Union Jack to the broken masthead, which was blown away at the battle of Camperdown. He was not ashamed to risk his life, nor the colours of his country.

God is not ashamed of His people, why should they be ashamed of Him ?

There is an artistic touch in the graphic words of the Holy Spirit. One such is the word " Kataischuno," which means to shame, to disgrace, and put to the blush. The

word is rendered " Dishonoureth " (1 Cor. xi. 4, 5), and
" Confounded " (1 Pet. ii. 6). The Lord assures His people
again and again they shall not be put to shame—that is,
disgraced or confounded. The following are some of the
reasons why believers shall not be ashamed :

1. Christ is the BASIS of it (Rom. ix. 33).
2. Redemption is its PROOF (Isa. xxix. 22).
3. Salvation is its EVIDENCE (Isa. xlv. 17).
4. Confidence is its ASSURANCE (Isa. l. 7).
5. Christ is its EXAMPLE (Isa. l. 7).
6. God's Word is its PROMISE (Isa. liv. 4 ; Rom. x. 11).
7. God Himself is its PLEDGE (Heb. xi. 16).

" NO TIME FOR CRITICISM "

" Redeeming the time."—Eph. v. 16.

" I am so fully occupied in praising the Lord, and thank-
ing Him for His goodness, that I have no time for criticism,"
so said a child of God in a city in New England. Critics are
always cavilers, they see more than there is, and they make
up the rest. We shall be fully occupied if we keep our own
doorstep clean. We often see in others what is in ourselves.
Let us be careful lest the mote seen in the brother's eye is
but the reflection of the beam in our own. Sometimes we
think a thing is, then we make a reality of an unreality, till
the unreality becomes a reality. Many a thing made in jest,
leads to the thing in earnest. Many who have been criticised
for doing a certain thing, do the thing for which they were
unjustly criticised. Critics are often ministers of sin. Spend
your breath in praising God rather than in prating about
your brethren.

We shall find our time fully occupied if we follow the
examples given below.

1. PRAY to the Lord THREE TIMES as DANIEL did (Dan.
vi. 10).
2. FOLLOW the Lord FULLY as Caleb and Joshua did
(Num. xiv. 24).
3. KEEP ON in the Lord's SERVICE as Nehemiah and
his fellow labourers did (Neh. iv. 6).
4. INTERCEDE for OTHERS as Epaphras did (Col. iv. 12).

5. CLING to the Lord TENACIOUSLY as David did, when he said, " my soul followeth hard after the Lord (Ps. lxiii. 8).

6. PRAISE the Lord CONTINUOUSLY as the Psalmist did, and as he says, " at all times " (Ps. xxxiv. 1).

7. SEARCH the SCRIPTURES daily, as the Berean Christians did (Acts xvii. 10-12).

NOT YIELDED

" *Kept back part of the price.*"—Acts v. 2.

A Christian Jewess, out on the Pacific Coast, said to the writer, " I have been a believer in Christ for twenty-seven years, but I never yielded my heart and life wholly to Him until a few years ago." A yielded life to Christ is essential if He would do anything effective with us.

1. A COMMAND.—" Yield yourselves unto God " (Rom. vi. 13).

2. A SPECIFICATION.—" Yield your members servants to righteousness unto holiness " (Rom. vi. 19).

3. A PROHIBITION.—" Neither yield ye your members as instruments of unrighteousness unto sin " (Rom. vi. 13).

4. A TEST.—" Know ye not that to whom ye yield yourselves servants to obey his servants ye are ? " (Rom. vi. 16).

" OBEDIENCE "

" *To obey is better than sacrifice.*"—1 Sam. xv. 22.

A story is told of a great captain who, after a battle, was talking over the events of the day with his officers. He asked them who had done the best that day. Some spoke of one man who had fought very bravely, and some of another. " No," he said, " you are mistaken. The best man in the field to-day was a soldier who was just lifting up his arm to strike an enemy ; but, when he heard the trumpet sound a retreat, checked himself, and dropped his arm without striking the blow. That perfect and ready obedience to the will of his general is the noblest thing that has been done to-day."

1. Obedience is the SECRET OF BLESSING (Deut. xi. 27).

2. Obedience is the BRINGER OF THE HOLY SPIRIT (Acts v. 32).

3. Obedience is the POWER OF SERVICE (Hag. i. 12-14).
4. Obedience is the LIFE OF HOLINESS (Rom. vi. 17).
5. Obedience is the MEANING OF FAITH (Heb. xi. 8).
6. Obedience is the SUSTAINER IN TRIAL (Isa. i. 19).
7. Obedience is the PURIFIER OF THE SOUL (1 Pet. i. 22).

OBEDIENCE : ITS SPIRIT

" Ye have obeyed."—Rom. vi. 17.

Gibbon, the historian, tells us of the marvellous advance of an Oriental conqueror named Abu, until at last one hundred thousand fanatical soldiers followed in his train, and he marched to the capital of the Caliph, and it seemed as if no power could resist his onset. But the Caliph sent a lieutenant with five hundred cavalry to meet him and to demand his surrender under the penalty of the annihilation of his army before sunset, and that if he refused he would give his body to the wolves. Abu laughed in scorn, and asked by what authority he made such demand, and by what means he expected to execute his threatenings. Then the officer called three soldiers, commanded one to stab himself to the heart with his dagger, a second to drown himself in the Tigris, and a third to hurl himself from the overhanging precipice. The three commands were instantly obeyed. " Now," said the soldier, " these are some of my master's followers. What are you to expect from an army that will follow a leader like that ? " The rebel chief was so impressed with this spectacle of confidence that he yielded to the command, and rightly felt that such a force was invincible.

This is the spirit of obedience. To the men who recognise it, no difficulty is too great, no task too insuperable to claim our instant response. This is the real foundation of missionary work—obedience to the Master's command, without compromise or qualification.

1. Obedience is the FIRST STEP IN SALVATION, as Christ declares, when He says, " He that heareth My Word . . . is passed from death into life " (John v. 24).

2. Obedience is the MARK OF BEING in the flock of Christ's sheep, for they hear and follow (John x. 27).

3. Obedience is the EVIDENCE WE LOVE CHRIST, for He

says, " If ye love Me, ye will keep My commandments "
(John xiv. 15, R.V.).

4. Obedience SECURES THE SPIRIT'S POSSESSION and power,
for He is given to those who " obey " (Acts v. 32).

5. Obedience SECURES GOD'S BENEDICTIONS, for He
assures us, if we are willing and obedient, we shall eat the
good of the land (Isa. i. 19).

6. Obedience results in the sounding out from us, to
others' blessing, what we have received (1 Thess. i. 6-9).

7. Obedience to Christ is the SECRET OF SUCCESS in service,
for it was when Peter obeyed, the multitude of fish were
caught (Luke v. 4-6).

ONE ACT MAY LEAD TO MANY CONSEQUENCES

" Offence of One . . . Grace of one man."—Rom. v. 15.

By a decree of Judge James H. Sisk, filed with the clerk
of Norfolk Superior Court in U.S.A., the town of Cohasset is
ordered to withhold from Llewellyn A. Litchfield, of that
town, payment of 1,500 dols. voted by the citizens at the
annual town meeting in March, 1924, for the loss of twenty-
three hives of bees and twenty chickens.

The bees had been poisoned by gathering honey from
the blossoms of fruit on a neighbouring farm, that had been
sprayed by the town warden. The chickens ate the dead
bees with equally fatal results.

The court ruled that the warden had merely done his
duty in spraying the fruit trees, and the town was not
responsible for the loss of bees poisoned by gathering honey
beyond the limits of their owner's property.

Suit has been brought by ten citizens of Cohasset to stop
payment of the money.

The above illustrates the fact that one act may lead to
many consequences. One sinner may destroy much good,
and one saint may scatter many blessings.

1. One THEUDAS led many astray (Acts v. 36, 37).

2. One WOMAN OF SAMARIA caused many to believe on
Christ (John iv. 39).

3. One ACT OF SIN blasted the whole of the human race
(Rom. v. 12).

4. One ATONEMENT for sin by Christ has provided salvation for all men (Titus ii. 11, R.V.).

5. One ANDREW was the cause of Peter's conversion (John i. 40, 41), and he was the means of three thousand being converted (Acts ii. 37-41).

6. One REHOBOAM was the instrument to lead many astray (1 Kings xiv. 21-30).

7. One ACT OF DAVID'S brought triumph to the host of Israel (1 Sam. xvii. 48-53).

ONE : THE ONLY ONE

" *None other Name.*"—Acts iv. 12.

A well-known English preacher in visiting Boston, admired the statue to Phillips Brooks, and says of it, " I don't think I ever saw anything nobler than the inscription on his monument. The statuary is a failure ; it is a representation of him in the act of preaching, with the Saviour standing behind him, and the servant is more imposing than the Master ; but the inscription is sublime. Phillips Brooks, ' the preacher of the Word of God and the friend of man.' I don't think any man can get a nobler title than that."

Phillips Brooks' statue overshadowed that of the Lord's. The same thing is being done all the time in actual life. Too many are taking the things of God for the advancement and glory of self. There is no sin so sinful as this. We shall not overshadow Christ if we take the Spirit's testimony in our testimony.

There are things said about Christ which cannot be said of any other. He stands alone in the exclusiveness of His Being, in the Holiness of His nature, in the Love of His compassion, in the tenderness of His mercy, in the goodness of His grace, in the exercise of His offices, in the vicariousness of His death, in the might of His resurrection, in the uniqueness of His priesthood, in the effectiveness of His Spirit, and the glory of His coming.

1. ONE STANDING IN THE MIDST.—" There standeth One among you " (John i. 26). He stands to save, to help, to bless, to succour, to teach, to reveal, and to equip.

2. ONE SHEPHERD TENDING.—" There shall be One

Shepherd " (John x. 16). The Good Shepherd can do what none other can do, because He is the Only One.

3. ONE MAN DIED.—" One man should die for the people " (John xi. 50 ; xviii. 14). God cannot die, but He who died for us is God.

4. ONE HOLY.—" Thine Holy One " (Acts ii. 27 ; iii. 14 ; xiii. 35). Being what He was, none could contaminate Him, and death could not detain Him.

5. " ONE MAN " (Rom. v. 15, 17, 18, 19).—The Federal headship secures the salvation and standing of all who are associated with Him.

6. " ONE OFFERING " (Heb. x. 12, 14).—He has given to God the " one sacrifice for sins," which answers for them, and puts them away.

7. " ONE LORD JESUS CHRIST " (1 Cor. viii. 6).—What an One He is ! And of Him the Holy Spirit has given us the summary, " Through whom are all things, and we through Him."

" ONLY UNFORGIVABLE THING "

" *Forgiving one another, even as God for Christ's sake hath forgiven you.*"—Eph. iv. 32.

" The only unforgivable thing," says one, " is a love which calls itself love, yet fails to forgive. Love can forgive all wrongs, intentional or unintended."

What a revelation we have of what true love is in the love of God !

In Christ—

1. Love is seen in its HIGHEST FORM (1 John iii. 16).

2. Love is revealed in its LOWEST STOOP (1 John iv. 9).

3. Love is made known in its GREATEST SACRIFICE (John iii. 16).

4. Love is manifest in its PUREST GRACE (1 John iv. 10).

5. Love is unrivalled in its SUBLIMEST ESSENCE (1 John iv. 8).

6. Love is bestowed in its MIGHTIEST POWER (1 John iv. 16).

7. Love is communicated in its INTENSEST BLESSING (1 John iv. 17-21).

Oh ! to know the love which is unknowable, but God only knows the love of God, yet we may know that which is beyond human ken, even as a swallow can drink of a mighty river and yet cannot drink the river.

OPPORTUNITY AND ABILITY

" *He gave talents . . . to every man, according to his several ability.*"—Matt. xxv. 15.

The parable of the talents has generally been considered to represent the natural abilities which we have, or the spiritual gifts the Spirit bestows, which are to be used in God's service. We suggest another interpretation—namely, the talents represent the opportunities the Lord gives us to serve Him, and that we are each to improve these opportunities " according to his several ability " (Matt. xxv. 15). The " several ability " embraces what we have as to qualification for the Lord's service from the human standpoint, and the power which operates within us effectually, from the Divine standpoint. The talents speak of the opportunities which are to be found wherever we are, and which are seized in the " ability " which makes them of use. Let us buy up the opportunity which the Lord has given us in this present time, for " the night is far spent and the day is at hand."

The Acts of the Apostles illustrate how opportunity was seized and improved.

1. PETER on the Day of Pentecost improved the occasion when the " multitude came together " (Acts ii. 6) to preach the Gospel.

2. PETER and JOHN seized the opportunity to aid the lame man, when they saw him in helplessness (Acts iii. 1-11).

3. THE APOSTLE did not allow the opportunity to pass, when he saw the rulers in an enquiring mood, to preach the Lord's message (Acts iii. 5-22).

4. When the APOSTLES were bidden to go to the people, and stand and preach " all the words of this life " (Acts v. 20), they did not lag, but responded at once.

5. When STEPHEN was arraigned before the council, he did not hesitate to proclaim the truth (Acts vii.).

6. When PHILIP the Evangelist was directed by the Spirit

to go and lead the eunuch to Christ, " he arose and went " ; yea, " he ran " to do as he was bidden (Acts viii. 27-31).

7. When PAUL saw the Athenians " wholly given to idolatry," his spirit was stirred within him, and he " preached Jesus and the Resurrection " (Acts xvii. 16-18).

PALESTINE : PROMISED LAND

" *The Lord's Land.*"—Hosea ix. 3.

The land of Palestine, which has been purchased and sanctified by the blood of Christ, should be a matter of concern to the child of God, and ever the subject of study to the student of Scripture. We can never forget that land, where, as Shakespeare says :

" Those holy fields,
Over whose acres walked those sacred feet,
Which . . . were nailed
For our advantage on the bitter Cross."

That is the land of prophecy, for it is yet to be the land where Israel is to enjoy the covenants Jehovah made with Abraham and David. So we may well sing of, and say to, that land :

" Thou land of the Cross and the Glory,
Whose brightness at last will shine
Afar through the earth—what a story
Of darkness and light is thine."

PALESTINE VARIOUSLY DESCRIBED

The Scriptures describe the land of Promise in various ways ; each of which has its peculiar association and meaning. Jehovah calls it " My Land " (Isa. xiv. 25), " The Land " (Lev. xix. 23), " Thy Land " (1 Kings viii. 36), " This Land " (Gen. xii. 7), " His Land " (Deut. xxxii. 43), " Land of Canaan " (Lev. xiv. 34), " The Promised Land " (Heb. xi. 9), " Pleasant Land " (Dan. viii. 9), " Good Land " (Deut. i. 25), " Land of Israel " (1 Sam. xiii. 19), " Land of Judah " (Isa. xxvi. 1), " Holy Land " (Zech. ii. 12), " The Lord's Land " (Hosea ix. 3), " Thy Land, O Immanuel " (Isa. viii. 8), " Land of the Hebrews " (Gen. xl. 15), " Glorious Land " (Dan. xi. 16), " A Land flowing with milk and honey " (Deut. vi. 3), " Your Land " (Lev. xix. 33), " The Land of your habitations " (Num. xv. 2), " Abundant Land " (Deut. viii. 1-10), " A land which the Lord thy God careth for " (Deut. xi. 12), and " The Land which the Lord thy God giveth thee " (Deut. xxv. 19), etc.

PALESTINE'S FUTURE

" *Concerning the Land of Israel.*"—Ezek. xxxvi. 6, etc.

Attention is being riveted upon the Land of Palestine. Politicians, men of letters, and men and women are concentrating their thoughts upon the Land of Promise. A Land without a people, and a People without a Land. Small parties used to visit this land. Now hundreds are visiting " those fields," as Shakespeare tersely remarked, where trod those holy feet " for our advantage." Only a short while since, in waiting for a train from Quebec to Montreal, there was a party of tourists, and upon their hand-bags, covered with stick-on labels from hotels, were to be read such names as Bethlehem, Nazareth, Beirut, and not least among them " Allenby Hotel, Jerusalem."

SEVEN THINGS TO REMEMBER

Generally speaking, there are seven things we need to remember in relation to the Jews and Palestine, and these are :

1. There is ONE PEOPLE whom Jehovah calls His " peculiar treasure unto Me above all people " (Exod. xix. 5).

2. There is ONE LAND, which He called " holy " (Zech. ii. 12), and promised to Israel for an " everlasting possession " (Gen. xvii. 8).

3. There is ONE CITY, which is called " The Beloved City " (literally " The Dearly Beloved "), and which Jehovah will make a " praise in the earth," and that is Jerusalem (Rev. xx. 9 ; Isa. lxii. 7).

4. There is ONE MOUNTAIN which has been honoured in the land of Palestine, and that is the Mount of Olives, for Christ's sacred feet last rested upon it. He ascended to Heaven (Acts i. 12), and it is upon that mountain His holy feet will stand when He returns in manifest glory to the earth, and which mountain will be the object of great and momentous convulsions (Zech. xiv. 4).

5. There is ONE TEMPLE, which is to be the scene of the greatest sacrilege ever committed in a holy place, and that temple will be the rebuilt one, in which the abomination of the Antichrist will be set up (Dan. ix. 27 ; Matt. xxiv. 15).

6. There is ONE THRONE upon which Jehovah has said a descendant of David is to sit for ever (2 Sam. vii. 10-17 ; Luke i. 31-33), and therefore is peculiarly honoured and magnified by Him.

7. There is ONE MAN in whom all God's plans are centred and He is a Jew, namely, Christ, for He is distinctly said to be of " the seed of David " (2 Tim. ii. 8) " of Israel " (Rom. ix. 5), and " the Son of Abraham " and " David " (Matt. i. 1).

PANACEA

" Who died for us."—1 Thess. v. 10.

Rev. Thomas Phillips, in speaking on Christ's atonement, related the following : " I will sum it up in a story which is the best theory of the Atonement I know. It is the story of Hannah Lamond and the golden eagle. Hannah Lamond took her child out into the hayfield and let it rest in the hay while she was busy hay-making. A golden eagle swept down from an inaccessible cliff, and carried away the child, back to the heights. The people working in the field were panic-stricken, and did not know what to do, but the mother rushed to the foot of the hill and began to climb a precipice which nobody had climbed before ; through thorns and brambles, tearing herself, bleeding, taking hold of little branches, though if they had broken she would have fallen and been smashed to pieces ; walking around the very brink of precipices and knowing nothing about them ; higher and higher, and up and up, until at last she clutched her child from the talons of the eagle, giving her life, giving her blood, but saving the child. There is something like that in the heart of God. ' The Lamb slain from the foundation of the world.' Man in the grip of sin ; in the talons of the evil of sin. God in Christ coming to snatch and deliver man from the grip of this terrible evil. That is our hope as we bring the eternal sacrifice of God to bear upon the sins and ills of this great city."

The only cure for the ills of mankind is found in Christ. How often we read, " He died," " suffered," " bare," " offered," " gave," " shed," " His blood."

Mark a passage where each of these words occur, and see in the different phraseology there is embodied the eternal fact of Christ's atoning death.

1. " DIED."—" Christ died for us " (Rom. v. 8). It does not say, " He lived for us," but " He died for us." Sin was the cause of that death, and now through His death we do not die for our sin.

2. " SUFFERED FOR US " (1 Pet. ii. 21, 23 ; iii. 18 ; iv. 1).—He suffered in spirit, soul, and body. His cry on the Cross proves the first, His agony in Gethsemane evidences the second ; and His wounded body proclaims the last.

3. " BARE."—" Who His own self bare our sins " (1 Pet. ii. 24). What He bore was " our sins," and He, " His own self," alone could do it.

4. " OFFERED."—" Offered Himself without spot to God " (Heb. vii. 27 ; ix. 14). " To God " the offering was made, and made " once." He alone was fit to do it, and He did it fittingly.

5. " GAVE."—" The Son of God, who loved me, and gave Himself up for me " (Gal. ii. 20). God the Son was the One who gave, and love made Him do it.

6. " SHED."—He " shed " His blood " for the remission of sins " (Matt. xxvi. 28). He emptied out His life, that we might be emancipated from the tryanny and thraldom of sin.

7. " BLOOD."—" The blood of Christ " (Heb. ix. 14). There is an eternal virtue in His blood, because of the Eternal One who shed it.

PARADOXES

" *As dying, and behold we live.*"—2 Cor. vi. 9.

A paradox is defined to be a " tenet or proposition contrary to received opinion, and seemingly absurd, but true in fact."

The Gospel of Christ is full of paradoxes ; for God's thoughts and ways are on a higher plane than human thoughts and ways, and therefore appear impossible and even absurd from the merely human standpoint, just as the statements and actions of an astronomer searching the heavens with a telescope would appear absurd to the wild savages in the heart of Africa. We give a few of these :

1. We SEE unseen things (2 Cor. iv. 18).

2. We CONQUER by yielding (Matt. v. 5, with Rom. xii. 20, 21).

3. We REST under a yoke (Matt. xi. 28-30).

4. We REIGN by serving (Mark x. 42-44).

5. We become GREAT by becoming little (Matt. xviii. 4).

6. We are EXALTED by being humbled (Matt. xxiii. 12).

7. We become WISE by becoming foolish (1 Cor. i. 20, 21).

8. We become FREE by becoming slaves (Rom. vi. 17-22, with Rom. viii. 2).

9. We POSSESS all things by having nothing (2 Cor. vi. 10).

10. When we are WEAK, then we are strong (2 Cor. xii. 10).

11. We TRIUMPH by defeat (2 Cor. xii. 7-9).

12. We GLORY in our infirmities (2 Cor. xii. 5).

13. We LIVE by dying (John xii. 24, 25, with 2 Cor. vi. 9, 10).

PAST AND PRESENT TENSE

" Taken . . . shall come."—Acts i. 11.

In a mission school in Arabia the boys, all of mixed nationality, are bright students, and many of them true believers in Christ. A number are prevented from open confession through their Arab parents, and others who hold them, until they come of age, in a grip of iron. The school begins every morning with an hour's Bible lesson, attended by all. Sometimes the boys' answers to questions show real intelligence. " What is the past tense ? " asked a teacher one morning of a small pupil. " The ' absent ' tense," he replied quickly. " Jesus Christ went to heaven, and He's been in the ' absent ' tense ever since,' until He comes again in the present, which may be very soon " ! The words of the men, as Christ went away, suggest many things.

1. A WONDERFUL RECEPTION.—" Taken up " may be read " Received up." That reception to the right hand of the Father was after Christ had atoned for sin by His death, and risen from the dead by the power of God (Acts i. 11).

2. A WONDERFUL REDEEMER.—" This same Jesus." The One of the eternal past, of Bethlehem's manger, of Nazareth's home, of Bethany's love, of Gethsemane's agony, of Gabbatha's sufferings, and Golgotha's agony.

3. A WONDERFUL COMPANY.—" Ye have seen Him go." Those who had companioned with Him were witnesses of what the world had never seen (Acts x. 38-43).

4. A WONDERFUL CORRESPONDENCE.—" Shall so come in like manner as ye have seen Him go away." He went away in the act of blessing (Luke xxiv. 50-53), and He will come back in the same way (Phil. iii. 20, 21).

5. A WONDERFUL ASSURANCE.—" Shall . . . come." God's " shall's " are His post-dated cheques. He will honour all His promises, fulfil all His pledges.

PATIENCE

" *Add to your faith . . . patience.*"—2 Pet. i. 6.

Sir Robertson Nicoll says on patience as a Christian grace, " Patience, of which our Lord speaks, is not the mere patience of nature. It is the patience of grace. It is the patience of hope and faith. It is not mere doggedness and resolution. It is something more than fortitude ; it is the patience which not only keeps our true selves, but makes our true selves. It is a great thing to have the courage necessary to resist trouble. It is a far greater thing to have the patience that takes something out of trouble, something which makes a new character, something which anneals the spirit, something which gives a new power of discerning and loving and reverencing. To remain under pain and trouble, and to live in spite of them, is something, but far greater is the achievement which permanently enriches the soul."

By this patience we are filled with the blessed assurance that God places us where we are. With not a few the desire to escape from their present environment is passionate and paramount. " Set me anywhere rather than here. The conditions of my life are unbearable, and yet the force of circumstances keeps me where I am. There is no door open to me. I have been beating blindly against an iron wall." Of this comes rebellion, of this may come madness.

But once be sure that the Lord is in this place once realise His presence, His will, His love, and all things become different.

1. Patience is An Inheriting Grace. " Who through patience inherit the promises " (Heb. vi. 12).

2. Patience is A Productive Grace. " Bring forth fruit with patience " (Luke viii. 15).

3. Patience is A Needed Grace. " Ye have need of patience " (Heb. x. 36).

4. Patience is An Enduring Grace. " Run with patience the race set before you " (Heb. xii. 1).

5. Patience is A Christ-appreciated Grace. " I know thy . . . patience " (Rev. ii. 2).

6. Patience is An Expecting Grace. " I waited patiently for the Lord " (Ps. xl. 1).

7. Patience is A Qualifying Grace. " Gentle unto all men, apt to teach, patient " (2 Tim. ii. 24).

PAUL AND THE PHILIPPIAN JAILOR
Acts xvi. 19-40.

When Catherine Evans, a Quaker heroine of the seventeenth century, was imprisoned within the gloomy walls of the Inquisition, in the island of Malta, for preaching the Gospel, she was put into an inner prison, which had only two small holes in it for light and air. Friar Malachi told her on one occasion that unless she abandoned her faith she would never go out of that room. To this she fearlessly replied, " The Lord is sufficient to deliver me, but whether He will or not, I will not forsake the Living Fountain to drink at a broken cistern." Paul and Silas also were not to be deterred in their ministry by persecution, suffering and imprisonment. To such souls

" Stone walls do not a prison make,
Nor iron bars a cage."

Paul and the Philippian jailor ! What a contrast between the two ! The former, like a beneficent lighthouse, sending out his gladdening rays across the troubled waves of humanity ; and the latter, like a helpless barque, at the mercy of wind and waves being driven on to the rocks of doom.

We see the apostle in three characters—as the persecuted evangelist, as the praising saint, as the proclaiming herald.

1. THE PERSECUTED EVANGELIST.—The persecutions which met Paul and Silas were as a fan to flame their love into ardent devotion to the cause of evangelism.

2. THE PRAISING SAINT (25).—What did Paul and Silas sing ? The 103rd Psalm ? They were much like Madame Guyon, who was imprisoned in the castle of Vincennes, in 1695 ; she not only sang, but wrote songs of praise to her Lord. " It sometimes seems to me," she said, " as if I were a little bird whom the Lord had placed in a cage, and that I had nothing to do but sing. The joy of my heart gave brightness to the things around me. The stones of my prison looked to my eyes like rubies."

3. THE PROCLAIMING HERALD (31).—Paul had an answer to the jailor's cry of distress, and a message to all his house (32). The " Lord Jesus Christ " was the content of his message, and " the Word of the Lord." That " word " must ever be the rock on which we build in life, the hand which holds us in trial, the oil which makes us burn in testimony, the sword with which we fight in conflict, the rule by which we square our conduct, the plan by which we go in service, and the authority by which we speak.

PAUL'S AFFLICTIONS

" We be afflicted."—2 Cor. i. 6.

Our American friends have the reputation, or some of them, of being large in their appreciation of their own country, large in their expectations, and large in their generosity. The following reported incident certainly illustrates their " expectations " :

A Presbyterian Church in a Western town of America was looking out for à minister, to whom it offered a salary of 1,600 dollars a year. " The sort of man we want," said an elder of the Church, " is one who is eloquent as Chrysostom, zealous as the Apostle Paul, pious as Thomas à Kempis, learned as the Admirable Crighton, suave as Chesterfield, diplomatic as Talleyrand, a good mixer, and a good tenor singer." The Church had between sixty or seventy members and the town had a population of fewer than a thousand. " We don't want any one who is out for a soft place," added the elder, " for ours is a hard job."

No true servant of Christ ever had a soft job. Take Paul as an example.

1. He was CRITICISED by his friends (2 Cor. x. 10-13).
2. BUFFETTED by Satan (2 Cor. xii. 7).
3. SNEERED at by authorities (Acts xxvi. 28, R.V.).
4. STONED by his enemies (Acts xiv. 19).
5. SURROUNDED by warring obstacles (2 Cor. xi. 23-28).
6. FORSAKEN by his brethren (2 Tim. iv. 10, 11).
7. DISTURBED by mere professors (Phil. iii. 18, 19).

PEACE PERSONIFIED

" *Prince of Peace.*"—Isa. ix. 6.

Andrew Carnegie once called at the White House, to pay a visit to President Roosevelt, and said, " I called merely to pay my respects to the Great Pacificator." No greater compliment could be paid to President Roosevelt than to call him the great pacificator. His name will go down to posterity as the mover in the proceedings which ended the war between Japan and Russia.

There is another who has a greater right to the title of prince of peace, even the Lord Jesus. He is

1. The PROVIDER OF PEACE, for He gives the blessing of His own peace (John xiv. 27).

2. He is the PURCHASER OF PEACE, by the blood of His atoning cross (Col. i. 20).

3. He is the PERSONIFICATION OF PEACE, for " He is our Peace " (Eph. ii. 14).

4. He is the PROMISER OF PEACE, for as we observe the conditions He has laid down, His own peace will guard our hearts and minds in Himself (Phil. iv. 6, 7).

5. He is the PATHWAY OF PEACE, for as we walk in the pathway of His Word, we enjoy the peace His Word imparts (Ps. cxix. 165).

6. He is the PATTERN OF PEACE, for He was ever saying, " Peace be still " (Mark iv. 39), and thus illustrates His own beatitude (Matt. v. 9).

7. He is the Prospect of Peace, for He shall adjust all the discordant notes of nature, hush the noise of war, and placate every disturbing element (Luke ii. 14), for " This Man shall be the Peace " (Mic. v. 5).

" PEARL BEYOND ALL PRICE "

" He loved . . . He gave "—John iii. 16.

The ladies of England during the Great War, gave their pearls in aid of the Red Cross. It is said, " 3,715 have been given by the British Empire." Among those given was one sent by a mother, who wrote a touching letter, and said, " I send it in memory of a pearl beyond all price, already given—my only son." Tears and blood, and love, and sacrifice, and prayers and heartaches, and memory are identified with that pearl-gift. What a pearl of a gift in that gift of the pearl !

The " only son " who gave and was given for his king and country reminds us of God's only Son who was given for us. Seven times He is said to be " The Only Begotten," or the " Begotten."

1. The Fact of His Being.—" The Holy Thing which is Begotten shall be called the Son of God " (Luke i. 35, R.V.). As God He could not be begotten, for as the Eternal Son He is Deity ; as man, He was not begotten by man, for He is " The Seed of the woman," but He was begotten by the Holy Spirit.

2. The Glory of His Being.—" We beheld His glory, the glory of the Only Begotten of the Father " (John i. 14). That glory has a sevenfold colour, namely, love is its substance, grace is its attitude, salvation is its aim, eternal life is its gift, peace is its blessing, miracle was its evidence, and God is its revelation.

3. The Glory of His Union.—" The only Begotten Son, which is in the bosom of the Father " (John i. 18). The " bosom " is the seat of affection and nearness, hence we find the Gospel opens with the Son in the Father's bosom, and ends with a disciple in the Son's bosom (John xxi. 20).

4. The Glory of His Love.—" He gave His only Begotten Son " (John iii. 16). The Father's giving is the

Son's giving. Love always gives itself out in benefit to others, and never looks at consequences to itself.

5. THE GLORY OF HIS NAME.—Not to believe in the " Name of the Only Begotten Son of God " (John iii. 18) is the greatest sin that can be committed, for the " Name " is expressive of God Himself, and of His love and grace.

6. THE GLORY OF HIS MISSION.—" God sent His Only Begotten Son, that we might live through Him " (1 John iv. 9). That life He came to procure by His death and resurrection. That life has God as its Source, the Cross as its means, union with God as its blessing, and the Spirit of Power as its working.

7. THE GLORY OF HIS KEEPING.—" He that was begotten of God keepeth him " (1 John v. 18, R.V. marg.). Christ is the One that " WAS " begotten, and the believer is the one that " IS " begotten of God."

Thus we see God made one Son like to all, that all sons might be made like to One.

" PERFECT PEACE "

" *Thou wilt keep him in perfect peace* " (*marg.*, " *peace, peace* "), " *whose mind is stayed on Thee, because he trusteth in Thee.*"—Isa. xxvi. 3.

Peace is the opposite of discord, strife, conflict, and opposition ; therefore, it denotes harmony, oneness, and accord. When applied to the individual, it signifies a state of health, wholeness, completeness, and well-being. The word for peace is derived from " Shalom," which means oneness, or wholeness, and so completeness. The margin of the A.V. gives, " Peace, peace," and comes under the figure denoting duplication, where we find a noun repeated for an adjective, and hence the word means " much peace," or " great peace." By the words " peace, peace," we have the thought in the text—" perfect peace."

" Perfect peace " must come from the perfect God, through the perfect sacrifice of Christ's atonement, assured by the perfect Word of the Spirit's assurance, enjoyed by the God-given grace of faith, and the garrisoning presence of the God of Peace.

A desirable blessing. Who would not desire the blessing of " perfect peace " ? There are three colours to this rainbow of blessing.

1. BLOOD-PURCHASED PEACE.—Peace with God is not a product of earth's growth, is not an obtainment of man's endeavour, is not a bestowment of man's giving, is not a gem of self's finding, is not a virtue of angel's bringing, is not a diamond in earth's mines, nor an outcome of a magician's art. It is a making of Christ's blood of atonement (Col. i. 20). He has given to God for us what we could never give ourselves ; hence He gives to us what no man could give, and what we could never give ourselves.

I once listened to a coloured pastor in Canada preaching the Gospel, and he said something to this effect : " Man was united to God by a golden chain of love in the Garden of Eden, Satan and man by his sins has severed the golden link which bound him to God. Now the question arose, ' How could man be united to God again ? ' Man tried to weld the broken links together by the efforts of his doing, but the broken links would not unite, so man had to give up in despair ! But the Lord Jesus undertook to unite the broken links, and this He did by shedding His precious blood, and now the golden chain is more firmly fused than ever before, for no power of man nor Satan can break the blood-fused links."

The illustration is not perfect in its logic, but it points the fact that Christ's atoning blood is the power that brings man to God and makes him one with Him.

2. FAITH-OBTAINED PEACE.—Faith is the hand which takes what grace proffers ; hence we read, " Therefore, being justified by faith, we have peace with God, through our Lord Jesus Christ " (Rom. v. 1). The " Therefore " takes us back to chapter iv. 25, where we read, " Who was delivered for (on account of) our offences, and raised again for (on account of) our justification " ; hence, when we believe on the Lord Jesus Christ, our faith is accounted for righteousness. Our sin being reckoned to Christ, Christ the Righteousness of God is reckoned to us. As Luther has tersely said, " He was my sin, and I am His righteousness."

Before Esther went into the presence of Ahasuerus, she

was not sure of the mind of the king towards her ; hence she said, " If I perish, I perish," but when the king in grace held out the golden sceptre, she touched it with the hand of faith, for she knew that his favour was towards her. There is no uncertainty about God's favour towards us, for the grace and love of God are extended towards us in the extended hands of Christ on the Cross, and the moment we take Him as our Saviour by the act of our faith, we receive the benefit of His atoning death.

3. CHRIST-PLEDGED PEACE.—" Peace I leave with you, My peace I give unto you " (John xiv. 27). Here is the double peace again. The legacy of the dying Saviour, " Peace I leave with you " ; and the gift of the gracious Lord, " My peace I give unto you." Canon Girdlestone has well said, " On examining the passages where the word ' peace ' occurs in the New Testament, we cannot but be struck with the prominence, which it assumes ; and the more carefully the subject is analysed, the more clearly will it be perceived that the peace with God, wrought for the Christian through Christ's blood and sustained in his heart by the agency of the Holy Spirit, is not freedom from enmity, though that is an essential part, but also an absolute oneness or fellowship between the Father and His children, a spiritual relationship, producing a completeness in the nature of man."

We have this fact of oneness and rest in Christ's double promise of rest, in Matt. xi. 28, 29. He not only says, " Come unto Me, and I will give you rest " ; but, Be yoked with Me in the will of God, and ye " shall find rest unto your souls." Perhaps if we were to read " life " (as we may) instead of " soul," we should see a deeper meaning. Rest to the whole life is only possible as we are yoked with Christ in God's will, for God's will is always our weal. There is no real well-being, but by being well in the sweetening will of God.

PERSONALITY QUESTIONING

" Is it I ? "—Matt. xxvi. 17-25.

In Bach's Matthew Passion music, whose libretto was prepared under the Master's own guidance, there is a great passage wherein, at the Last Supper, Christ has just said :

" One of you shall betray Me." And they all begin to say, the recitative tells us, although at once passing the words over into the mouths of the chorus, " Is it I ? Is it I ? Is it I ? " and there begins the wonderful chorus of The Believers : " 'Tis I. My sins betray Thee, who died to make me whole." The effect of this is to transport the listener to a realm where he no longer hears an old story of the past retold, but looking down, as it were upon the whole stream of time, sees the betrayal, the divine tragedy, and the triumph, in one.

The one passage in the above quotation, of arresting importance, is : " 'Tis I. My sins betray Thee, who died to make me whole." We condemn Judas too readily for his betrayal of Christ, but many of us are worse traitors. Someone remarked to the late Joseph Parker, " I wonder that Christ could ever choose Judas." " Ah ! " the doctor responded, " there is a greater wonder than that, and that is, that He should ever choose me." If we know anything of our own hearts, we know we out-Judas Judas in the latent possibilities of our own evil hearts.

The above reminds us sins of all kinds are identified with our Lord who died for them. How pregnant, powerful, far-reaching, do we find our Lord's sacrifice for sins. How many phases of sin we find in that great Passional chapter, Isaiah liii. Listen and ponder some of the sayings.

1. " GRIEFS."—" Surely He hath borne our griefs," sicknesses in all their malady.

2. " SORROWS."—" Man of sorrows " . . . " Carried our sorrows." Pains as caused by sin.

3. " TRANSGRESSIONS."—" Wounded for our transgressions." Sins, expressing the going beyond the boundary of God's will.

4. " INIQUITIES."—" Bruised for our iniquities." He had to suffer for our stepping aside, and inequalities.

5. GUILT OFFERING.—" Thou shall make His soul an offering (a guilt offering) for sin." He was made a guilt offering.

6. " POURED OUT."—" Poured out His soul (life) unto death." His life given for us.

7. BURDEN.—" He bare the sin of many." He was our sin, in all its weight and woe.

PERSONAL KNOWLEDGE

" I know."—2 Tim. i. 12.

It has been said, men are four.

There is the man who does not know he does not know ; he is a fool, avoid him.

There is the man who knows he does not know ; he is simple, teach him.

There is the man who does not know he knows ; he is asleep, awake him.

There is the man who knows he knows ; he is wise, listen to him.

One of the lamenting cries of Christ was, " If thou hadst known " (Luke xix. 42) ; but because the Jews did not know, they " crucified the Lord of Glory " (1 Cor. ii. 8).

How frequently Paul sounds out the clarion note, " I know."

1. " I know " of SIN.—Regarding the evil nature within, he testified, " I know that in me (that is, in my flesh) dwelleth no good thing " (Rom. vii. 18).

2. " I know " of SALVATION.—In relation to the Lord he witnesses, " I know Him whom I have believed " (2 Tim. i. 12, R.V.).

3. " I know " of SANCTIFICATION.—In looking at his life he could say, " I know nothing against myself " (1 Cor. iv. 4, R.V.).

4. " I know " of SATISFACTION.—Of his circumstances and condition, he joyfully affirms, " I know how to be abased, and I know how to abound ; everywhere and in all things I am instructed both to be full and to be hungry, both to abound and to suffer need " (Phil. iv. 12).

How happy are we, indeed, when we have no anxiety about the past, no doubts in the present, and no dismay regarding the future ; for if we know the Lord, we can joyfully go on our way singing :

" I know not where His islands lift
    Their fronded palms in air ;
I only know I cannot drift
    Beyond His love and care."

PERSONAL TOUCH

" The Lord is my Light, and my Salvation, the Lord is the Strength of my life, of whom shall I be afraid? "—Ps. xxvii. 1.

The things which we make our own, are the things which benefit and bless. This is especially true in relation to a personal faith in the Lord Jesus. Martin Luther, the young monk in the monastery at Erfurt, had long been troubled, desiring peace, but never finding it. He found a counsellor in old David Staupitz, who one day quoted to him that article of the Creed : " I believe in the forgiveness of sins."

" Yes," answered Luther, " I believe it."

" Ah ! " cried the old man, " I see what you lack. You believe in the forgiveness of the sins of David and Peter ; but this is not enough. God's command is that you believe that your own sins are forgiven."

Then the light broke into Luther's soul—when he put " my " into the Creed, made it personal, and appropriated the mercy of God in Christ.

Psalm xxvii is full of personal pronouns, speaking of the personal touch with the Lord. The Psalm is full of " I's," " Me's," and " My's." See how the personal touch is brought out in the following " Me's."

1. " HIDE ME " (5).—Troubles cannot harm us, when we make Jehovah our abiding place.

2. " SET ME " (5).—When the Lord sets the believer on the rock, who can reach him ?

3. " ANSWER ME " (7).—The personal prayer brings a personal answer. " Lord help me," causes the me to be helped.

4. " LEAVE ME NOT " (9).—How can He leave us, when He says, " I will never leave thee " ?

5. " TAKE ME UP " (10).—Jehovah, the unchanging One, can never fail us, for He never alters.

6. " TEACH ME " (11).—We are well taught, when He teaches. He teaches the way to walk in, the will to rest in, and the Word to trust on.

7. " DELIVER ME NOT " (12).—He loves us too well, to let our enemies have us. He routs them, when we cry to Him.

PICK-UP MAN

" Is anything too hard for the Lord ? "—Gen. xviii. 14.

While Americans are regarded as the most wasteful people on earth, we see evidences that there is not so much waste in New York after all. For instance, there is the pick-up man, who is after peach stones and cigar butts and who occasionally finds something valuable. There is also a man who carries off empty cans for their solder, while another finds his speciality in the partially decayed fruits in the markets, which can be distilled into cheap wine. Another buys all the turkey heads he can find in the market—price three cents a pound—as they make such lovely soup for his boarding house.

There is another kind of waste, namely, the waste-man, who, like the prodigal, wastes his substance and himself in sin. Thank God there is a Pick-up Man who goes after lost humanity. At a recent meeting in New York, at a downtown meeting, there were ten " down and outs " who were seeking the Lord Jesus as their Saviour, and found Him. He, who cleansed bloody Manasseh, delivered demon-possessed Mary, forgave the woman of the city, saved thieving Zacchæus, arrested self-righteous Saul of Tarsus, and absolved the adulterous woman, is still the Lifter-up of fallen humanity. Christ meets men in their direst extremity, and makes them by His Divine execution trophies of His grace and evidences of His skill.

Many more hard things the God of grace can do. Think of the following :

1. He can BEAUTIFY A FILTHY Joshua (Zech. iii. 3, 4).

2. He can BLESS A CURSED Law-breaker (Gal. iii. 13).

3. He can BEGET a new life into the lifeless (Eph. ii. 1).

4. He can BENEFIT the undeserving (Ps. ciii. 2).

5. He can BETHELISE the homeless (Gen. xxviii. 19).

6. He can BETROTH the shameful (Hosea ii. 19).

7. He can BIND up the breaches of sin (Isa. xxx. 26).

PITEOUS CRY

" *Seeking rest and findeth none.*"—Matt. xii. 43.

" I can find no rest in this world. I am mad. God forgive me."

This was the letter left by Mr. James Edon, 39, art master at Southend Secondary School, who was found dead with his throat cut, at his house in Southend.

His wife, who made the discovery, had seen him shaving a few minutes previously. He had been medically attended for a nervous breakdown.

The above man was evidently deranged, but some who have been in the madness of sin have sent up piteous cries.

1. CAIN, the offering-refuser, said, " My punishment is greater than I can bear " (Gen. iv. 13).

2. SAUL, the Amalek-compromiser, cried in abject despair, " I have sinned " (1 Sam. xv. 24, 30).

3. BALAAM, the sin-dominated, owned he would see the Lord, " but not now," and " behold Him but not nigh " (Num. xxiv. 17).

4. JUDAS, the Christ-betrayer, in anguish of soul exclaimed, " I have betrayed the innocent blood " (Matt. xxvii. 4).

5. JOB, the soul-complainer, groping after the Lord said, " Oh, that I knew where I might find Him " (Job xxiii. 3).

6. THE PRODIGAL, the self-wanderer exclaimed in his dire distress, " I perish with hunger " (Luke xv. 17).

7. JONAH, the disobedient prophet wailed in his soul's distress, " I am cast out of Thy sight " (Jonah ii. 4).

PLACES OF CRISIS

" *Come see the place.*"—Matt. xxviii. 6.

A commercial traveller was boasting in a railway carriage of the places he had visited. A fellow-passenger asked him if he had visited a place called Calvary. The commercial man confessed he did not know such a place. Calvary is the place of all places.

Places named in Scripture are often places of momentous consequence.

Many places mentioned in the Bible have associated with them critical and crisis events. Three things are connected with the following places :

1. THE EDEN of man's innocence, sin, and judgment (Gen. iii. 24 ; Rom. v. 12).

2. THE FLOOD of iniquity, devastation, and the ark of salvation (Gen. vi. and vii ; Heb. xi ; 1 Pet. iii).

4. THE UR of the Chaldees of idolatry, calling, and separation (Gen. xii. 1 ; Heb. xi. 8).

4. THE EXODUS of Bondage, Redemption, and Deliverance (Exod. xiv. 30).

5. THE SINAI of Law, Provision, and Condemnation (Exod. xx. 1-21).

6. THE CALVARY of Love's giving, sin's damnation, and grace's claim (John iii. 16 ; Rom. viii. 1, 2 ; v. 20).

7. THE OLIVET of Ascension, Promise, and Advent (Acts i. 11 ; Zech. xiv. 1-4).

PLACES TO VISIT

" I will give thee places to walk among."—Zech. iii. 7.

" What places have you visited during your holiday ? " was the question put by one friend to another. Then followed a recounting of some of the places visited. Here are a number of places mentioned in the New Testament, as revealed in connection with the word " place."

1. PLACE OF HUMILIATION.—" No place " (" room," A.V. ; same word as " place ") for Him in the inn (Luke ii. 7). The Lowly One took the lowest place, that He might lift the lowly ones into the highest place.

2. PLACE OF RESIGNATION.—" When He was at the place " (Gethsemane) . . . " He prayed " . . . " Not My will, but Thine be done " (Luke xxii. 40-42). He not only prayed to be resigned, but He was resigned as He prayed.

3. PLACE OF CRUCIFIXION.—" The place called Calvary " (Luke xxiii. 33). At that place, love was revealed, grace was manifested, sin was abrogated, atonement was made, Satan was conquered, God was glorified, and peace was procured.

4. PLACE OF RECEPTION.—" I go to prepare a place for you. And if I go and prepare a place for you, I will come

again, and receive you unto Myself ; that where I am, there
ye may be also " (John xiv. 2, 3). He prepares for us a place,
and He prepares us for the place.

5. PLACE OF ILLUMINATION.—The Word of Prophecy is
a " light that shineth in a dark place " (2 Pet. i. 19). Fogs of
doubt, mists of unbelief, and the darkness of ignorance, are
all around us, and we need this Sure Light to guide our feet
and direct our ways.

6. PLACE OF CONDEMNATION.—" This place of torment "
(Luke xvi. 28). He went to " his own place " (Acts i. 25).
The place of sin's choice is the destiny of the sinner's doom.
Sin is the fire of hell, and the fuel that kindles God's wrath.

7. PLACE OF REVELATION.—" Found the place where it
is written " (Luke iv. 17). There is always a place written
in the Word, which guides our conduct in the place where
we may be found.

POWER OF TRIFLES

" Behold how great a matter a little fire kindleth."—Jas. iii.5.

A few years ago the Grand Trunk flyer in Canada going
East, was in hard luck, says the *Ottawa Citizen.* At Napance
the steam box on the big engine got overworked, or something,
and refused to continue the journey. The timely arrival of
a freight train helped. The cars were shunted to a siding
and the freight engine brought into commission on the
express, taking it as far as Brockville, when another large
engine was secured.

Now comes the peculiar part of the troubles of that train.
When about twenty miles out of Cornwall it ran into a sea
of peculiar flies. There were millions of them—perhaps
billions—but the train was going so fast it was impossible to
count them.

The cars became quite dark as the train ploughed through
the mass of insects and then the train came to another sudden
stop. The engine was full of flies. The little things were
ground into a mass in the driving rod. They were in everything on the engine.

The train had been ploughing through the flies at a mile
a minute for several miles. The track was covered with

crushed insects and the engine wheels balked at going round on it. After a little persuasion and a lot of cleaning up the train went upon its way again.

On arrival at Montreal the engine presented a truly curious spectacle. The bars of the cowcatcher were filled right up with flies. On the front of the engine they were several inches thick.

A few flies would have made no impression on that flyer of an express, but the many brought it to a standstill.

I have sometimes wondered what the combined efforts of God's people in any given city would accomplish ! Many an express train of sin and iniquity would be stopped.

1. The COMBINED SHOUT of the Israelites brought down the walls of Jericho (Josh. vi. 20).

2. The UNITED PRAYERS of the early Church secured the outpouring of the Holy Spirit (Acts i. 14 ; ii. 1-4).

3. The FOUR " TOGETHERS " of Ezra accomplished the service of the Lord (Ezra iii. 9, 11 ; iv. 3 ; vi. 20).

4. The persistent and UNITED ACTION of the builders under Nehemiah succeeded in building the wall, and completed the work (Neh. vi. 15).

PRAYER

" The God that answereth."—1 Kings xviii. 24.

We shall have no doubt that God answers prayer, if we accept what God says in His Word. Bishop Barnes says :

" I myself have no doubts as to the value of prayer." He is further reported, in his Gifford Lectures, in the *Aberdeen Press*, to have said : " A merely mechanical theory of the Universe I reject. God rules the world : the laws of Nature are His laws, and in no way constrain His freedom. Thus there is no reason to believe that God cannot grant favourable answers to the crudest petitionary prayers ; our experience alone can determine whether He thus acts as we seek His aid.

" I should even hesitate to declare that petitions for rain or fair weather were necessarily unavailing, there is no theoretical reason why God should not hearken to such prayer. I would pray for a friend's recovery from sickness with the knowledge that such prayers are often of no avail, and yet with hope that God in His goodness would grant my petition. With great confidence would I pray for strength against temptation, whether I myself or some other were in need."

God not only answers by fire, as He did on Mount Carmel, but He answers in a variety of other ways, as the following seven instances, recorded in Holy Writ, illustrate.

1. By HEALING from sickness, as in the case of Hezekiah (2 Kings xx. 1-7).

2. By DELIVERANCE from danger, as demonstrated in Hezekiah's victory over Sennacherib (2 Chron. xxxii. 20-22).

3. By SUCCESS in carrying through an enterprise, as He did Nehemiah, in building the wall of Jerusalem (Neh. iv. 4-6).

4. By POWER, as at Pentecost, when the power of the Spirit came on the disciples (Acts ii. 1-4).

5. By an EARTHQUAKE, as evidenced when the prison at Philippi was shaken, Paul and Silas were freed (Acts xvi. 25-29).

6. By an ANGEL, as seen in Peter's case, when he was brought out of prison (Acts xii. 5-18).

7. By RAIN, as revealed in the downpour which deluged the land through Elijah's petitions (James v. 17, 18).

PRAYER

" When they had prayed the place was shaken."—Acts iv. 31.

" Prayer," says Dr. A. F. Shauffler, " is either a prodigious force or a disgraceful farce. If a farce, you may pray much and get little ; if a force, you may pray little and get much." " If," said a plain, blunt farmer, in referring to a minister's prayer, " any son of mine should ask a favour as tamely as that minister spoke to his ' Father in heaven,' I should give him the stick."

Oh, that we might realise to the full :

" Prayer is the mightiest force that men can wield ;
A power to which omnipotence doth yield ;
A privilege unparalleled—a way
Whereby the Almighty Father can display
His interest in His children's need and care."

We see what a potent force was in the life of the early Christians. They lifted themselves up to the Lord in earnest prayers, and He moved them on by His Living power. What a power prayer is.

1. Prayer is a PROCURING POWER. It was in answer to and while they, the saints, were praying, the power of Pentecost came (Acts ii. 1, 2).

2. Prayer is a QUALIFYING POWER. After the early Christians had prayed, they " spake the Word of God with boldness " (Acts iv. 31).

3. Prayer is an EVIDENCING POWER. The mark by which Ananias was to recognise Saul of Tarsus as a believer, was, " Behold he prayeth " (Acts ix. 11).

4. Prayer is an ENLIGHTENING POWER. Of Cornelius it is said he " prayed to God alway," and the result was he had a vision (Acts x. 1-6, 30).

5. Prayer is a LIBERATING POWER. When Peter was shut up in prison, it was the prayers of the saints that brought him out of it (Acts xii. 5-17).

6. Prayer is the CONSECRATING POWER. While the early church at Antioch prayed and fasted, the Holy Spirit consecrated Paul and Barnabas to the consecrated service of the Gospel (Acts xiii. 1-3).

7. Prayer is an AWAKENING POWER. The prayers of Paul and Silas was the cause of the earthquake, which caused a heart-quake in the heart of the Philippian jailor (Acts xvi. 25-34).

PRAYER : AN ATTITUDE

" *I will therefore that men pray everywhere, lifting up holy hands, without wrath and doubting.*"—1 Tim. ii. 8.

Benjamin Jowett says of prayer : " Prayer is an act, performed at set times, in certain forms of words ; but prayer is also a spirit which need not be expressed in words—the spirit of contentment and resignation, of active goodness and benevolence, of modesty and truthfulness." In other words, Jowett says that prayer is an attitude of heart, as well as an act of worship, in expressed need. This attitude of heart is expressed in many ways in the Psalter.

1. It is a waiting upon the Lord in DEPENDENCE (Ps. xxvii. 14).

2. It is a being still before the Lord in CONTENTMENT (Ps. lxii. 1, marg.).

3. It is an expectation from the Lord in RELIANCE (Ps. lxii. 5).

4. It is a delight in the Lord in COMMUNION (Ps. xxxvii. 4).

5. It is a resting on the Lord in PATIENCE (Ps. xxxvii. 7).

6. It is a trusting with the Lord in SERVICE (Ps. xxxvii. 3).

7. It is a rising to the Lord in SATISFACTION (Ps. xci.).

PRAYER : ITS OUGHTNESS

" *Men ought always to pray.*"—Luke xviii. 1.

In a prominent place in the *Chicago Tribune* appeared the following :

" PRAYER BEFORE MEALS AN AID TO DIGESTION.

" Philadelphia, Pa., June 28—In addition to being an excellent religious practice, the saying of grace before meals is an aid to digestion, Dr. Gilbert Fitzpatrick, of Chicago, president of the American Institute of Homeopathy, told the eighty-second annual convention of the institute.

" Family squabbles, business problems, and other frictional disturbances tend to disrupt the process of digestion, Dr. Fitzpatrick added. Instead, he advocated laughter and cheer at, meal-time."

There are many reasons why we should pray. The following are some of them :

1. THE BEHEST OF PRAYER.—The commands of the Lord are for our obedience ; hence, we are to " pray without ceasing " (1 Thess. v. 17).

2. THE BENEFIT OF PRAYER.—The teaching of the parable is, God will undertake our cause if we plead with importunity (Luke xviii. 7).

3. THE BROTHERLINESS OF PRAYER.—" Epaphras . . . labouring fervently in prayer " (Col. iv. 12). There is no ministry so effective in helping others like prayer.

4. THE BENEDICTION OF PRAYER.—When prayer is coupled with thanksgiving and carefulness about nothing, it bestows the benediction of the peace of God (Phil. iv. 6, 7).

5. THE BETTERMENT OF PRAYER.—No one can truly pray without being the better for it, for coming to God, we are receivers from Him, for we become like that which we receive. The disciples received the Spirit in answer to prayer, and that caused a marked difference in their lives (Acts i. 14 ; ii. 1-4).

PRAYER : ITS PRIVILEGE AND POWER

" *In prayer.*"—Neh. xi. 17.

Dr. Rendle Harris, in *The Guiding Hand of God*, tells of a father in Oxford who was caused one evening to pray for his soldier son, absent on service in the South African War. Under the same impelling, he continued in prayer till the morning broke. Then came relief, and he went to rest. It transpired that in the distant land his son had been brought very seriously wounded into hospital. The doctor had at first declared there to be no hope, but yielding to the nurse's pleading, they had together fought throughout the night to draw that life into safety, and at dawn the crisis had been passed. It was in the " self-same hour " that his father had felt that he could cease his intercession. Prayer, when it becomes a reality, opens the eyes and directs the gaze upon the unseen. The secrets of the Lord are ours.

Several times we find the words " In prayer.".

1. ARTICULATED PRAYER.—" Whiles I was speaking IN PRAYER " (Dan. ix. 21).

2. PRIVILEGED PRAYER.—" Whatsoever ye shall ask IN PRAYER " (Matt. xxi. 22).

3. CONTINUED PRAYER.—" Continued all night IN PRAYER " (Luke vi. 12).

4. UNITED PRAYER.—" One accord IN PRAYER and supplication " (Acts i. 14).

5. EXAMPLED PRAYER.—" Laboured fervently IN PRAYERS " (Col. iv. 12).

6. INTENSE PRAYER.—" Continuing IN PRAYER " (Rom. xii. 12).

7. WATCHFUL PRAYER.—" Continue IN PRAYER, and watch in the same " (Col. iv. 2).

PRAYER OF FAITH

" The Prayer of Faith."—James v. 15.

There are many things which are said to be " of faith." There is the " walk of faith " which companions with the company of God (2 Cor. v. 7) ; there is " the Word of faith " which listens to the voice of God (Rom. x. 8) ; and there is " the prayer of faith " which hands everything over to God (Jas. v. 15).

The word " prayer " in the sentence " the prayer of faith," is peculiar in its inwardness, it indicates the condition of the one who prays, and therefore signifies that the one who prays is right with God.

There are only two other instances where the same word is rendered " prayer." Once when it says of Christ, " He prayed," and the other place where we read, " They prayed and fasted " (Luke ix. 29; Acts xiii. 1-3). Wrapped up in the soul of the word there is implied the faithfulness of a consistent life in the one who prays, therefore no one prays " the prayer of faith " who does not live in the life of faithfulness. Burns happily expresses the thought in the *Cotter's Saturday Night*, when he says,

> " They never sought in vain,
> Who sought the Lord aright."

The Prayer of Faith is :

1. SECRET IN ITS FELLOWSHIP.—" When thou prayest, enter into thy closet . . . pray to thy Father which is in secret " (Matt. vi. 6).

2. SUBMISSIVE IN ITS ATTITUDE.—Christ prayed saying, " Thy will be done " (Matt. xxvi. 42, 44).

3. SUPPLICATING IN ITS SERVICE.—" Prayed for them " (Acts viii. 15).

4. SINCERE IN ITS REQUEST.—" I prayed in mine house " (Acts x. 30).

5. SANCTIFIED IN ITS DESIRE.—" When they had fasted and prayed " (Acts xiii. 3).

6. SYMPHONISING WITH OTHERS.—" If two of you shall agree on earth, as touching anything that they shall ask, it

shall be done for them of My Father which is in heaven " (Matt. xviii. 19).

7. Single-hearted in Its Devotion.—" We made our prayer unto God " (Neh. iv. 9).

PRAYER : RICHARD BAXTER'S TESTIMONY

" Whatsoever ye shall ask."—Matt. xxi. 22.

Richard Baxter has left this testimony : " Many a time when I have been brought low, and received the sentence of death in myself, when my poor, honest, and praying neighbours have met, and, upon their fasting and earnest prayers I have recovered. Once, when I had continued weak three weeks, and was unable to go abroad, the very day they prayed for me, being Good Friday, I recovered, and was able to preach, and administer the sacrament the next Lord's day ; and was better after it, it being the first time I ever administered it. And ever after that, whatever weakness was upon me, when I had, after preaching, administered the sacrament to many hundreds of people, I was much revived and eased of my infirmities."

If we ask rightly we shall obtain bountifully. If we ask wrongly, we shall obtain disastrously.

1. Asking in Prayer.—" Ask and it shall be given you " (Matt. vii. 7-11). Have something to ask for, and get what you ask, then the benefit of asking will be enjoyed.

2. Asking for Help.—" Give to every man that asketh of thee " (Luke vi. 30). Better to make mistakes in giving, than to have the mistakes of an ungenerous nature.

3. Asking for Water.—" Askest drink of Me." " . . . Thou wouldest have asked of Him " (John iv. 9, 10). Water from earth's resources fails, but Christ's reservoir is lasting and satisfying.

4. Asking for Light.—The jailor " called (asked) for a light " (Acts xvi. 29). He needed light in a twofold sense. To see how things were, and to see his spiritual need.

5. Asking for Wisdom.—" If any man lack wisdom, let him ask of God " (Jas. i. 5). To be wise through God's Word is to have a wisdom worth having.

6. Asking for Filling.—Paul's " desire " (same word

as " ask "—*aiteo*, Col. i. 9) for the saints at Colosse was that they might be " filled " with the knowledge of God's will.

7. ASKING FOR A MURDERER.—The people were incited to " ask " for Barabbas, and their sad choice is recorded against them (Matt. xxvii. 20 ; Acts iii. 14).

PRAYER THAT PRAYS : OR, AN ALPHABET OF PRAYERFUL AND PERSONAL PRAYERS

" *Pray without ceasing.*"—1 Thess. v. 17.

The Indians say that when a man kills a foe, the strength of the slain enemy enters into the victor's arm. We know that when the enemy of prayerlessness is killed, strength comes to the one that prays.

How many prayers we have recorded, and how many blessings there are which come to us as we pray. Let the following prayers illustrate.

" ABIDE WITH US."—The Prayer for Companionship (Luke xxiv. 29).

" BLESS ME."—" Bless me, even me also, O my Father " (Gen. xxvii. 34). Individual Prayer.

" COME UNTO ME."—" Let Thy tender mercies come unto me, that I may live " (Ps. cxix. 77). Prayer for Life.

" DELIVER ME."—The Prayer for Victory (Ps. xxxi. 15).

" EXAMINE ME."—A Prayer for Testing (Ps. xxvi. 2).

FORGIVENESS.—A Prayer for Forgiveness (Ps. xxv. 18). " Forgive all my sins."

" GUIDE ME."—The Prayer for Leading (Ps. xxxi. 3). " For Thy Name's sake . . . guide me."

" HELP ME."—The Prayer for Aid (Matt. xv. 25).

" INTEGRITY . . . PRESERVE ME." —Prayer for Uprightness (Ps. xxv. 21).

" JUDGE ME."—Prayer for Discretion (Ps. liv. 1).

" KEEP ME."—The Prayer for Preservation (Ps. xvii. 8).

" LEAD ME."—The Prayer for Direction (Ps. cxxxix. 24).

" MAKE ME."—The Prayer for Adjustment (Ps. cxix. 35).

" NEVER BE ASHAMED."—" Let me never be ashamed." A Prayer for Constancy (Ps. lxxi. 1).

" OPEN MINE EYES."—The Prayer for Illumination (Ps. cxix. 18).

" PRESERVE ME."—The Prayer for Keeping (Ps. xvi. 1).
" QUICKEN ME."—The Prayer for Revival (Ps. cxix. 25).
" REDEEM ME."—Prayer for Release (Ps. xxvi. 11).
" SAVE ME."—The Prayer for Rescue (Matt. xiv. 30).
" TEACH ME."—The Prayer for Instruction (Ps. xxvii. 11).
" UNITE MY HEART."—The Prayer for Communion (Ps. lxxxvi. 11).
" VISIT ME."—A Prayer for Visitation (Ps. cvi. 4).
" WATCH."—" Set a watch, O Lord, before my lips " (Ps. cxli. 3). Prayer for Prevention.
XTREMITY.—" Remember me " (Luke xxiii. 42).

The above prayers impress one in several ways. They are brief in utterance, direct in petition, personal in plea, humble in tone, dependent in faith, conscious of need, and earnest in manner.

PRAYER : THE GREATEST MINISTRY OF ALL

" *Ye also helping together by prayer for us.*"—2 Cor. i. 11.

A station in the China Inland Mission was peculiarly blessed of God. Inquirers were more numerous and more easily turned from dumb idols to serve the living God than at other stations. The difference was a theme of conversation and wonder. In England Dr. J. Hudson Taylor was warmly greeted at a certain place by a stranger who showed great interest in his mission work. He was so particular and intelligent in his questions concerning one missionary and the locality in which he laboured, seemed so well acquainted with his helpers, inquirers, and the difficulties of that particular station, that Dr. Taylor's curiosity was aroused to find out the reason of this intimate knowledge. He now learned that this stranger and the successful missionary had covenanted together as co-workers. The missionary kept his home brother informed of all the phases of his labour. He gave him the names of inquirers, stations, hopeful characters and difficulties, and all these the home worker was wont to spread out before God in prevailing prayer.

There is no ministry so effective and helpful as the intercession of prayer. Think of some of the results as brought out in the Book of Acts.

1. Prayer brought the POWER OF PENTECOST (Acts ii. 4).

2. Prayer brought RENEWED GRACE to the disciples in need (Acts iv. 31).

3. Prayer brought DISCRETION and DIRECTION to the early church in missionary work (Acts xiii. 3).

4. Prayer SUSTAINED Paul and Silas in suffering and persecution, and made them a blessing to others (Acts xvi. 25).

5. Prayer BROUGHT Peter OUT OF PRISON by means of angelic ministry (Acts xii. 5).

6. Prayer brought CONSOLATION to the church in Ephesus, when Paul left it (Acts xx. 36).

7. Prayer brought HELP to Saul of Tarsus in his need (Acts ix. 11).

PRAYER : THREE KINDS

" *Master, have mercy upon us !* "   " *Where are the nine ?* "— Luke xvii. 13, 17.

" *Pharisee . . . prayed with himself.*"—Luke xviii. 11.

" *God be merciful to me a sinner.*"—Luke xviii. 13.

Bishop Jeremy Taylor appropriately has described three kinds of prayers :

> " Many, in direst trouble, pray ;
> But when that trouble's over they
> Forget to give the praise that's due
> To the good God who helped them through.

> " Some, like the Pharisee, oft pray
> Thus with themselves, thankful that they
> Are not so bad as those ' than whom
> I thank Thee that I better am.'
> ' Better in what ?   That thou'rt a sham ?
> Wouldst thou do better in their room ? '

> " But, like the publican, I'd rather
> Beat on my breast, and cry, ' Oh ! Father,
> A sinner I ; have mercy, Thou !
> From my worse self, oh, save me now ! "

1. PRAISE-LESS PRAYERS.—Thankless ones like the lepers, who returned not to thank the Lord for their cleansing :

such are disgraceful in their want of gratitude. Those who are wanting in praise will be wanting in blessing.

2. PHARISAICAL PRAYERS.—The Pharisee prayed " with himself," about himself, but not for himself. His prayer began, continued, and ended in himself.

> " I, I, I, I, I, itself ;
>   The inside and the outside,
>   The what and the why,
>   The when and the where,
>   The low and the high,
>   All I, I, I, I, itself I."

3. PUBLICAN'S PRAYER.—His prayer was for mercy, because he knew he was a sinner ; yea, what he actually prayed was, " God be propitiated to me, the sinner " (Luke xviii. 13, R.V., marg.), or as it might be rendered, " God make an atonement for me, the sinner." The word " merciful " is translated " make reconciliation " in the Revised Version of Heb. ii. 17. It reads, " Make propitiation " (atonement) " for the sins of the people," and refers to the high priest on the Day of Atonement, in his making an atonement for the sins of the people (See Leviticus xvi.).

PREACHER'S THEME

" *We preach Christ crucified.*"—1 Cor. i. 23.

In one of the old-fashioned mansions in the United States there is still be be seen a brass-bound clock upon the staircase landing, with the hands fixed at the minute and hour when Washington died. The grandfather of the present owner was a pall-bearer at the funeral of the great republican, and set the hands where they have since remained. Even so, the preacher's finger must ever point the multitude to Jesus Christ and Him crucified.

" Christ crucified " :

1. EXPRESSES the outshining of God's love (John iii. 16).

2. EXHIBITS the wonder of God's grace (2 Cor. viii. 9).

3. ENFOLDS the revelation of God's Word (John xix. 24, 28).

4. EXTINGUISHES the self of man's evil (Gal. ii. 20).

5. ENDOWS the believer with God's salvation (Acts iv. 10-12).

6. EXCLUDES the world of Satan's rule (Gal. vi. 14).

7. ENRICHES the saint with God's riches (Eph. i. 3-7).

PRESENCE MADE A DIFFERENCE

" *My presence shall go with thee.*"—Exod. xxxiii. 14.

It is said, every day, without fail, there is one express train that runs into London dead on time. It is so punctual that it has been dubbed by the members of the " Black Bag Brigade," the " Infallible Express." For a long time it was a mystery to the scores of business men, ´ stockbrokers and doctors and outer residents of London, why, when other trains failed, this one was invariable in its habits. And then one day the secret leaked out. The managing director of the line travels to town every morning by the " Infallible Express."

The presence of the man of the line made the difference. When we have the Lord with us, He makes all the difference.

1. His presence is an ESSENTIAL PRESENCE, for we cannot do without Him (Exod. xxxiii. 15).

2. His presence is an EXHILARATING PRESENCE, for He causes all nature to sing (1 Chron. xvi. 33).

3. His presence is an EXULTING PRESENCE, for in it there is " fulness of joy " (Ps. xvi. 11).

4. His presence is an ENVIRONING PRESENCE, for He hides us in the secrecy of His pavilion (Ps. xxxi. 20).

5. His presence is an EXPRESSIVE PRESENCE, for things melt and are moved before Him (Ps. xcvii. 5).

6. His presence is an ENCOMPASSING PRESENCE, for we cannot get away from it (Ps. cxxxix. 7).

7. His presence is an EMANCIPATING PRESENCE, for it delivers from enemies and bondage (Isa. lxiii. 9).

8. His presence is an ENABLING PRESENCE, for He equips for His service, as we live in the consciousness of it (Luke i. 19).

9. His presence is an ENRICHING PRESENCE, for times of refreshing come from Him (Acts iii. 19).

PROOF OF DISCIPLESHIP

" *By this shall all men know that ye are My disciples, if ye have love one to another.*"—John xiii. 35.

" In one of my early journeys I came," writes a missionary, " with my companions to a heathen village on the banks of the Orange River. We had travelled far, and were hungry, thirsty, fatigued ; but the people of the village rather directed us to halt at a distance. We asked for water, but they would not supply it. I offered three or four buttons left on my jacket for a drink of milk, but was refused. We had the prospect of another hungry night at a distance from water, though within sight of the river. When twilight came on, a woman approached from the height beyond where the village lay. She bore on her head a bundle of wood, and had a vessel of milk in her hand. The latter, without opening her lips, she handed to us, laid down the wood, and returned to the village. A second time she came with a cooking vessel on her head, and a leg of mutton in one hand and water in the other. She sat down without saying a word ; prepared the fire and put on the meat. She remained silent until we affectionately entreated her to give a reason for such un-looked-for kindness to strangers. Then the tears rolled down her cheeks, and she replied :

" ' I love Him whose you are, and surely it is my duty to give you a cup of cold water in His name. My heart is full, therefore I can't speak the joy I feel at seeing you in this out-of-the-world place.'

" On learning a little of her history, and that she was a solitary light burning in a dark place, I asked her how she kept up the light of God in the entire absence of the communion of saints. She drew from her bosom a copy of the Dutch New Testament which she had received from Mr. Helm, when in his school some years before. ' This,' she said, ' is the fountain from whence I drink ; this is the oil that makes my lamp burn.' "

Christ is the reason why we should love one another.

1. Because He gave HIMSELF for us (1 John iii. 16).
2. Because He gives the EXAMPLE (John xiii. 14, 15).
3. Because He COMMANDS us to do so (John xiii. 34).

4. Because He has FORGIVEN us (Eph. iv. 32 ; v. 1).

5. Because we are ONE WITH EACH OTHER (Rom. xii. 10).

6. Because we have PASSED FROM DEATH UNTO LIFE (1 John iii. 14).

7. Because this is THE EVIDENCE WE KNOW Him (1 John iv. 7, 8).

" PUT TO SHAME OR NOT "

" *He that believeth on Him shall not be confounded,*" or *put to shame.*—1 Pet. ii. 6.

Judge Avory in condemning Hatry, the forger, to penal servitude, said, " I am unable to imagine any worse case than yours under this statute and, therefore, upon the forging and uttering counts of the first indictment the sentence of the court is that you be detained in penal servitude for 14 years."

When justice put the sinner to shame, what shame rests upon him !

The word " Kataischuno " in the following Scriptures means to be disgraced, overwhelmed with shame, and to be confounded and dishonoured.

1. FAITH'S ASSURANCE.—" He that believeth on Him *shall not be ashamed* " (Rom. x. 11). When we know what God says, we have a firm foundation on which to rest.

2. HOPE'S POWER.—" Hope *maketh not ashamed* " (Rom. v. 5). When hope goes up the stairs of Love's providing, it has a heaven-born courage, which enables it to look out into the future with confidence.

3. APOSTLE'S BOAST.—" If I have boasted anything to him of you, *I am not ashamed* " (2 Cor. vii. 14). If what we say of others is true, truth is always something in which we can glory.

4. GOD'S CHOICE.—" God hath chosen the foolish things of the world to *confound* the wise " (1 Cor. i. 27). The Lord chooses for His purpose very unlikely instruments to carry out His will.

5. CHRIST'S VICTORY.—" All His adversaries *were*

ashamed " (Luke xiii. 17). Those who tried to worst Christ were always worsted by Him.

6. SCRIPTURE'S PROMISE.—" As it is written . . . whosoever believeth on Him shall not *be ashamed* " (Rom. ix. 33). When we have God's " shall not " we may not question His word.

7. BELIEVER'S POWER.—When we have a " good conscience " within, and a " good conversation " (R.V., " manner of life ") without, we have a power which speaks for itself, and those who oppose us " *may* " well " *be ashamed* " (1 Pet. iii. 16).

QUESTIONS WE ASK

" What ? "—John viii. 5. *" What ? "*—Luke xv. 4, 8.

" We are born questioners from the cradle to the grave. The cradle and the grave are themselves the intensest marks of interrogation. As we begin, so we go on. The putting of questions is a continuing sign of life. It is the inquisitive child that gathers knowledge. Without the spur of curiosity there is mental atrophy," says the *Times*.

" The scientist makes his discoveries by a pertinacious questioning of a reticent Nature. He is a great man if he manages to spell his way through a few lines in her infinite book of secrecy. Endeavour in every form can be seen as putting questions to circumstance and making the best of the answer. And the answer is rarely one that is self-explanatory or wholly satisfying. Sometimes it is the Irishman's answer of a counter-inquiry ; sometimes an enigma which prompts further questioning and further effort.

" It often seems as if the questions which matter most are those to which there is least hope of a reply. And yet we can never cease to ask them. No man who is not content to lose the whole sense of moral value can bring himself to give up asking why he came into the world, what he is doing in it, and what is to become of him when he goes out of it.

" He is under compulsion to pour his eager questions into the darkness and to frame some working hypothesis out

of the echoes which come back to him. In his weakness he
often tires of trying to read the riddle, and complains that

> ' of the myriads who
> Before us passed the door of Darkness through,
> Not one returns to tell us of the Road,
> Which to discover we must travel too.'

He has forgotten for the moment that the answered riddle is
a gathered flower, and that ' gathered flowers are dead.' It
is the mark of the live soul that it should be unwearied in its
questioning, and resolved to take no blank negation for an
answer."

The most pertinent questions that were ever asked were
those asked by Christ. Let us recall seven questions which
He put, and which begin with the word " What ? "

1. " WHAT THINK YE OF CHRIST ? " (Matt. xxii. 42).—
What we " think " proves what we are ; therefore, right
thoughts about Christ evidences what we are, and our
relations to Him.

2. " WHAT IS A MAN PROFITED IF HE SHALL GAIN THE
WHOLE WORLD ? " (Matt. xvi. 26).—To lose one's life in sin
is to lose one's self in eternity.

3. " WHAT WILL YE THAT I SHOULD DO UNTO THEE ? "
(Matt. xx. 32). When we have an answer to Christ's request,
we find He replies to our answers in all things, as the blind
men found when they received their sight.

4. " WHAT REASON YE IN YOUR HEARTS ? " (Luke v. 22).—
When our reasoning blinds our minds, Christ's questions
search us, and show our folly.

5. " WHAT IS WRITTEN IN THE LAW ? " (Luke x. 26).—
The law shows us God's demands and our inability to meet
them. We find ourselves convicted of sin, and ourselves put
to shame, by the commands of God's righteousness.

6. " WHAT SEEK YE ? " (John i. 38).—Those who seek
after Christ have something and Someone worthy of their
quest. Unless we seek Him, we shall miss everything that
is worth having.

7. " WHAT MANNER OF COMMUNICATIONS ARE THESE ? "
(Luke xxiv. 17).—Christ listens to what we have to say,
especially the things which relate to Himself. Let us be
careful what we say, for He is listening.

READY FOR CHRIST'S COMING

" Ready, for in such an hour as ye think not the Son of Man cometh."—Matt. xxiv. 44.

When Shackleton was driven back from his quest of the South Pole, he left his men on Elephant Island, and promised to come back to them. Working his way as best he might to South Georgia, he tried to get back to his men to fulfil his promise, and failed, tried again and failed. The ice was between him and the island ; he could not get near it. He had promised his men to come, and he was not able to come, but he could not rest ; though the season was adverse, though they told him it was impossible to get there, that the ice barrier was thick between, in his little boat, " Yalcho," he tried it again.

It was the wrong time of the year when he tried, but, strange to say, he got nearer the island ; there was an open avenue between the sea and the place where he had left his men ; he ran his boat in at the risk of being nipped, got his men, all of them, on board, and came out again before the ice crashed to. It was all done in half an hour. When the excitement was partly over, he turned to one of the men, and said : " Well, you were all packed and ready ! " and the men said : " You see, boss, Wild (the second in command) never gave up hope, and whenever the sea was at all clear of ice he rolled up his sleeping-bag, and said to all hands, ' Roll up your sleeping-bags, boys ; the boss may come to-day.' " " And so it came to pass," said Shackleton, " that we suddenly came out of the fog, and from a black outlook ; in an hour all were in safety, homeward bound."

Aye ! my friends, you and I must keep awake, and my message to you this day is, " Roll up your sleeping-bags." " My soul, wait thou only upon God, for my expectation is from Him." Keep awake, be alert : the Lord may come to-day. It may not be till to-morrow, it may not be till next week, but you may be quite sure that He in whom you trust with all your mind and with all your heart will not fail you.

As the elementaries in education were the three R's— reading, 'riting, and 'rithmetic, so there are SEVEN R's in relation to the coming of Christ. He, " The Lord our God shall come."

1. He will come as the REMOVER of His people from the world. As it was said of Enoch, " He was not, for God took him," so it shall be said of them (Heb. xi. 5 ; 1 Thess. iv. 17).

2. He will come as the RESURRECTION to awaken those who have fallen asleep ; for Christ is the great " I am," as " The Resurrection," to raise the dead to life and immortality (John xi. 25 ; 1 Cor. xv. 51-55).

3. He will come as the REDEEMER to complete our salvation ; for we are sealed with the Holy Spirit unto the Day of Redemption (Eph. iv. 30 ; Rom. viii. 23).

4. He will come as the RECEIVER, to welcome us to Himself ; for His promise is, " I will come again and receive you unto Myself." (John xiv. 3).

5. He will come as the RESTORER, to fulfil Jehovah's covenant to Israel, to give Abraham's seed the Land of Promise, and the Throne of David to his posterity (Acts iii. 20, 21).

6. He will come as the RULER, to reign in righteousness, when all wrongs will be righted, and disabilities will cease (Acts xvii. 31).

7. He will come as the RECONCILER of humanity, when strife and lawlessness will be stamped out, and all things will be reconciled to Himself (Col. i. 20).

RECEPTIVITY OF THE CHRISTIAN LIFE

" *As ye . . . received Christ Jesus the Lord, so walk ye in Him.*"
—Col. ii. 6.

General Bramwell Booth used to tell the following concerning Cecil Rhodes, who had been with the General to visit one of the social schemes of the Salvation Army at work. On the return journey by train (the General states), " I leaned across and said, ' Mr. Rhodes, are you a happy man ? ' I shall never forget how he threw himself back against the cushions of that first-class compartment, gripped the arm of the seat, and, looking at me with that extraordinary stare of his, exclaimed, ' Happy ? I—happy ? Good God, no.' Later, Rhodes said, ' You are right ; you have the best of me, after all. I am trying to make new countries, you are making new men.' "

How many public men and women are unhappy ? It is only those who are " new creatures in Christ Jesus " that are truly happy. The Happy Man is the One described in Ps. i. The happy one has Christ for his Saviour, God as his Father, the Holy Spirit as his Power, the love of God as his Inspiration, the Word of God for his guide, the joy of the Lord as his strength, the peace of God as his garrison, holiness as his life, purity as his indweller, and the coming of Christ as his hope.

The secret of attainment in the Christian life is obtainment. The word rendered " receive " in the following Scriptures is " Obtain " in 1 Cor. ix. 25.

1. CHRIST RECEIVED.—" As many as received Him . . . become sons " (John i. 12). We become children of God by receiving the Son of God.

2. THE HOLY SPIRIT RECEIVED.—" Whom the world cannot receive " (John xiv. 17), but the believer in Christ can receive Him, and this is as definite as receiving Christ.

3. POWER RECEIVED.—" Ye shall receive power, the Holy Spirit coming upon you " (Acts i. 8). The blessing of Pentecost is power, and that power is in the Spirit.

4. CHRIST'S WORDS RECEIVED.—" They have received them " (John xvii. 8). The words of Christ are weights for ballast, and wealth for blessing.

5. MINISTRY RECEIVED.—" The ministry which I received of the Lord Jesus " (Acts xx. 24). A ministry received from Him is a ministry received by others.

6. GRACE RECEIVED.—" Of His fulness have all we received, and grace upon grace " (John i. 16). All kinds of grace, for every kind of need.

7. ANSWERS RECEIVED.—" Ask, and ye shall receive " (John xvi. 24). " Whatsoever we ask we receive of Him." (1 John iii. 22). God changes things in answer to prayer.

RECOGNISED

" I am glad on your behalf."—Rom. xvi. 19.

Bishop Harrington C. Lees was asked to sign a paper for a wounded soldier. He asked him if he was a " private." " Lance-corporal, sir," was the reply. " I beg your pardon," the Bishop replied, " I had not noticed your stripe."

We often fail to notice in others what the Lord recognises, and if the Lord recognises others, surely we ought to recognise them. How quick Paul was to recognise the grace of the Lord in others !

1. HELPING PRISCILLA AND AQUILA.—" My helpers in Christ Jesus " (Rom. xvi. 3).

2. LABOURING MARY.—" Mary, who bestowed much labour on us " (Rom. xvi. 6).

3. SUCCOURING PHEBE.—" She hath been a succourer of many and of myself also " (Rom. xvi. 2).

4. APPROVED APPELLES.—"Appelles approved in Christ " (Rom. xvi. 10).

5. WORKING TRYPHENA AND TRYPHOSA.—" Tryphena and Tryphosa, who labour in the Lord " (Rom. xvi. 12).

6. ABOUNDING PERSIS.—" Beloved Persis, who laboured much in the Lord " (Rom. xvi. 12).

7. KINDLY GAIUS.—What a host Paul says when he says, " Gaius my host " (Rom. xvi. 23).

There are others who are named and appreciated in Romans xvi.

RECOGNITION IN THE LIFE TO COME

" Then shall I know, even as also I am known."—i Cor. xiii. 12.

It is often asked, " Shall we know each other in the next life ? " We cannot say *how* it will be, but we know God says it shall be. We are assured the quickened or raised body should contain identically some material particle or particles of the old body, however entering into new chemical or organic combinations. It may be well to avoid such defini-tions, even such a word as " material." What we know is that the old companion of the soul will join it again after the long parting—both joyous, free, and glorified, but still the same—the same after all the differences. So may we gaze in peace on the image of the departed, and say :

> " On high
> A record lives of thine identity !
> Thou shalt not lose one charm of lip or eye ;
> The hues and liquid lights shall wait for thee,
> And the fair tissues wheresoe'er they be.
> So shall the beauty its old rights maintain,
> And they sweet spirit own these eyes again."

The following are a few proofs of the identity of the individual in the life to come with what we were known here.

1. CHRIST DECLARES THE LIFE OF RECOGNITION when He says " God " is the God of the Living and not of the dead (Luke xx. 38).

2. SPIRIT PROCLAIMS IT, for those who have been " shall see His Face " (Rev. xxii. 4).

3. GOD REVEALS IT, for those who have lived in the " earthly house " will be " clothed with a house from heaven " (2 Cor. v. 1, 2).

4. OLD TESTAMENT SAINTS ANNOUNCED IT, for they looked for a life to come, and acted accordingly (Heb. xi. 13-16).

5. THE TRANSFIGURATION ILLUSTRATES IT.—The Moses and Elijah of the past are known as the same persons on the mount of transfiguration (Luke ix. 30).

6. PAUL WAS ASSURED OF IT, for he speaks of sleeping and living saints being together, " By the Word of the Lord " (1 Thess. iv. 15-18).

7. CHRIST'S RESURRECTION CONFIRMS IT, for " This same Jesus " will be known as He was known (Acts i. 11).

REJOICING CONTINUALLY

" *Rejoice evermore.*"—1 Thess. v. 16.

The grace of God can make us sing when suffering (Acts xvi. 25), rejoice when persecuted (Acts v. 41), bless when cursed (Matt. v. 44), content when buffeted (2 Cor. xii. 7-9), merry when saved (Luke xv. 24), joyful when tried (2 Cor. vii. 4), and lifted up when cast down (2 Cor. iv. 9-11).

Payson, in his last days, said : " Christians might avoid

much trouble and inconvenience if they would only believe what they profess, that God is able to make them happy without anything else. They imagine that if such a dear friend were to die, or such-and-such blessings were to be removed, they would be miserable. Whereas God can make them a thousand times happier without them. To mention my own case : God has been depriving me of one blessing after another, but as every one was removed He has come in and filled up its place, and now when I am a cripple, and not able to move, I am happier than I ever was in my life before, or ever expected to be ; and if I had believed this twenty years ago, I might have been spared much anxiety."

Determination in exultation is a sign of grace. If we practise well, we shall sing harmoniously.

1. THE ONE WE PRAISE.—" I will praise Thee, O Jehovah " (Ps. ix. 1). He is the Faithful and unchanging One. We can rest in the solidarity of His love, and rely on the sovereignty of His grace.

2. THE REASON OF OUR SONG.—" I will sing unto Jehovah, because He hath dealt bountifully with me " (Ps. xiii. 6). His bounties are lasting love, living grace, and lifting power. We have something about which we can sing.

3. THE POWER OF WHICH WE CHANT.—" I will sing of Thy power " (Ps. lix. 16). He gives power to be, to do, to suffer, to witness, to fight, and to rest in Himself. He never calls us to do anything without qualifying us for it.

4. THE MERCIES WHICH COME.—" I will sing of the mercies of the Lord " (Ps. lxxxix. 1). His mercies are continuous in their blessing, faithful in their service, loving in their kindness, holy in their ministry, and suitable in their application.

5. THE HEART WHICH SINGS.—" O God, my heart is fixed. I will sing and give praise " (Ps. cviii. 1). The heart which is tuned to praise is the heart that is fixed on the Lord, and is content with the Lord.

6. THE INSTRUMENT WITH WHICH WE SING.—" I will sing a new song unto Thee, O God ; upon a psaltery, and an instrument of ten strings, will I sing praises unto Thee " (Ps. cxliv. 9). The ten strings of our body should praise Him—our eyes by looking to Him, our ears by their atten-

tion, our hands by our work, our feet by our walk, our tongue by our speech, and our heart by our love.

7. WHERE WE SING.—" I will sing unto Thee among the nations " (Ps. lvii. 9). We praise Him truthfully and triumphantly when we live for Him holily.

RESPONSIVENESS OF THE LORD TO FAITH

" Thou wilt."—Luke v. 12.

Gipsy Smith relates how his daughter commenced a meeting for young people, and one night there appeared a ragged urchin, who had a pair of pants whose legs were not of corresponding size, and out of which was hanging part of another garment called a " shirt." The boy's hair was like an electrified haystack, and his face was as black as a coal-miner's. It was the custom of the class, when the roll was called, for each member to repeat a text. When each member had done this, " Zillah " (Miss Smith) turned to the black-faced boy, and said, " Of course, my boy, you not being in the habit of attending our class, have not a text."

" Ain't I, though ; I 'ave."

" Well, we shall be glad to hear it."

Remember the boy's face was black—very black. Lifting up his grimy face to the teacher's, and his black eyes twinkling, he said : " Lord, if Thou wilt, Thou canst make me clean."

The following " Thou wilt's " in the Psalms, reveal the expectancy of faith, as confirmation of the leper's cry.

1. BLESSING.—" For Thou, Lord, wilt bless the righteous " (Ps. v. 12). The blessings of forgiveness, peace, deliverance, power, holiness, joy, alone can come from Him.

2. PROTECTION.—" O Lord, with favour Thou wilt compass him as with a shield " (Ps. v. 12). He surrounds as a wall of fire, as an army, as a hedge, as mountains round a city, as a shield, and as a fortress.

3. REVELATION.—" Thou wilt show me the path of life " (Ps. xvi. 11). He will reveal the way out of difficulty, doubt, despair, danger and death.

4. CONFIDENCE.—" Thou wilt hear me " (Ps. xvii. 6). To those who truly pray, the Lord has always an answer. He who knocks at Heaven's gate, always finds an open door.

5. ILLUMINATION.—" Thou wilt light my candle " (Ps. xviii. 28). He will not leave us in the dark, and He will also supply the " lamp " (R.V.) of our being with the oil of the Spirit.

6. COMFORT.—" Thou wilt make all his bed in his sickness " (Ps. xli. 3). The Lord as the Bed-maker will surely supply the feathery bed of His love, the soft pillow of peace, the blankets of comfort, and the eiderdown of cover-all.

7. REVIVAL.—" Wilt Thou not revive us again ? " (Ps. lxxxv. 6). Of course, He will. There is no need to ask the question, when He is ready to answer every question.

RESULTS : FAITHFUL TO THE LORD, NOT LOOKING FOR THEM

" *Labour in the Lord.*"—1 Cor. xv. 58.

James Gilmour, in his diary, after years of labour in Mongolia, writes : " In the shape of converts I have seen no results. I have not, as far as I am aware, seen any one who even wanted to be a Christian."

This is the cry of anguish of no laggard or unspiritual, but of an earnest and consecrated soul. He had started out full of faith and expectation, as is evident in the following extract from his diary—" Several huts in sight ! When shall I be able to speak to the people ? O Lord, suggest by the Spirit how I shall come among them, and guide me in gaining the language, and in preparing myself to teach the life and love of Christ Jesus."

Do not these extracts tell us it is harder, more soul-suffering work, to plod on with the plough of the Word, the seed of the Word, and the harrow of prayer, than to handle the sickle of harvest and the sheaves of reaping ? " I trust any boy to reap," said an old farmer once, " but I always sow the seed myself." Let tired and plodding workers take fresh heart and new courage, if they have the consciousness of faithful service and consecrated testimony. On the other hand, let no lazy worker (?) take this meat for his comfort, for it is not meant for him. Often such an one laments his leanness and unfruitful labour, when he has need to confess his laziness and repent of his un-Christlikeness in service.

" Labour in the Lord " can never be in vain, for the Lord is in such labour.   The word which proceeds out of His mouth cannot return void, for His Word is always vital. The flaming sword of His utterance will surely cut and convert.   The blood of His atonement will undoubtedly bless, and doubly so when it is given with the bleeding hands of sacrifice, the wounded lips of prayer, the tear-stained face of sympathy, and the lacerated feet of service.   It is when the worker ceases to bleed, that he ceases to bless.   The agonised prayer of Gethsemane, the cross of self's crucifixion, and the Upper Room of Pentecost are precursors to the blessing of others.

What is the labour in the Lord, that can never be in vain ? (1 Cor. xv. 58).

1. When we are MOVED by the " Love of Christ " (2 Cor. v. 14).

2. When we go forth BEARING THE PRECIOUS seed of God's Word (Ps. cxxvi. 6).

3. When we are CO-WORKERS WITH GOD (2 Cor. vi. 1).

4. When we are ENERGISED by the POWER OF GOD'S SPIRIT (Col. i. 29).

5. When we WITNESS with a " Thus saith the Lord " (Jer. xxix. 10, 25).

6. When we AIM to be well-pleasing to the Lord (2 Cor. v. 9, R.V.).

7. When we know EXPERIMENTALLY what we tell others (1 Tim. i. 12-16).

RUBBISH

" Much Rubbish."—Neh. iv. 2, 10.

A booklet on the slogan of litter was published sometime ago containing poems, slogans, notices both witty and earnest, photographs of litter-collecting apparatus and of disfigurement by litter, and songs and playlets for the education of children and the " thoughtless tripper."

A handbill on litter concludes : " This is literature, not litter ; so when you have read it please hand it on to some one else, or burn it—Don't Throw It Down."

The litter baskets at Weston-super-Mare bear the following notice :

" You can go where you will without fear ;
  But there's one thing we wish to make clear,
  Be you walker or sitter, we object to your litter ;
  Take it home, or else put it in here."

Two of the best-known slogans are : " If each before his own door swept, the village would be clean " ; and " Dirt and papers in pretty places, slam park gates in people's faces."

There is " much rubbish " in the religious world that needs to be removed or burnt.

1. The RUBBISH OF SELF CONCEIT.—Many are like Theudas, who are " boasting " they are " somebody " (Acts v. 36).

2. The RUBBISH OF UNREALITY.—There are those in our church circles still, who belong to the company of Ananias and Sapphira, who profess one thing, and act another (Acts v. 10).

3. The RUBBISH OF SIMONY.—Like Simon the Sorcerer, who thought Spiritual power could be obtained by money (Acts viii. 18-23).

4. The RUBBISH OF SECTARIANISM.—Like Peter the Sectarian, who had to have a vision from heaven to convince him of his wrong conception of what was clean and unclean (Acts x. 13-16).

5. The RUBBISH OF NOISE.—Like those who could cause confusion and uproar at Ephesus by crying, " Great is Diana " (Acts xix. 27-29).

6. The RUBBISH OF SHOW.—Like those in Paul's day, who thought if they mentioned the " name of Jesus," and went through certain antics, they would accomplish spiritual results (Acts xix. 11-20).

7. The RUBBISH OF AGNOSTICISM.—Like those at Athens, who were identified with " an unknown god " (Acts xvii. 22-28).

SABBATISM

" There remaineth a rest."—Heb. iv. 9.

The rest to come is aptly described in the following quotation :

The verb " Sabbatise " never occurs in the New Testament, but the cognate noun " Sabbatism," the keeping of the Sabbath, occurs there once—in the Epistle to the Hebrews (iv. 9) : " There remaineth therefore a rest "—" a Sabbath rest " (R.V.)—" for the people of God." Here is a grand thought which was the very soul of the ancient Day of Rest, and which, like all else that was precious in the Jewish order, has been given a larger significance in the Christian usage. Observe the argument of the sacred writer. His epistle is a demonstration to those Hebrews of the superiority of the new order to the old—how the ideals and hopes of the Jewish Faith had been realised and fulfilled in the Gospel ; and here he cites the Lord's promise to His people in the wilderness that He would give them rest (cf. Ps. xcv. 11). The rest which they thought of was the end of their wanderings and their happy settlement in the good land. But when they came thither, they found no rest. It was rather the beginning of weary centuries of strife and sin and sorrow. Since, then, Joshua (cf. ver. 8, R.V.) did not give them rest, it was another day that the promise had in view—that great day when the Lord will bring His people home to the Eternal Rest. " There remaineth therefore a Sabbath rest for the people of God."

And here is the idea of the Day of Rest under both the old dispensation and the new. The ancient Sabbath was not merely a commemoration of the Creator's rest from His work on the seventh day, nor is the Lord's Day merely a commemoration of His Resurrection. They are both prophetic, pointing us forward to the glad homegathering.

This is the blessed hope which should occupy our hearts whenever we assemble on the Holy Day. It is written (Heb. x. 25) : " Let us not forsake the assembling," rather " the gathering of ourselves together " ; and it is very instructive that the phrase occurs only once again, where Paul says (2 Thess. ii. 1) : " We beseech you by the coming of our Lord Jesus Christ and our gathering together unto Him." Our gathering together each Lord's Day is a prophecy of our gathering together at last in our Father's House.

So, let us, in the light of that rest,

1. Look for Christ LONGINGLY (2 Tim. iv. 8).
2. Watch for Him FAITHFULLY (Matt. xxiv. 46).
3. Wait for Him PATIENTLY (1 Thess. i. 9, 10).

4. Work for Him DILIGENTLY (Luke xix. 13).
5. Obey Him WHOLLY (1 Thess. v. 23).
6. Expect Him PRAYERFULLY (Rev. xxii. 20).
7. Use our Talents CONTINUALLY (Matt. xxv. 19).

SACRIFICE

" *Neither count I my life dear unto myself.*"—Acts xx. 24.

In the old legends of Japan, they tell that when the great bell of Kyoto was being cast the precious metals would not mix, and finally the founder reported that it was impossible to fulfil his contract. The Mikado sent him word that if he did not finish the bell he would lose his head. His daughter heard this, and went to the oracle to ask how she could help her father, and the answer was that if a virgin's blood were mingled with the precious metal the casting would be complete. And so she waited until the metal was about to be poured into the mould, and then she leaped headlong into the fiery mass, and her blood mingled with the silver and the brass. The bell came forth in perfect form, and its strange and mighty tones can be heard to-day for miles and miles, in soft and far-resounding echoes, the most wonderful bell in all the world. Beloved, God's highest work can never be consummated until it reaches the heights and depths of sacrificial love. Oh that we might cast ourselves into the glorious work to which our Master gave His life, His all, and there shall come forth, as from yonder bell, echoes that will repeat the story of the redeeming love to every land and every tongue, and voices that will come back with the answering shout that will welcome back our coming King.

If our allegiance to Christ does not cost anything, we need to question our confession.

1. LOVE'S DEVOTION.—Mary gave her conserved box of precious spikenard to her Lord (John xii. 3).

2. LOVE'S SERVICE.—The good Samaritan gave loving attention to the man who fell among thieves (Luke x. 33-37).

3. LOVE'S RISK.—David's three mighty men risked their lives in getting what their Lord desired (1 Chron. xi. 17-19).

4. LOVE'S SURRENDER.—Jonathan loved David so well that he gave up his rights to him (1 Sam. xviii. 1-4).

5. LOVE'S WATCH.—Rizpah watched over the bodies of her slain sons, so that no birds could mutilate them (2 Sam. xxi. 10).

6. LOVE'S CONCERN.—John the Apostle is essentially the Apostle of Love. How often he speaks of those to whom he writes as " My little children," or, " My dear children " (see seven times in John's first epistle " My little children "—ii. 1, 12, 28 ; iii. 7, 18 ; iv. 4 ; v. 21).

7. LOVE'S CARESS.—The Beloved One in the Song of Solomon is addressed by the Bride as the One, who caresses her. Pure love understands the embrace of real affection (S. of S. ii. 6).

SADDENING SIGHTS

" *And when the woman saw . . . that it was a delight to the eyes.*"—Gen. iii. 6.

One has said, " Gaze not on beauty too much, lest it blast thee ; nor too long, lest it blind thee ; nor too near, lest it burn thee. If thou like it, it deceives thee ; if thou love it, it disturbs thee ; if thou hunt after it, it destroys thee. If virtue accompany it, it is the heart's paradise ; if vice associate with it, it is the soul's purgatory. It is the wise man's bonfire, and the fool's furnace."

Here are some sad sights, which brought saddening results.

1. EVE looked on the forbidden tree, and ruined her race (1 Tim. ii. 14).

2. " SONS OF GOD " saw the fair daughters of men and committed sin (Gen. vi. 2).

3. " LOT " saw the well watered plains of Sodom and got into the wicked city (Gen. xiii. 10-12).

4. " ACHAN " saw the Babylonish garment and committed sacrilege by taking what was consecrated to the Lord (Josh. vii. 21).

5. AARON saw the golden calf, and with the people worshipped it (Exod. xxxii. 5).

6. THE SPIES saw the sons of Anak, and gave way to fear and unbelief (Num. xiii. 28, 32, 33).

7. THE ISRAELITES saw the giant Goliath, and were " sore afraid " (1 Sam. xvii. 24).

" SAINT : WHAT IS HE ? "

" Called Saints."—1 Cor. i. 2.

A saint is one who is " sanctified in Christ Jesus," that is one who is set apart to God, in Christ.

" A little child on a summer morning stood in a great cathedral church. The sunlight streamed through the beautiful stained glass windows and the figures in them of the servants of God were bright with brilliant colour. A little later the question was asked, ' What is a saint ? ' and the child replied, ' *A saint is a person who lets the light shine through.*' "

An active saint is described in Gal. vi. 1-16.

1. A SPIRITUAL BROTHER.—" RESTORE." It requires a spiritual condition of soul to be able to " restore " one who has erred. If we consider our own liabilities, it will prevent us from being hard and critical.

2. A SPIRITUAL BEARER.—To " BEAR " one another's burdens will show we are having fellowship with Him who bore our sins, carried our sorrows, and who shoulders our cares.

3. A SPIRITUAL BUILDER.—To " PROVE " our own work is to test it with the plummet of God's Word, and to measure it with the reality of faithfulness.

4. A SPIRITUAL BESTOWER.—" COMMUNICATE." To pass on what we have received to others, is to retain what we have got, and to be a helper to them.

5. A SPIRITUAL BENEFACTOR.—" WELL DOING." To be " doing well " is to be " well " in our own spiritual life, and to be " doing well " to others.

6. A SPIRITUAL BEACON.—To " DO GOOD " to others is to be like our Lord, who went about " doing good." This is to keep our own good, and find a double good.

7. A SPIRITUAL BENEFIT.—" WALK according to this rule." To " walk " means to make progress, and " this rule " implies we keep in the road the Lord directs.

SALVATION

" Salvation is of the Lord."—Jonah ii. 9.

It was a problem for poor Jonah, when he was in the whale, how to get out again ! The Lord alone solved the problem, when Jonah confessed, " Salvation is of the Lord."

A writer in the London *Westminster Gazette* makes the following statement : " The world is full of problems, but most of them are man-made and essentially unimportant. They do not belong to the eternal verities ; many of them are petty side issues, and not even *en route* to the great achievement. There is only one major problem in the whole world, and that is the salvation of the individual soul. We do not mean salvation in any narrow theological sense ; we mean salvation in the largest and broadest human sense."

The writer makes the confession that the " major problem " is the salvation of the individual soul, although he would not limit it " in any narrow theological sense." We don't want a " theological " salvation, but all men need a Biblical one. Could Mr. Francis W. Hirst have a better salvation than the expanded one of Titus ii. 11-14 ?

1. The SOURCE of Salvation.—" The grace of God " as focussed and found in Christ.

2. The TEACHING of Salvation.—" Teaching us " to deny ungodliness and worldly lusts.

3. The OUTLOOK of Salvation.—" Looking for that Blessed Hope and the glorious appearing of our great God and Saviour " (R.V.).

4. The PRICE of Salvation.—" Who gave Himself for us."

5. The PURPOSE of Salvation.—" That He might redeem us from all iniquity " ; that is, everything that is crooked, and not found in the will of God.

6. The END of Salvation.—" Purify unto Himself a peculiar people " ; that is, a people for Himself, as His treasure, and for everything that He desires.

7. The EMPLOYMENT of Salvation.—" Zealous of good works." " Good works " mean a heart of love, a hand of help, and a benediction to the undeserving.

SATAN

" *The dragon, that old serpent, which is the devil, and Satan.*" Rev. xx. 2.

A line of sandwich men were walking along one of the principal streets in the City of London, and each board on the backs of the men had an announcement about Satan. The book of a well-known novelist on *The Sorrows of Satan* was being shown in a cinema. The announcement boards asked a series of questions, such as, " Where is Satan ? " " Is Satan in London ? " " Are you sorry for Satan ? " " What is Satan doing ? "

The above four questions are answered for us in the Holy Scriptures.

" Where is Satan ? " He is " the prince of the power of the air " (Eph. ii. 2).

" Is Satan in London ? " He is not in more than one place, personally, all the time, for " he is said to be walking about " (1 Pet. v. 8).

" Are you sorry for Satan ? " We are sorry that he cannot be sorry, and he would not if he could. Milton makes Satan say, in speaking of hell, " I, myself, am hell." Fixedness of character determines fixedness of destiny.

" What is Satan doing ? " What is he not doing ? At least, he is doing the following seven things :

1. He TAKES AWAY the Word of God from those who hear it (Mark iv. 15).
2. He TEMPTS TO SIN (1 Thess. iii. 5).
3. HURLS his darts to wound (Eph. vi. 16).
4. SEEKS to devour (1 Pet. v. 8).
5. BEGUILES by his wiles (Eph. vi. 11).
6. ENDEAVOURS to trap by his " snares " (1 Tim. iii. 7).
7. And aims to DECEIVE (Rev. xx. 2).

SCRIPTURES' CLAIM

" *All Scripture is given by inspiration of God.*"—2 Tim. iii. 16.

The great Lord Shaftesbury once spent a few hours in the house of a country clergyman. As he was looking at the books in the study, he saw one which was labelled, *Bishop Watson's Apology for the Bible.* He thought that the binder had made a mistake in the lettering, so he pulled out the book ; but there, sure enough, were the words, on the title page, " Bishop Watson's Apology for the Bible." He put back the book, and said with indignation, " The Bible needs no apology." And his Lordship was right !

The Bible may need interpretation, explanation, yea, even vindication. But " Apology ! " Never !

Remember a few things the Scriptures claim.

1. They are DIVINE in Origin (2 Tim. iii. 16).
2. LIVING in Nature (Heb. iv. 12).
3. POWERFUL in Operation (Acts. xix. 20).
4. ASSURING in Statement (1 John v. 11-13).
5. SOUL-SAVING in Reception (1 Thess. i. 8-10).
6. SANCTIFYING in Work (John xvii. 17).
7. CHRIST-REVEALING in Revelation (Heb. x. 7).

SCRIPTURE'S INFALLIBILITY

" *The mouth of the Lord hath spoken it.*"—Jer. ix. 12.

The late Mr. Spurgeon has some excellent remarks on " The Infallibility of Scripture." He says : " If ' the mouth of the Lord hath spoken it,' we have in this utterance the special character of immutable fixedness. Once spoken by God, not only is it so now, but it always must be so. The Lord of Hosts hath spoken, and who shall disannul it ? The rock of God's Word does not shift, like the quicksand of modern scientific theology. One said to his minister, ' My dear sir, surely you ought to adjust your beliefs to the progress of science.' ' Yes,' said he, ' but I have not had time to do it to-day, for I have not yet read the morning papers.' "

No less than twenty-four times do we find the words " I, the Lord, have spoken it," in Ezekiel. If the Scriptures are pondered, it will be found that this sentence occurs in the following connections :

1. DISTINCT in its Accomplishment (v. 13, 15, 17 ; xii. 28).
2. DEFINITE in its Application (xvii. 21, 24 ; xxxiv. 24).
3. DISCONCERTING in its Fulfilment (xxi. 32 ; xxii. 14 ; xxiii. 34).
4. DELIBERATE in its Act (xxi. 17, R.V.).
5. DETERMINED in its Justice (xxiv. 14 ; xxviii. 10 ; xxxvi. 5, 6 ; xxxviii. 17, 19 ; xxxix. 5, 8).
6. DESIGNED in its Prophecy (xxvi. 5, 14 ; xxx. 12).
7. DENOTING in its Promise (xxxvi. 36 ; xxxvii. 14).

SEEING CHRIST IN OTHERS

" *Beholding your good conversation in Christ.*"—1 Pet. iii. 16.

" Have you learned to know Jesus Christ ? " asked a missionary of a Hindu. " No ; but I have seen Him," was the startling answer.

The best witness we can give to our Lord is when our lives witness for Him.

1. HIS POWER is seen when we are made strong to walk for Him, as the LAME MAN evidenced (Acts iv. 14).

2. HIS CONSECRATION is seen when we gladly lay our all at His feet, as BARNABAS did (Acts iv. 36, 37).

3. HIS COURAGE is seen when He speaks through UN-LEARNED FISHERMEN, and was made known to the Council in Jerusalem (Acts iv. 13).

4. HIS LOVE is seen when we give something of cost, as MARY revealed when she broke the box of spikenard on the Saviour (John xii. 3).

5. HIS PATIENCE is seen when we endure as JOHN did, in his banishment to the Isle of Patmos (Rev. i. 9).

6. HIS JOY is seen when Christians endure suffering joyfully, like the early Christians, who rejoiced they were " counted worthy " to suffer for the sake of the Lord (Acts v. 41).

7. HE HIMSELF is seen when He lives out His life in us, and we can say with Paul, " I live, yet not I, but Christ liveth in me " (Gal. ii. 20).

SEEKING : SEEKING MINISTRY

" *I will seek that which is lost and will bring again that which was driven away.*"—Ezek. xxxiv. 16.

One night in the Scottish highlands, when the snow was deep upon the mountain side, a shepherd found that two of his flock were still out in the storm. Calling his faithful collie, or shepherd's dog, he roused her from her warm kennel, where she was lying with her young, and, pointing through the open door, he held up two fingers, and said, " Go." Well she understood his meaning, and gave one pitiful look at her pups, and then one appealing glance at him, but there was no relenting in his look. Quietly and promptly she passed out through the open door in the dark and wintry night. It was late in the night when the shepherd was roused by a scratching on the door, and as he opened it, there was one of the lost sheep, and the tired dog dragged herself through the door and lay down once more in her kennel with her young. He carefully nursed the tired sheep, and then again he called the faithful dog, and pointing his finger through the open door, he called, " One is still lost. Go."

Tenderly she gazed once more at her young. Longingly she clung to her little brood, pleadingly she gazed into the shepherd's eyes, and seemed to say, " Must I go again ? " But still there was no reprieve in that glance. There was but one message, and that was, " Go." And slowly she dragged herself again to the door and went forth into the darkness. The dawn had come before the shepherd was again awakened to find the lost sheep there, and the poor dog scarcely able to drag herself to her corner and lie down to die. As she pressed her little ones to her breast, and gasped out her last breath, he gently patted her head, and tried his best to say, " Good and gentle servant, you did your best." She was but a dog. For her there was no heaven, no crown of bright reward, no higher motive than obedience. Beloved, with so much more for us, shall we be less faithful than a shepherd's dog ?

1. SEEK AND FIND, like Saul who went after the asses (1 Sam. x. 2).

2. SEEK DILIGENTLY, like the woman who found the piece of silver (Luke xv. 8).

3. SEEK LOVINGLY, like the shepherd who sought the lost sheep until he found it (Luke xv. 4).

4. SEEK DEFINITELY, like Christ, who came to seek and to save that which was lost (Luke xix. 10).

" SELF-SACRIFICE "

" *The sacrifice of Himself.*"—Heb. ix. 26.

Describing an effort of a devoted wife who wanted to save her husband from fear, caused by gas during the War, an author says : " Calm, clear-eyed, infinitely tender, mastering herself to save him, she walked by his side through the cold shadows—understanding sometimes, pitying always, but faltering never, learning with each painful step Love's ultimate lesson, the lesson of self-sacrifice."

Life is the opportunity to sacrifice self. This is no mere sentiment, but the crucifixion of self. True sacrifice costs something, but it blesses in its bleeding.

1. Self-sacrifice GIVES ITS BEST, as Abraham gave Isaac (Gen. xxii. 2 ; Heb. xi. 17).

2. Self-sacrifice is WILLING TO LOSE, as Jonathan did for David (1 Sam. xviii. 4).

3. Self-sacrifice FACES DIFFICULTIES, as Rebecca did when she went to meet Isaac (Gen. xxiv. 58-66).

4. Self-sacrifice is WILLING TO SPEND and be spent in the Lord's service, as Paul was (2 Cor. xii. 15).

5. Self-sacrifice is REGARDLESS OF ITS COMFORT, like Gideon and his 300 men (Judges vii. 5).

6. Self-sacrifice is willing to RISK ITS LIFE, as Esther was willing to " perish " to save her people (Esther iv. 16).

7. Self-sacrifice is UNCONCERNED ABOUT CONSEQUENCES, even as Christ, who, to put away our sin, sacrificed Himself (Heb. ix. 26).

SEPARATION

" They are not of the world . . . Kept them from the evil."— John xvii. 15, 16.

" The place of separation from the world, and to the Lord, is the place of power," so said one in calling for the believer to enter into the meaning of Christ's prayer.

1. SEPARATED NATION.—Israel was separated to Jehovah (Deut. xxxii. 8), and so are believers in Christ (1 Pet. ii. 9).

2. SEPARATED WORSHIPPERS.—" The God of Israel hath separated you " (Num. xvi. 9). Priestly character and conduct are essential for consecrated service.

3. SEPARATED WARRIORS.—" The Gadites separated themselves unto David . . . men of war fit for the battle " (1 Chron. xii. 8). When we are separated to the Lord, we can fight for Him.

4. SEPARATED PRIESTS.—" Aaron was separated that he should sanctify the most holy things, he and his sons " (1 Chron. xxiii. 13). Those who are sanctified, sanctify. Those who are holy, communicate what they are to others.

5. SEPARATED READERS.—" The seed of Israel separated themselves . . . and read in the Book of the Law of the Lord their God " (Neh. ix. 1-3). When our spirits are separated to the Lord from evil, we read His Word to find out His will.

6. SEPARATED SAINT.—Abram separated himself from Lot, and Lot from Abram. The one went to the world of Sodom, and the other to the Lord. " The Lord said unto Abram after that Lot was separated from him " (Gen. xiii. 9, 11, 14).

7. SEPARATED LIVES.—" Separated you from other people . . . Separated from you . . . unclean " (Lev. xx. 24-27). Because they were a " severed " people to the Lord, the people of Israel were to keep from things and men that were unclean.

SEPARATION KEEPS FROM CONTAMINATION

" Touch not the unclean thing."—2 Cor. vi. 17.

It is said, a certain nobleman's daughter died of typhus fever of the most malignant type ; and when inquiry was made as to how she had caught the infection, it was discovered that it was through a beautiful riding habit presented to her by her father. This riding habit, bought from a London tradesman, had been made in a miserable attic, where the husband of a seamstress was lying ill of fever, and it had been used by her to cover him in his shivering fits. The highest are not proof against infection that originates among the lowest.

Separation from sin and sinners is the only safety from contamination. Here are some weighty *nots*, which are the Spirit's positive commands.

1. SIN.—" Let not sin therefore reign in your mortal body " (Rom. vi. 12). Having quit the old master (Sin), we must not give any service to him.

2. WORLD.—" Be not conformed to this world " (Rom.

xii. 2). The maxims and methods of the world are not for the following of the saints.

3. SEPARATION.—" Be ye not unequally yoked together with unbelievers " (2 Cor. vi. 14). The unclean animal, under the law, was not to be yoked with a clean one (Deut. xxii. 10) ; so in grace.

4. SERVICE.—" Let us not be weary in well-doing " (Gal. vi. 9). Faintness and weariness in the Lord's service tell us there is something wrong with the inner life.

5. HOPE.—" Be not moved away from the hope of the Gospel " (Col. i. 23). To be moved away from the truth of the Lord's Coming, shows we are drifting to the gorge of despair.

6. SLOTHFULNESS.—" Let us not sleep " (1 Thess. v. 6). To be asleep to our privileges is to be lacking in carrying out our responsibilities.

7. DILIGENCE.—" Neglect not the gift that is in thee " (1 Tim. iv. 14). A neglected fire is a fireless grate. If we do not stir up the fire of God's grace, it will burn low in our lives.

SEVEN COMINGS MENTIONED IN JOHN VI

Ralph Erskine once made the trite and telling remark, " All God's commands are God's enablings." He never tells us to do anything without giving us the power to do it.

1. A MISTAKEN COMING.—Coming to make Christ King. " When Jesus, therefore, perceived that they would come and take Him by force to make Him a King, He departed again into a mountain Himself alone " (15). Christ would not receive the kingdom at the hands of men, but He will receive it at the hands of His Father (Dan. vii. 13, 14 ; Rev. xix. 16.

2. AN OPPORTUNE COMING.—Coming of Christ to the disciples. " They see Jesus walking on the sea, and drawing nigh unto the ship " (19). His comings are always timely, and on time. He is never late, and He always comes with a purpose.

3. A CURIOSITY COMING.—Coming of the multitude after Christ. " The people . . . came to Capernaum, seeking for Jesus " (24). He saw they thought more of miracles than of Himself. Loaves and fishes were essentials with them.

4. A COMPASSIONATE COMING.—The coming of Christ to earth. Seven times He is said to have " come down from heaven " (33, 38, 41, 42, 50, 51, 58). He came to meet us in our need, and He brought all the supplies we needed with Him.

5. A SATISFYING COMING.—The coming of a needy one to Christ. Christ says, " He that cometh to Me shall never hunger " (35). The heart of man's need can only be met by Him who is the Bread of Life.

6. A DRAWING COMING.—The reason of our coming is because the Father draws us. " All the Father giveth Me shall come to Me " (37, 44, 45, 65). We come because He draws, and but for His drawing we should never come.

7. AN ASSURED COMING.—He assures and we accept. " Him that cometh to Me I will in no wise cast out " (37). No case will be turned away. The door is always open to those who knock. The prodigal not only found an open door when he came to his father, but an open heart of love, and open arms of welcome.

SIMPLICITY

" The Lord preserveth the simple."—Ps. cxvi. 6.

The beautiful Hebrew melodies of Byron are noted for their simplicity, for notwithstanding Byron's faults, he, more than any other man, had preserved the Saxon purity of the English tongue. Stanzas of his could be found that contained no foreign word. His verses could be understood by everyone, by the rude peasant, and you thought you were listening to the wandering minstrel in the time of Alfred the Great. Take the *Destruction of Sennacherib.*

" And there lay the steed with his nostril all wide ;
  But through it there rolled not the breath of his pride.
  And the foam of his gasping lay white on the earth
  And cold as the spray of the rock-beating surf."
This is all pure Saxon. Take the next stanza :
" And there lay the rider distorted and pale,
  With the dew on his brow and the rust on his mail."

There is only one foreign word here. Compare this with the newspaper English. The newspaper man, had he to report this circumstance, instead of saying, " And there lay the rider, distorted and pale ; With the dew on his brow and the rust on his mail," would have said, " The gallant officer was placed hors de combat and presented a ghastly appearance. The morning brought evidence that there were symptoms of rapid decomposition, and his arms and accoutrements were undergoing the disintegrating process of oxidation."

1. Simplicity IN PRAYER is the art of asking, as seen in Solomon, when he asked for wisdom and knowledge (2 Chron. i. 10).

2. Simplicity IN HELP is the art of giving, as evidenced in the children of Israel in their giving of material for the work of the Tabernacle (Exod. xxxv. 29).

3. Simplicity IN SPEAKING is the art of being understood, as Paul declared in his preaching to the Corinthians, " I came not with excellency of speech " (1 Cor. ii. 1).

4. Simplicity IN FAITH is the art of trust, as the Apostle said, " We trust in the Living God " (1 Tim. iv. 10).

5. Simplicity IN LOVE is the art of heart-mating, as illustrated in Jonathan's love for David (2 Sam. i. 26).

6. Simplicity IN GREATNESS is the art of goodness, as exemplified in Barnabas, who when he saw the grace of God, was glad, and the reason was because he was " good " (Acts xi. 23, 24). For as Emerson says, " Nothing is more simple than greatness ; indeed, to be simple is to be great."

SINGING UNTO THE LORD

" *Sing unto the Lord.*"—Ps. xxx. 4.

Longfellow tells of three God-sent singers who came to earth to touch the hearts of men and bring them back to heaven again. The first, a youth with a golden lyre and a soul on fire playing the music of our dreams. The second, a bearded man singing in the market place, and stirring the hearts of listening crowds. The third, a man in the fulness of years singing in cathedrals dim and vast. Those who heard the three singers felt there was discord, as the music awakened different echoes in each heart. But the great

Master said, " I see no best in kind but in degree. I gave a various gift to each."

> " There are the three great cords of might,
> And he whose ear is tuned aright
> Will hear no discord in the three,
> But the most perfect harmony."

Singing unto the Lord is :

1. The voice of TRIUMPH (Exod. xv. 1).
2. The expression of GRATITUDE (Ps. xiii. 6).
3. The soul of APPRECIATION (Ps. xxxiii. 1-5).
4. The eye of RECOGNITION (Ps. xlvii. 1-9).
5. The outcome of CONSECRATION (Ps. lvii. 7-11).
6. The heart of JOY (Zeph. iii. 17).
7. The evidence of the Spirit's FILLING (Eph. v. 19).

SINNER'S RIGHT

" *As many as received Him, to them gave He the right* (*marg.*) *to become the children of God.*"—John i. 12, R.V.

" There is only one thing to which a sinner has a right," said a preacher once, and one looking at himself in his deservings as a sinner would naturally say, " And that is hell " ; but the servant of Christ did not say so. One who was listening, and under the conviction of sin, responded in his heart, and said, " Ah ! I wonder what that thing can be ? " We may imagine how startled he was when he heard the ringing words, " The one thing to which a sinner has a right is the Blood of Christ." Let us see what the Word tells us about the rights the Blood of Christ's atoning death gives.

1. THE RIGHT OF REMISSION.—" Without shedding of blood there is no remission," but since the Blood has been shed, there is no omission. The past is not " under the Blood," as we sometimes sing, but blotted out by it (Heb. ix. 22).

2. THE RIGHT OF ADMISSION.—We have boldness to " enter into the holiest of all by the Blood of Christ " (Heb. x. 19). Every hindrance has been swept out of the way, so now we have access into the Father's presence, and can lay our petitions before Him.

3. THE RIGHT OF MANUMISSION.—Manumission signi-

fies the giving of liberty to bondmen. It is by the Blood of Him who loved us that we are " loosed from our sins " (Rev. i. 5, R.V.).

4. THE RIGHT OF DISMISSION.—Dismission means a sending away. The meaning of the word " forgiveness " is a sending away, so that we have forgiveness by means of Christ's Blood (Eph. i. 7).

5. THE RIGHT OF INTROMISSION.—Intromission signifies the act of permitting to enter, hence those who have washed their robes in Christ's Blood have " the right to the tree of life " (Rev. xxii. 14, R.V.).

SMOKING AND HABIT

" *The old man with his deeds.*"—Col. iii. 9.

A Baptist minister in Melbourne, who once lived in Glasgow, was convinced that smoking was wrong in the following way. He found he had not brought with him his tobacco when away from home on one occasion. The consequence was, he was fidgety and morose. While in this condition, the question came to him, " Am I such a helpless slave to tobacco that I find myself in this condition, that I can't do without it ? " He determined he would not be mastered by habit, so he sought Divine grace, and never lit a pipe again. What helpless slaves the majority of smokers are ! When they have not got the tobacco they are like fish out of water. What an irksome thing unholy habit is. It is like the word itself. If you take away the " h " from " habit " you still have " a bit " ; if you take away the " a," you still have a " bit " ; if you take away the " b " you still have " it."

Habit

A Bit

Bit

It

It clings like the fabled habit, which became a part and parcel of the wearer, and he could not get rid of it. The test of anything, as to its rightness or wrongness, is, Does it master me, or am I master of it ?

There are twelve things in Ephesians iv we are to " put

off," " put away," for they belong to the old habits of the old man.

1. A walk after VANITY (17).
2. The OLD manner of LIFE (22, R.V.).
3. The profanity of " LYING " (25).
4. The wrath of " ANGER " (26).
5. The grab of DISHONESTY (28).
6. The corrupt speech which DEFILES (29).
7. The " BITTERNESS " of a sour spirit (31).
8. The " WRATH " of a bad temper (31).
9. The " ANGER " of passion (31).
10. The " CLAMOUR " of hard words (31).
11. The " EVIL SPEAKING " of gossip (31).
12. The " MALICE " of ill intent (31).

SNARES

" The snare of the devil "—2 Tim. ii. 26.

An extraordinary condition of things was once caused by the surface of the sea being thickly coated with 1,500 tons of oil pumped from the American steamer *Piave*, which was some time since lying a wreck on the Goodwins off the English coast.

Gulls, and other sea birds, which frequent the district in large numbers at certain seasons, have been entrapped and distressed.

Settling on the water and attempting to dive in search of food—chiefly sprats—they found themselves in difficulties, their heads, beaks, and feathers becoming coated with the oil. The more they flapped their wings, the more the thick, slimy substance enveloped them.

Many birds were washed ashore, presenting a pitiable sight ; and they were so exhausted that they could be easily picked up. People took them home, washed them with paraffin, and released them, but they were soon as helpless as before.

While the birds were in their own element they were safe, but when a foreign one was introduced it proved their undoing, and even when they were washed and released they were soon as helpless as before. How like sinners when they get the oil of iniquity and selfish love upon the wings of their lives, they find themselves in the slime of helpless bondage.

1. LUST.—Balaam was slimed with the greed of lust (2 Pet. ii. 15).

2. COVETOUSNESS.—Judas with the love of gold (John xii. 6).

3. WORLD.—Demas with the love of the world (2 Tim. iv. 10).

4. ERROR.—Hymeneus with the love of error (1 Tim. i. 20).

5. PRIDE.—Diotrephes with the love of pre-eminence (3 John 9).

6. AMBITION.—Simon Magus with the love of power (Acts viii. 19-23).

7. SELF.—Theudas with the love of self (Acts v. 36).

Beware of the devil's oil of the world and the flesh and sin, for it will clog the energies of the soul, the feathers of self-betterment, and the rising wings of liberty.

SOME CONTENTS OF THE BOOK

" *It is written.*"—Rom. iii. 10 ; Heb. x. 7.

Sir William Jones, the eminent Orientalist, says, " The Bible contains, independently of its Divine origin, more true sublimity, more exquisite beauty, more pure morality, more important history, and finer strains both of poetry and excellence, than could be collected within the same compass from all other books that ever were composed, in any age, or in any idiom."

Ponder some of the revelations of the Book as found in connection with the words, " It is written."

" It is written "

1. That MAN is a sinner (Rom. iii. 10).

2. That CHRIST is the Atoner for sin (Heb. x. 7-10).

3. That the JUSTIFIED " live by faith " (Rom. i. 17).

4. That the NATURAL MAN cannot understand spiritual things (1 Cor. ii. 9).

5. That GOD expects His people to be holy (1 Pet. i. 16).

6. That God's THINGS are supreme (Luke iv. 4, 8, 10).

7. That CHRIST would be smitten for others (Matt. xxvi. 24).

SOMETHING SURE AND LASTING

" *The Word of the Lord endureth for ever.*"—1 Pet. i. 23, 25.

His Word is fixed, immutable truth. When Science has spoken its last word, and its teachings have become fixed, final and unalterable, we might then seriously consider whether some of our interpretations of Scripture should be abandoned in the light of knowledge which is beyond question immutable. But so-called scientific facts are continually changing. The late Dr. Griffith Thomas, in an address delivered in London in the year 1922, said : " Suppose someone comes to me and says, ' I have brought you the last book on botany.' I reply, ' Of course, you mean the latest book.' ' No,' he says, ' the last,' and he adds that no other book will ever be written on botany. Well, I should try to be polite but, of course, I should not believe him. The last book on any science cannot be written. But here in the Bible we have not the latest, but the last word on sin, on redemption, on holiness, on immortality, and this Book has been before the world for nearly two thousand years."

When we turn to the Sacred Page, we find the fixedness and lastingness of God's Word is variously described.

1. It is SETTLED in its SOURCE.—" Thy Word is settled in heaven " (Ps. cxix. 89).

2. It is SATISFYING in its CONTENTS.—" Thy Word was unto me the joy and rejoicing of my heart " (Jer. xv. 16).

3. It is SURE in its PROMISES.—" I will hasten My Word to perform it " (Jer. i. 12).

4. It is SOUL-SAVING in its CERTAINTY.—" The engrafted Word which is able to save your souls " (James i. 21).

5. It is SECURE in its GUIDANCE.—" Thy Word is a lamp unto my feet " (Ps. cxix. 105).

6. It is SANCTIFYING in its INFLUENCE.—" Sanctified by the Word of God " (1 Tim. iv. 5).

7. It is SUPREME in God's ESTIMATION.—" Thou hast magnified Thy Word above all Thy Name " (Ps. cxxxviii. 2).

SOUL-LESS MAN

" *Without natural affection.*"—2 Tim. iii. 3.

" Tell me, have you ever tried to analyse this interest of

yours in human beings and crowded cities, this hatred of solitude and empty spaces ? " asked one of another. The other was a man who could do unholy things without feeling.

The reply given was as follows : " I think it is because I have no soul." A soul-less man is devoid of principle, and lacking in conscience.

A soul-less man, is :

1. A WALKER in the self-righteous " way of Cain " (Jude 11 ; 1 John iii. 12).

2. A RUNNER in the greedy path of Balaam's error and sin (Jude 11 ; Num. xxii. 7).

3. A CONFEDERATE with the proud " gainsaying " of Korah (Jude 11 ; Num. xvi. 1).

4. A COMPANION of the traitorous Judas (Matt. xxvi. 14-16 ; xxvii. 3-10).

5. AN ASSOCIATE of Esau in the greed of his appetite (Heb. xii. 16 ; Gen. xxv. 33).

6. A TALKER with Diotrephes the prater (3 John 9).

7. A WIND-BAG with Goliath the boaster (1 Sam. xvii. 46).

STANDING FOR GOD AND THE RIGHT

" *Stand upright on thy feet.*"—Acts xiv. 10.

A distinguished general said to Luther, as the latter was about to enter the presence of his judges at the Diet of Worms : " Poor monk ! Thou art now going to make a nobler stand than I or any other captains have ever made in the bloodiest battles. But if thy cause is just, and thou art sure of it, go forward in God's name, and fear nothing. God will not forsake thee."

Of John Knox, the Scottish Luther, it was said by one who stood by his grave : " Here lies one who never feared the face of man."

Sir Francis Drake, being in a dangerous storm in the Thames, was heard to say, " Must I who have escaped the rage of the ocean be drowned in a ditch ? " Mr. Spurgeon said : " Will you, experienced saints, who have passed through a world of tribulation, lie down and die of despair, or give up your profession because you are at the present moment passing through some light affliction ? Let your past preservation inspire you with courage, and constrain you to brave all storms for Jesus' sake."

It is a good thing to know where we stand, and take our stand on the stand where the Lord has placed us.

1. To stand ON THE ROCK of the Lord's personality, is to find our feet on safe ground (Ps. xl. 2).

2. To stand IN THE GRACE of God is to be able to approach with confidence into His presence (Rom. v. 2).

3. To stand IN THE ARMOUR of the Lord's equipment, is to withstand the assaults of the enemy (Eph. vi. 11-17).

4. To stand AGAINST THE THREATS and persecution of the world, we need the power of the Holy Spirit (Acts v. 20-42).

5. To stand FAST IN THE LORD is to do what the Lord wishes (Phil. iv. 1).

6. To stand ON THE WATCH is to be ready for an emergency (Hab. ii. 1).

7. GOD ALONE CAN MAKE US stand, for He alone has the ability required (Rom. xiv. 4).

STRAW AND BRICKS

" *Ye shall no more give the people straw to make bricks.*"—
Exod. v. 7.

" In connection with the preparation of Acheson graphite, it is remarkable that the inventor found the key to the method in the Bible, where we read that the Egyptians used straw in the process of making bricks," wrote Dr. A. C. Brown, of the Royal Technical College, in the *Glasgow Herald*.

" While reading the account of the trials of the Israelites, of how they complained bitterly that bricks could not be made without straw, it is difficult to realise that they were faced with a problem in colloid chemistry. Such, however, was the case.

" It was the practice to soak straw in water for some time, and to use this liquid in working up the clay, because the resultant mass was found by experience to be much more plastic and easily worked than if water alone had been used.

" Straw contains tannin, and it was the presence of this tannin in the straw infusion which brought about the increased plasticity. It is still the practice to add tannin to clay when an increase in plasticity is desired."

What the Egyptians found in the straw, to enable them to make bricks with "increased plasticity," so we may say of faith. It is that grace which gives us plasticity in the things of God. See how this is brought out in the lives of some of the Old Testament saints mentioned in Hebrews xi.

1. Faith gave plasticity to ENOCH'S FEET, for it enabled him to walk with God (5).

2. It gave plasticity to NOAH'S HANDS, for it moved him to work for God (7).

3. It gave plasticity to ABRAHAM'S EYES, for it caused him to see things in the future (8-10).

4. It gave plasticity to ISAAC'S and JACOB'S TONGUES in leading them to bless their sons "concerning things to come" (20, 21).

5. It gave plasticity to MOSES' HEART, for he was attracted to choose the things that were invisible (23-30).

6. It gave plasticity to GIDEON'S ARM to equip him to use it against the Midianites (32).

7. It gave plasticity to DANIEL'S SOUL, and strengthened him to rest in repose in the lions' den (34).

SUBSTITUTION

" For the transgression of My people was He stricken."
Isa. liii. 8.

There is an English rendering by Mr. Alfred Percival Graves, in his *A Celtic Psaltery*, of an ancient (probably tenth century) Irish poem on the subject of "Eve." Mr. Graves's version of the first stanza runs :

"I am Eve, great Adam's wife,
'Twas my guilt took Jesus' life.
Since of Heaven I robbed my race,
On His Cross was my true place."

It is a good thing to own to our "true place," that we may know what it meant to Him who took our place.

"Bearing shame and scoffing rude,
In my place condemned He stood."

If we ponder that blood-drenched and sacrificial chapter, Isa. liii, we shall find :

" He was acquainted with grief,"
" Bore our griefs,"
" Carried our sorrows,"
" Wounded for our transgressions,"
" Bruised for our iniquities,"
Chastised for " our peace,"
Secured our healing by " His stripes,"
Laden with our " iniquity,"
" Cut off,"
" Stricken " for His people,
Made an " offering for " our " sin,"
And was " numbered with the transgressors."

SUFFERING FOR CHRIST

Read Acts xx. 16-24, 36-38 ; xxi. 3-34 ; xxiii. 11-35.

A Hindoo woman applied to a Baptist missionary for Christian baptism ; the missionary pointed out the sufferings which would surely come in the renouncing of her heathenish creed, but she replied : " I am willing to bear it all ; I am ready to sacrifice all to my Lord. Surely I cannot endure anything in comparison to what He suffered for me."

Paul suffered much for Christ.

Suffering for and with Christ is one of the great privileges of the child of God ; it is one of the things which is well pleasing to the Lord, and evidences that we are following in the steps of Christ (1 Pet. ii. 20-23, R.V.).

We can only pick out the prophesied references to the suffering of the apostle.

PAUL'S WITNESS AND WORK (Acts xx. 18-21, 24-27).

See how these are summarised in the following personal references.

HUMILITY before the Lord (19).
SUFFERING for the Lord (19, 22-24, 26, 27).
FAITHFULNESS to the Lord (20).
TESTIMONY in the Lord (21, 24, 25).
RESPONSIBILITY to the Lord (28).

WARNING from the Lord (29-31).
COMMENDATION to the Lord (32).
WORKING for the Lord (33-35).
PRAYING to the Lord (36, 37).

Paul's one dominating purpose was to serve the Lord, irrespective of what the consequences might be. When the Roman General Pompey was warned against the danger of his returning from Egypt to Italy, to meet a new trouble in his own land, his heroic answer was, " It is a small thing that I should move forward and die. It is too great a matter that I should take one step backward and live." Life is never well lived when it is held to be more dear than duty. So let us

> " Discharge aright
> The simple dues with which each day is rife ;
> Yea, with all thy might,
> Ere perfect scheme of action thou devise
> Life will be fled,
> While he who acts as conscience cries
> Shall live, though dead."

WARNINGS GIVEN TO PAUL

Paul was warned by the Holy Spirit that " bonds and afflictions abide me " (xx. 23 ; marg., " wait for me ") ; the Church at Ephesus " wept sore " as they listened to his words and parted from him (xx. 37), a message " through the Spirit " came from the disciples at Tyre that he " should not go up to Jerusalem " (xxi. 4), Agabus prophesied that his hands and feet would be bound in Jerusalem (xxi. 10-12), and Paul would not listen to the prayers of the saints, but chided them for trying to keep him back from going forward (xxi. 12-15).

Sometimes it is well to listen to our friends, but there are other times when inward conviction must be resolved in outward action.

PLOTTERS AGAINST PAUL

After Paul had arrived in Jerusalem (xxi. 17), and the charges made against him were found to be false (xxi. 21-25), then the plotters began to move against him. The " Jews of Asia " stirred up the people and laid hands on him (xxi. 27), the people laid hands on him and sought to kill him (xxi. 30-34). Afterwards certain Jews banded themselves under a curse to slay him (xxiii. 11-35). Amid all this Paul was encouraged by the Lord's visit to him, who said to him, " Be of good cheer," and that He would be with him in Rome, as He was in Jerusalem (xxiii. 11).

With the Lord's " good cheer," what have we to fear ?

TAKING THE PLACE OF OTHERS

" I sat where they sat."—Ezek. iii. 15.

" Science emphatically denies what is known as action at a distance. That one body may act upon another at a distance, through a vacuum, without the mediation of anything else, scientists declare to be an absurdity. A thing cannot act where it is not. That one body should operate upon and affect another body without mutual contact is inconceivable. But if this principle of distant action is impossible in the material universe, it is even less so in the spiritual realm. One soul can only move another by mutual contact."

We have many illustrations in God's Word, that the contact of sympathy is essential to the accomplishment of benefit.

1. THE TOUCH OF LOVE.—The Father not only " saw " the prodigal in the distance, but He fell on his neck and kissed him in love (Luke xv. 20).

2. THE TOUCH OF STRENGTH.—The Shepherd not only found the sheep, but put it on His shoulders and carried it home (Luke xv. 5).

3. THE TOUCH OF CLEANSING.—Christ not only beheld the leper, but He put forth His hand and touched him (Mark i. 41).

4. THE TOUCH OF SYMPATHY.—The Samaritan did more than look on the fallen man, he poured oil and wine into his wounds (Luke x. 34).

5. THE TOUCH OF LIFE.—Elisha not only pitied the widow and her son, but he stretched himself on the child till life came back again into the body (2 Kings iv. 34).

6. THE TOUCH OF HELP.—Peter did more than say, " look on us " to the lame man, he took him by the hand and lifted him up (Acts iii. 4-7).

7. THE TOUCH OF IDENTITY.—Christ not only pitied us, He took our nature that in our nature He might remove our sin (Heb. ii. 14).

"TELL ME WHAT YOU KNOW OF HIM"

"That I may know Him."—Phil. iii. 10.

"Tell me what you know of Him and I will tell you where you are in your Christian experience," so said one to another.

There is too great a disproportion between theorising upon and practicing holiness ; too much neglect of " perfecting holiness " after its inception through the incoming Holy One. " Be ye holy in all manner of living," exhorts the Apostle Peter. Samuel Rutherford, called the " Seraphic Rutherford," is an illustrious example of holy living. Rutherford's letter is a classic of celestial beauty and the sweetness of Paradise reflected in the life transformed by the grace of God. He says, " Brother, I speak of Christ to you. Oh ! if ye saw in Him what I see ! A river of God's unseen joys has flowed over my soul. I urge upon you communion with Christ, a growing communion. There are curtains to be drawn aside in Christ that we never saw, and new foldings of love in Him. There are so many plies to it. Therefore dig deep."

Do you know Him ?

1. As the KEEPER to keep from falling (Jude 1, 24).
2. As the REST-GIVER to keep from anxiety (Matt. xi. 29).
3. As the SATISFIER to fill the heart (Ps. lxxiii. 25).
4. As the SECRET of the Christian life (Gal. ii. 20).
5. As the HEAD to dominate the whole body (1 Cor. xi. 3).
6. As the BAPTISER with the Spirit (John i. 33).
7. As the STRENGTHENER to equip (Phil. iv. 13, R.V.).

THINGS GOD CANNOT DO

"God cannot . . ."—Titus i. 2.

In Ireland a teacher once asked a little boy if there was anything God could not do. The little fellow said, " Yes, He cannot see my sins through the blood of Jesus Christ."

1. "HIMSELF HE CANNOT SAVE" (Matt. xxvii. 42).—

Christ placed Himself under a necessity and an impossibility. In order to save us from the consequence of sin, He could not save Himself from the Cross, or the necessity of dying for sin.

2. " THE SCRIPTURE CANNOT BE BROKEN " (John x. 35).— The sacred writings cannot be gainsaid nor altered. They are immutable, unchanging, and imperishable.

3. " HE CANNOT DENY HIMSELF " (2 Tim. ii. 13).— Being the Faithful One, He binds Himself under the law of keeping to His Word. He would not go back from it if He could, and He could not if He would.

4. " GOD CANNOT LIE " (Titus i. 2).—His promise is unbreakable, His Word is impregnable, and His truth is invulnerable, and all because He is the Embodiment of Truth.

5. " THINGS WHICH CANNOT BE SHAKEN " (Heb. xii. 27). Things which the Eternal God makes permanent must be like Himself. (See the seven things specified in Hebrews xii. 22-24).

6. " A KINGDOM WHICH CANNOT BE MOVED " (Heb. xii. 28).—Earthly dynasties fall, earthly monarchies are deposed, and earthly crowns perish, but the heavenly kingdom is an everlasting one.

7. " GOD CANNOT BE TEMPTED OF EVIL " (James i. 13).— There is no response to evil in Him. The Holy One is not only blind to evil, but blinds the evil by His holiness.

" TONGUE LIKE A BELL-CLAPPER "

" *The tongue is a little member . . . a fire . . . a world of iniquity.*" James iii. 5, 6.

A bell-clapper is known by the noise it makes, and not by the music it gives. " He has a tongue like a bell-clapper," said one in speaking of another, and perhaps the one who said it had a clapper too !

Tongue-ology is the worst of the 'ologies. It parades its own worth and importance at the expense of others. The only consciousness of which it is conscious is its own consciousness. The personal pronouns are its stock-in-trade. I's, me's, my's, and mine are ringing all the time. The

noise of the clatter of its own matter is the only matter worthy
to be printed.

1. Its favourite TEXT is, " Is not this great Babylon which
I built ? " (Dan. iv. 30).

2. Its PRAYER is, " I thank God I am not as other men are "
(Luke xviii. 11).

3. Its AIM in life is, " I go a-fishing " (John xxi. 3).

4. Its OPINION is, like Naaman's, " I thought " (2 Kings
v. 11).

5. Its BOAST is, like Goliath's, " Am I a dog ? " (1 Sam.
xvii. 43).

6. Its POPULAR PHRASE, " I told you so," and its expectation is, " That's what I expected ! " (Ps. xxxi. 22).

7. Its COMPLAINT, like Jonah's, is, " I do well to be
angry " (Jonah iv. 9).

The only place for I, is, as Paul says, on the Cross—" I
am crucified with Christ " (Gal. ii. 20).

TRAITOR

" Lifted up his heel against me."—Ps. xli. 9.

Josiah Royce says of " a traitor " : " The first condition
is that a traitor is a man who has had an ideal, and who has
loved it with all his heart and soul. His ideal must have
seemed to him to furnish the cause of his life. It must have
meant to him what Paul meant by the grace that saves. He
must have embraced it, for the time, with full loyalty. It
must have been his religion, his way of salvation.

" The second condition that my ideal traitor must satisfy
is this, having thus found his cause, he must, as he now
knows, in at least some one voluntary act of his life have been
deliberately false to his cause. So far as in him lay, he the
worst, it is the traitor, and it is not the community, that
must, at least in that one act, have betrayed his cause." We
are traitors all, and traitors many times, for who of us has
been true all the time. Verily, we have to say, with
McCheyne, " The only door we can enter is by the sinner's
door."

Generally speaking, a traitor is one who is false to a trust.

1. A Traitor is A TRESPASSER. He is described as one who

has not been faithful in that which " was delivered him to keep " (Lev. vi. 4).

2. A Traitor is A TRANSGRESSOR, that is one who goes beyond the prescribed boundary of God's law ; hence Ezra charged those who had taken strange wives (Ezra x. 10), when he said, " Ye have transgressed " (Deut. xxv. 5).

3. A Traitor is A TRAFFICKER, for his own ends, like Achan, who took the consecrated things of the Lord for himself (Josh. vii. 20).

4. A Traitor is A TRUCKLER in Divine things, like Ananias and Sapphira, who were not real in their profession (Acts v. 1).

5. A Traitor is A TURN-COAT, like Rehoboam, who "took counsel " with the old men, and then turned against their counsel (2 Chron. x. 6, 13).

6. A Traitor is A TRICKSTER, like Ahab, who ran after Elijah for his convenience and then acted in direct opposition to him (1 Kings xviii. 1-46).

7. A Traitor is A TRUTHLESS DISCIPLE, like Judas, who consorted with the Lord, and yet betrayed Him (Luke xxii. 48).

TRAITS OF A TRUE CHRISTIAN
" He was a good man."—Acts xi. 24.

Rudyard Kipling wrote about the late Lord Roberts :

> " Clean, simple, valiant, well-beloved,
>   Flawless in faith and fame,
> Whom neither ease nor honours moved
>   An hair's-breadth from his aim.

> " Never again the war-wise face,
>   The weighed and urgent word
> That pleaded in the market-place—
>   Pleaded and was not heard ! "

Comment is superfluous on such a tribute, but we may point the tribute by saying, would that every believer in Christ was

1. " CLEAN " in the shrine of his heart (Ps. li. 10).

2. " SIMPLE " in the singleness of his faith (Ps. cxvi. 6).

3. " VALIANT " in the courage of his testimony (Heb. xi. 34).

4. " BELOVED " in the help of his service (Col. iv. 9).

5. " BLAMELESS " in the life of his behaviour (Phil. ii. 15).

6. UNMOVABLE in his " aim " to please his Lord (2 Cor. v. 9, R.V.).

7. EARNEST in the pleading of his confession (Acts xxiii. 1).

TREASURES IN CHRIST

" *In Whom are hid all the treasures of wisdom and knowledge.*"
—Col. ii. 3.

" Walk in," were the words which greeted us as we approached the Public Library in Columbus, Ohio, and as we neared the door of the building, we saw a further inscription on each side of the steps, namely, " All my treasures are within." How like the Lord in His love when He says to the sinner in so many words, " Walk in," or to put the same thing in His own words, " I AM the Door, by Me if any man enter in he shall be saved " (John x. 9). The effective Cause of our being able to " enter in " is found in the two little words, " By Me." The preposition " dia " rendered " by " with the genitive, signifies a producing cause, so that the words would be better rendered, " By means of Me." How much those words in their meaning, mean ; and how they remind us of Him who bled on Calvary, for it is only by means of His atoning blood that it is possible for us to enter in. And much we find when we enter in. How can we enter in ? How does a person enter any building ? By an act of their will which moves their steps. So faith is an act of the will, which moves the individual to enter the place of safety, even Christ, for He is God's salvation and ours.

" All my treasures are within." The treasures of the Public Library, referred to above, were said to be " within." Certainly all the treasures of wisdom, knowledge and all spiritual blessings are in Christ.

The Believer in Christ is blessed with all spiritual blessings in Him (Eph. i. 3).

And among the many are :—

Acceptance, which can never be questioned (Eph. i. 6).

Bounty, which can never be withdrawn (1 Cor. iii. 21-23).

Comeliness, which can never be marred (Ezek. xvi. 14).
Deliverance, which can never be excelled (2 Cor. i. 10).
Election, which can never be broken (Eph. i. 4 ; Rom. viii. 30).
Fulness, which can never be exhausted (Col. ii. 9, 10, R.V.).
Grace, which can never be limited (2 Cor. xii. 9).
Hope, which can never be disappointed (Heb. vi. 18, 19).
Inheritance, which can never be alienated (1 Pet. i. 3-5).
Joy, which can never be quenched (John xv. 11).
Kingdom, which can never be overturned (Heb. xii. 28).
Love, which can never be darkened (John xiii. 1).
Might, which can never be overcome (Eph. i. 19 ; 2 Cor. x. 4).
Nearness, which can never be reversed (Eph. ii. 13).
Ordination, which can never be removed (John xv. 16 ; Eph. ii. 10).
Purity, which can never be defiled (Song of Sol. iv. 7).
Quietness, which can never be disturbed (John xiv. 27 ; Isa. xxxii. 17).
Righteousness, which can never be tarnished (2 Cor. v. 21).
Salvation, which can never be cancelled (Heb. v. 9).
Triumph, which can never be clouded (2 Cor. ii. 14).
Union, which can never be severed (1 Cor. xii. 12).
Victory, which can never be altered (Heb. ii. 14 ; 1 John v. 18, R.V.).
Wisdom, which can never be baffled (1 Cor. i. 24).
'Xcellence, which can never be destroyed (Deut. xxxiii. 29).
Youthfulness, which can never be interrupted (Ps. ciii. 5).
Zeal, which can never be hindered (John ii. 17 ; Isa. ix. 7).

All these blessings have been given to us by our LOVING FATHER ; they have been purchased by our LOVING SAVIOUR ; they are received by a LIVING FAITH ; and enjoyed as we experience the LEADING of the HOLY SPIRIT.

These blessings are all in Christ as the place in which God has treasured them, therefore if we would know them as ours experimentally, we must " Abide in Him."

UNCHANGING ONE

" *I am Jehovah, I change not.*"—Mal. iii. 6.

" Our knowledge," says Sir David Bruce, " was constantly increasing, our ideas about things constantly changing, and what was looked on to-day as absolute, immutable truth, was seen to-morrow in the light of some newer knowledge to be but a crude beginning." There is thus no finality in many of the teachings of science. The ideas of scientific men about things are constantly changing. The text books of to-day soon become obsolete, and new editions containing new scientific doctrines are issued. Ideas which to-day are regarded as immutable truth have to give place to other ideas which in their turn are abandoned as a result of fresh investigation and fresh study. Yet we are asked by Liberal Evangelicals to believe that " God has been teaching the world, not only by His Church, but also by men of science and by critical scholars," and we are to " claim all knowledge as part of God's revelation." If the teachings of scientists and critical scholars were really the revelation of God, they would be fixed and immutable. God is unchangeable. He does not reveal one thing to-day and something wholly opposite to it to-morrow. " The Word of the Lord endureth for ever."

1. His Word is UNCHANGING in its TRUTH (Matt. xxiv. 35).

2. His Love is UNCHANGING in its AFFECTION (John xiii. 1).

3. His Power is UNCHANGING in its STRENGTH (2 Cor. xii. 9).

4. His Promises are UNCHANGING in their WORTH (2 Cor. i. 20).

5. His Life is UNCHANGING in its BLESSING (John x. 28, 29).

6. His Priesthood is UNCHANGING in its CHARACTER (Heb. vii. 16-25).

7. Christ Himself is UNCHANGING in His NATURE (Heb. i. 12).

" UNDER NEW MANAGEMENT "

" Spiritual Things."—1 Cor. ii. 15.

The writer recently passed a building which had been closed for some time, upon the outside of which was announced, " These premises will shortly be opened under new management." The old management had not worked, it was therefore wisdom to have a new one. Darby's version of 1 Cor. ii. 12, 13, is suggestive, it reads : " But we have received, not the spirit of the world, but the Spirit which is of God, that we may know the things which have been freely given to us of God : which things also we speak, not in words taught by human wisdom, but in those taught by the Spirit, communicating spiritual things by spiritual means." Mark the " means " by which the " spiritual things " are to be communicated. The things of the Spirit can only be made known by the Spirit of the things.

1. He alone can create a thirst for the " SPIRITUAL DRINK " from " the Spiritual Rock " (1 Cor. x. 4).

2. He alone can make us conscious of the need of the " SPIRITUAL BLESSINGS " of the Gospel (Eph. i. 3).

3. He alone can give us " the SPIRITUAL UNDERSTANDING " to know the things of God and the God of the things (Col. i. 9).

4. He alone can enable us to discern the THINGS that are SPIRITUAL in contrast to the things that are carnal (1 Cor. ii. 15).

5. He alone can build us into " the SPIRITUAL HOUSE " (1 Pet. ii. 5).

6. He alone can cause us " to offer up SPIRITUAL SACRIFICES " (1 Pet. ii. 5).

UNDER THE JUNIPER TREE

" *He lay and slept under a juniper tree, behold, then an angel . . . came.*"—1 Kings xix. 5-7.

" Lord save us from getting under the juniper tree," so prayed a good mother, and there was a responsive " Amen." And another has said : " There is a temptation to look for a juniper tree. But let us all keep away from the juniper tree ; our place is not under a tree, but in the open field. Let us not faint. Let us go forth to the work that waits with the hope that maketh not ashamed. We own that there are disquieting weaknesses in our Church work, but let no man forget the great multitude of faithful souls who make the Church and care for the Church, who are the reserves of the

238

Church, who, when clearly called, will come forth to do greater things than they have ever accomplished. Above all, let us not forget that Christ loves the Church and gave Himself for the Church. We have not, indeed, faith for the moment to care for the Church as we should have cared for it, to work for it as we should have worked, to pray for it as we should have prayed. We have allowed energy and effort which should have been consciously directed all the while to the strengthening of the Church to turn elsewhere and to ebb away."

One thing of special moment is, Jehovah sends His angel to meet the prophet in his need.

Our needs as sinners, saints, and servants are many, but there is One who can meet them all.

1. RECOGNITION OF NEED.—" I have need to be baptised of Thee " (Matt. iii. 14). John felt he needed a Sin-bearer and a Baptiser. Christ's work for us, and the Spirit's work in us, we all need.

2. KNOWLEDGE OF NEED.—" Your Father knoweth what things ye have need of " (Matt. vi. 8). His knowledge of our need is His guarantee that He will meet it.

3. MEETER OF NEED.—" He healed them that had need " (Luke ix. 11 ; Matt. ix. 12). Christ can heal our need and meet the need of all. His blood and power are the panacea for all maladies.

4. TIME OF NEED.—" Grace to help in time of need " (Heb. iv. 16). His grace is sufficient and always timely. He is never late nor lacking.

5. FELLOWSHIP OF NEED.—" Assist her in whatsoever business she hath need of you, for she hath been a succourer of many, and of myself also " (Rom. xvi. 2). No member in the Body of Christ can say, " I have no need of you " (1 Cor. xii. 21).

6. CONFESSION OF NEED.—" I am poor and needy " (Ps. xl. 17 ; lxx. 5 ; lxxxvi. 1 ; cix. 22). A consciousness and a confession of need is the first step to having it supplied.

7. SUPPLIER OF NEED.—" My God shall supply all your need, according to His riches in glory by Christ Jesus " (Phil. iv. 19). He loves to meet our necessity, according to His riches.

239

UNPRODUCTIVE HEAPS, PRODUCTIVE

" *The desert shall rejoice and blossom as the rose.*"—Isa. xxxv. 1.

" The mining district of South Lancashire is dotted with great mounds of refuse from the pits," one writes about them.

" Large stretches of what might be arable land are occupied with these useless heaps, which are unpleasant alike to the eye and to the nose. It occurred to a public-spirited firm at Atherton that something might be done. Merely to level the heaps would not suffice ; it would only enlarge the desert area.

" The firm, therefore, decided to remove the top layer of soil from certain fields, spread the pit refuse evenly to a good depth, and then replace the soil. They have dealt in this way with about fifty acres of land, and they are well satisfied with the results. The land is now under the plough and is yielding good crops, while the whole appearance of the district has been greatly improved.

" For this Atherton experiment proves that our mining districts need not be hideous, and that the obnoxious waste heaps may not only be levelled, but turned to good account. What has been done in Atherton can be done, and should be done, in many other places, and the saddest spots in the Black Country need not be regarded as irreclaimable. It will cost money, but the money would be well spent, and there is an abundance of unemployed labour that might be turned on to the task.

" In the near future, when factories are driven by electricity from central power-stations, and the smoke-cloud is lifted from the industrial districts, even the Black Country may be green once more."

What marvels we find the Lord can do with the wastes of wasted mankind.

1. He can take polluted Corinthians and WASH them white (1 Cor. vi. 11).

2. He can take " the woman " who is a sinner, and make her into a SAINT (Luke vii. 37).

3. He can arrest a persecuting Saul and reproduce a PATTERN SERVANT (1 Tim. i. 12-16).

4. He can pluck a burning brand, and cause him to be a bright SAMPLE OF HIS LOVE (Zech. iii. 2-5).

5. He can compassionate a wayward prodigal, and turn him into a WORTHY SON (Luke xv. 17-22).

6. He can pick up idol worshippers, and cause them to be WORSHIPPERS of the living God (1 Thess. i. 9).

7. He can quicken dead Ephesians, and UNITE them with the life-giving Christ (Eph. ii. 1-7).

VIRGIN BIRTH

" Behold, a virgin shall conceive, and bear a son, and shall call His name Immanuel."—Isa. vii. 14.

Many preachers of the Gospel are not only loosening the truth about the Virgin Birth, but they are losing it altogether. Those who question the incarnation of Christ, and deny its historicity, are making a grievous mistake, for, as J. Patterson-Smyth says : " One can but designate this hazy attitude as a grievous mistake. Nothing has occurred to justify it. In the long run it must affect belief in Christ's Divinity. For this is the lesson which history has taught us, that whoso loosens men's belief in the virgin birth of the Lord, is loosening the keystone to the doctrine of the Incarnation."

It is often said, Matthew and Luke alone record the virgin birth of our Lord ; but we need to remember, " *The Church did not believe the Virgin Birth because it was put into the Gospels, but it was put into these Gospels because the Church believed it.*"

The Virgin Birth cannot be denied without questioning the Eternal Sonship of Christ, for the " Word became flesh " (John i. 14) ; and without denying the prophecy that a virgin should bring forth a child, who would be " the Son " (Isa. ix. 6), and whose goings forth have been from eternity (Micah v. 2). Denial of the Virgin Birth gives the lie direct to the angel Gabriel, who said Christ would be the Product of the Holy Spirit (Luke i. 35) ; and beside this, a whole list of Scriptures in which the miraculous conception is implied have to be ignored, such as follows :

1. A SON SENT.—" God sent forth His Son, made of a woman " (Gal. iv. 4).

2. A Saviour Provided.—" God sending His Son in the likeness of sinful flesh, and for sin " (concerning sin) " condemned sin in the flesh " (Rom. viii. 3).

3. A Lord Identified.—" Our Lord made of the seed of David according to the flesh " (Rom. i. 3).

4. A Rich One Beggared.—" He was rich, yet for your sakes became poor " (2 Cor. viii. 9).

5. A Humble Servant.—" Took on Him the form of a servant," and was " made in the likeness of men " (Phil. ii. 7).

6. A God Manifested.—" God was manifest in the flesh " (1 Tim. iii. 16).

7. A Captain Sharing.—" The children are partakers of flesh and blood, He took part of the same " (Heb. ii. 10-14).

" WAKE THEM UP "

" Awake thou that sleepest."—Eph. v. 14.

During the Great War, a Frenchman, an Englishman and an Irishman found three Germans asleep, and the Frenchman said, " Let's shoot them " ; the Englishman said, " Let's take them prisoners " ; but the Irishman said, " Let's wake them up and have a scrap."

There are a great many Christians who need waking up. Waking up to their privileges in Christ, that they may fulfil their responsibilities.

The force of the apostolic words " Let us " is, let us do a certain thing without questioning and without hesitation.

1. Separation.—Seeing " the night is far spent," and " the day is at hand," let us cast off the works of darkness and put on the armour of light (Rom. xiii. 12). The clothes of the old man of sin are to be cast away as useless and worn out, and the armour of Him who is Light is to panoply us.

2. Walk.—" Let us walk honestly, and put on the Lord Jesus Christ " (Rom. xiii. 13, 14). To walk in the realm of honesty means to be open to the light, and free from any ulterior motives—namely, to be transparent. To be clothed with Christ signifies He is seen and heard.

3. Following.—" Let us therefore follow after peace " (Rom. xiv. 19). The association of these words is in relation

to our conduct towards each other. Our conduct will be reviewed at the judgment-seat of Christ, when we shall each have " to give account of himself to God " (12)—hence, we are not to judge or despise each other, but to " follow after peace."

4. REAPING.—" LET US not be weary in well-doing, for in due season we shall reap, if we faint not " (Gal. vi. 9). We shall reap in kind what we sow.

5. ALERTNESS.—" LET US not sleep " (1 Thess. v. 6). To be in a state of spiritual slumber, as the word " sleep " means, is to evidence we are in a wrong condition of soul. To be awake, is to show we are alert to the Lord's will.

7. WATCHFULNESS.—" LET US watch and be sober " (1 Thess. v. 6). We need a watchful eye to see what the enemy is after, a watchful heart to keep the garden of our inner being, and a watchful spirit to be ready for our Lord.

8. SOBRIETY.—" LET US, who are of the day, be sober " (1 Thess. v. 8). Because of what we are, we ought to be different to others.

WATCHING

" Watch."—Matt. xxiv. 42.

At the corner of four cross-roads in Pimlico, London, there is a window next to a second-hand store, and here a woman watches almost day and night. She keeps her constant vigil for the return of her soldier-son, who went to France with the first batch of Royal Fusiliers in 1914. Three years later he was " reported missing," and soon after the Armistice notification of his presumed death was received by the family. But the watching mother is convinced her boy will return. For several years she has peered across the roads, and every evening the oil-lamp gleams on the table by the window. The blinds are not drawn, and she watches till sleep overcomes her.

Oh ! that such vigilance might characterise our watching for the return of Christ ; for, if it did, it would show we are :

1. WAITING.—" Waiting " for His return (1 Cor. i. 7).

2. LOOKING.—That we are " looking " for the Blessed Hope (Titus ii. 13).

3. LOVING.—That we " love " His appearing (2 Tim. iv. 8).

4. PATIENCE.—That we have the " patience of hope " (1 Thess. i. 3).

5. HASTING.—That we are " hasting " the fulfilment of things to come (2 Pet. iii. 12-14).

6. PURIFYING.—That we are purifying ourselves (1 John iii. 3).

7. EQUIPPED.—That we are casting off the works of darkness, and putting on the armour of light (Rom. xiii. 11-14).

WHAT IS A CHRISTIAN ?

" *A man in Christ.*"—2 Cor. xii. 2.

What is a Christian ? The most concise and comprehensive sentence is the statement of the Apostle Paul, when he refers to himself as " a man in Christ."

A second question arises in answer to the one " What is a Christian ? " and that is, " What kind of a man is the one who is in Christ ? "

1. He is a QUICKENED MAN. " You hath He quickened " (Eph. ii. 1). Quickened from the death of sin, and made alive to God by means of the death of Christ.

2. A man in Christ is a CHRIST-SAVED MAN. " By grace are ye saved through faith " (Eph. ii. 8). His grace alone can save, His blood alone can cleanse, His peace alone can quicken, and His power alone can keep.

3. A man in Christ is a WORD-ASSURED MAN. Christ says, " These things I say that ye might be saved " (John v. 24, 34). God's Word is the cause of faith, it is the controller of faith, and the food which makes faith strong in its confidence, and holy in its consecration.

4. A man in Christ is a SPIRIT INDWELT MAN. " Know ye not that ye are the temple of God " (1 Cor. iii. 16).

5. A man in Christ aims to be a GOD-PLEASING MAN. " We make it our aim to be well-pleasing unto Him " (2 Cor. v. 9, R.V.).

6. A man in Christ is a LOVE-INSPIRED MAN. " The love of Christ constraineth us " (2 Cor. v. 14).

7. A man in Christ is a GOD-GLORIFYING MAN. " Glorify God in your body and spirit which are His " (1 Cor. vi. 20).

WHAT IS MAN ?

" What is man, that Thou art mindful of him, and the son of man, that Thou visitest him ? "—Ps. viii. 4.

" How large are we in reality ? On an asteroid, giants as large as Mont Blanc ; on the sun, small as ants ; in the universe, invisible particles ; under a microscope, with a magnifying power which gives an enlargement twenty thousand times that of the object, we should be nearly forty miles high. This conception does not satisfy chemistry. In her sight we are solar systems revolving at enormous speed, nebulæ composed of innumerable billions of atoms, and molecules endowed with marvellous and eternal energies, incessantly drawing together and separating. Each atom, each molecule is, perhaps, proportionately, as far from the next as Jupiter from the earth. Of what size does an atom appear to an angel ? Of what size do we appear to the God of Space, who sees each one of the innumerable atoms of which we are composed ? In any case, humanly speaking, we are immeasurably great in His sight."

Man is very small when compared with God ; but when we take God's thought about men, he is great, too. What is man ?

1. In NATURE, man is an indestructible spirit ; for he is created in the image of God (Gen. i. 27 ; James iii. 9, R.V.).

2. In SIN, man is a dead sinner ; for he is dead in trespasses and sins (Eph. ii. 1-5).

3. In CHRIST, man is a redeemed believer ; for he is liberated by His Blood (Rev. i. 5, R.V.).

4. In GOD, man is a privileged child ; for he possesses the nature and name of the Father (1 John iii. 1-3).

5. In the SPIRIT, man is a communing saint ; for the Spirit is the Element of a holy life (Gal. v. 16, 22, 25).

6. In the BODY, man is a united member ; for he is one with the Head and Body (1 Cor. xii. 12, 13).

7. In the GLORY, man will be a glorified being ; for he will be like his Lord (1 John iii. 2 ; Phil. iii. 20, 21).

WHAT IS OUR ATTITUDE TO CHRIST'S COMING ?

" To wait for His Son from heaven."—1 Thess. i. 10.

To Samuel Rutherford, the coming of Christ was a purifying hope. Hear his soul's cry for the Bridegroom : " Watch but a little, and ere long the skies shall rend, and that fair, lovely Person, Jesus, will come in the clouds, fraught and loaded with glory. Oh, when shall we meet ? Oh, how long is it to the dawning of the marriage day ? O sweet Lord Jesus, take wide steps ! O my Lord, come over the mountains at one stride ! O my Beloved, flee like a roe, or a young hart, on the mountains of separation. Oh that He would fold the heavens together like an old cloak, and shovel time and days out of the way, and make ready in haste the Lamb's wife for her Husband. Since He looked upon me, my heart is not my own ; He hath run away to heaven with it."

What should be our attitude in relation to the coming of our Lord ?

1. WATCH for Him ardently, as He has commanded in Luke xii. 36, 37.

2. WAIT for Him patiently, as the Spirit enjoins in 1 Cor. i. 7.

3. WITNESS for Him faithfully, for He bids us to " Hold fast the confession of our hope " (Heb. x. 23, R.V.).

4. WISH for Him prayerfully, as John the Seer did when he said, " Come, Lord Jesus " (Rev. xxii. 20).

5. WORK for Him diligently, for He bids us to be " Redeeming the time " (Eph. v. 16).

6. WAR for Him valiantly, by putting on " the armour of light " (Rom. xiii. 11-14).

7. WALK with Him dependently, for God alone can keep us blameless till Christ comes (1 Thess. v. 23, 25).

WHAT THE LORD IS TO HIS OWN

" To whom then will ye liken Me ? "—Isa. xl. 25.

There is no case so hard in life, but we shall find it described in The Book, and also the antidote of God's grace to meet it. We could hardly imagine a condition of things to make it essential to give such a warning as the following,

" Trust ye not in a neighbour ; put not confidence in a friend ; keep the doors of thy mouth from her that lieth in thy bosom. For the son dishonoureth the father, the daughter riseth up against her mother, the daughter-in-law against her mother-in-law ; a man's enemies are the men of his own house."

Here is a descriptive environment which would try the patience of Job, and make any Elijah get under a juniper tree. A neighbour not worthy of trust is bad, a friend unreliable as a confidant is worse, and not to be able to have fellowship with one's wife is worst, and what is worse than the worst, is not to find any reliable ground of confidence in one's own offspring.

Well for God's people who are found in such a plight if they do as the prophet did, and say, " But as for me, I will look unto Jehovah " (Micah vii. 5-7, R.V.), or " In Jehovah will I keep watch " (marg.). When the earthly fails we always find the heavenly still reliable. Amid all the changes of life, expected and not expected, there is One who says, " I am Jehovah, I change not."

In Him there is a rock for stability, a friend who is constant, a covenant that is sure, an arm that is strong, a love that is true, a grace that is sufficient, a promise that is kept, a supply that is full, a place that is undisturbed, a power that is omnipotent, a joy that is certain, and a presence that sustains.

The Lord is a :

1. ROCK FOR STABILITY.—" Thou art my Rock " (Ps. lxxi. 3).

2. FRIEND FOR CONSTANCY.—" A Friend that loveth at all times " (Prov. xvii. 17).

3. LOVER FOR AFFECTION.—" Behold what manner of love " (1 John iii. 1).

4. GRACIOUS LORD FOR SUFFICIENCY.—" My grace is sufficient for thee " (2 Cor. xii. 9).

5. HIDING PLACE FOR PROTECTION.—" Thou art my Hiding Place " (Ps. xxxii. 7).

6. POWER FOR STRENGTH.—" I am full of power by the Spirit of the Lord " (Micah iii. 8).

7. PRESENCE FOR RELIABILITY.—" I am with thee " (Isa. xli. 10).

WHAT MATERIAL ARE YOU SENDING ON ?

" *Those things which are before.*"—Phil. iii. 13.

A story of much significance is related of a worldly, selfish young woman, who on one occasion dreamed that she was in heaven.

As she was being shown through the Holy City, examining and admiring the many beautiful residences, she paused before one exceptionally beautiful. Turning to her guide, she said, " For whom is this beautiful place ? "

" Why, that's for your gardener," answered the guide.

" For my gardener ? Why, he would not know what to do in such a spacious dwelling. He would be entirely lost in a mansion like this ! Why, he lives in such a little bit of a cottage on earth ; he might do better, I give him reasonable wages, but he gives so much of it away to the poor, miserable people, that he has hardly enough to keep his wife and family, let alone any comforts or luxuries."

Walking on apace, they came to a little bit of a cottage.

" And whom is this being built for ? " asked the young woman.

" Why, that is for you," answered the guide.

" For me ! " she exclaimed in wonder and surprise. " Why, that cannot be for me ! I have always been accustomed to a mansion for a house. I could not adjust myself to such a small house."

Still plainly but sadly answered the guide : " It is for you. Our great Architect does the very best He can with the material that is sent up to Him."

Where are you laying up your treasure ?

What does the coming of Christ mean for those who are looking for Him ?

1. RECEPTION BY CHRIST.—His promise is, " I will come again and receive you to Myself " (John xiv. 3). What a reception !

2. LIKENESS TO CHRIST.—" We shall be like Him, for we shall see Him as He is " (1 John iii. 2).

3. TRANSLATION TO BE WITH CHRIST.—We shall be caught up to meet Him, and ever to be with Him (1 Thess. iv. 13-18).

4. REWARDED BY CHRIST (Luke xix. 13), for the Lord will come to reckon with His servants, and give to His faithful ones compensation.

5. PLACED BY CHRIST.—We shall not all occupy the same place, for there will be those who will have " a full reward " and an " abundant entrance " and there are those who will not (2 John 8 ; 2 Pet. i. 11).

6. TESTED BY THE LORD.—Our lives will be scrutinised, and our work will be sifted, and for what comes through the fire we shall be rewarded (1 Cor. iv. 4, 5, R.V.).

7. MOTIVES WILL BE EXAMINED BEFORE CHRIST.—For it is at His judgment seat we shall be "well-pleasing" to Him or not (2 Cor. v. 9, 10, R.V.).

WHAT'S IN A NAME?

" I have called thee by thy name."—Isa. xliii. 1.

" I spent an hour and a half riding across London," says a writer in the *Daily News*, " and chuckled the whole way from merely looking at the names over the shops. Leaving out the variations on the good old Jewish name of Cohen, there flashed past me a butcher named Portwine, and a public-house, ' The Green Man,' built of brown enamelled bricks. Over the windows of a cleaners', etc., shop was the sign, ' We dye to live,' a humorous way of attaining immortality ; while the name exhibited over a fish shop was ' Fry Bros.' "

There are seven names, or titles, by which believers are called.

1. " CHILDREN " for relationship. " Called the children of God " (1 John iii. 2, R.V.).

2. " SAINTS " for position and practice. " Called saints " (1 Cor. i. 2). Not " called TO BE saints," but saints by calling.

3. " CHRISTIANS " for association. " Disciples were first called Christians at Antioch " (Acts xi. 26).

4. " BRETHREN " for Fellowship. " For which cause He is not ashamed to call them brethren " (Heb. ii. 11).

5. " SHEEP " for character. " He calleth His own sheep by name " (John x. 3).

6. " SERVANTS " for employment. " He called His own

servants and delivered unto them His goods " (Matt. xxv. 14 ; Luke xix. 13).

7. " FRIENDS " for companionship. " I have called you friends " (John xv. 15).

WHAT WILL HE FIND ?

" When He cometh shall find watching."—Luke xii. 37.

On one occasion a number of soldiers in Ireland received an order to have their kit-bags ready for examination. As it was a very hot day, one of the soldiers had filled his kit-bag with straw, but had forgotten what he had done. He had done this to save himself from carrying the heavy burden of his kit. It may be imagined the consternation of the man when he saw the straw ! How will it be with us when we stand before the judgment-seat of Christ ? What will be found in the kit-bag of our life when we stand before Him ? Will there be the straw of mixed motive, the straw of self-seeking, the straw of love of ease, the straw of unfaithfulness, and the straw of pride ? Oh ! that there may be found in the kit-bag of our life :

1. The " TEN POUNDS " of practical use of the pound of the Gospel (Luke xix. 13).

2. The TALENTS of improved opportunities for the Lord (Matt. xxv. 20).

3. The WORK of endurance as seen in the test of trial (1 Pet. i. 7).

4. The RIGHT of abundant entrance into the kingdom (2 Pet. i. 11).

5. The ASSURANCE of a " full reward " (2 John 8).

6. The FINDING of a denied life (John xii. 25, 26).

7. The CLAIM of the Lord's special service (Luke xii. 35 ,36).

8. The ABIDING WORK of truth (1 Cor. iii. 14).

9. The FAITHFULNESS of endurance (James i. 12).

" WHOSOEVER "

" Whosoever believeth in Him."—John iii. 16.

A converted lad in talking to a man, who did not believe Christ loved him, got his Testament and said, " Does yer see that word marked wid red ink ? "

" Yes, I see it."

" Well, what is she ? "

" It's ' whosoever.' "

" Well, what does that mean ?"

" I guess it means just what it says, but you see with me it is different ! I was raised to do right, my father was a Methodist minister, and he taught me to pray and read the Bible. I knew what was right, but with my eyes open I went right into sin, and God can never forgive one who sins against the light."

" Say, read der whole verse," said Jimmie.

" I know it without reading it, I learned it at my mother's knee before I could talk plain."

" Well, git busy and say it then."

" God so loved the world "—.

" Loved der what ? "

" The world."

" Go on."

" That He gave His only begotten son "———.

" Dat's Jesus, ain't it ? "

" Yes, that is who it means."

" Go on."

" God so loved the world that He gave His only begotten Son, that whosoever "———.

" Who ? "

" Whosoever."

" Don't that mean you ? "

" I'm afraid not."

" Den dis is der way ter read it," said Jimmie. " Dat whosoever, 'cept Dave Beach, kin have everlasting life. Not on your fottygraff, it ain't writ dat way."

" Well, in another place it says that if you know to do right and do it not, it's sin."

" And dat makes yer a sinner, don't it ? "

" Yes, it does, and a bad one, too," said Dave.

Jimmie put his thumb into his mouth to wet it and turned leaf after leaf. At last he said, " Read dat."

Dave took the book and looked hard and long in silence.

" Read her," said Jimmie.

Dave read very slowly. " This is a faithful saying and

worthy of all acceptation, that Christ Jesus came into the world to save sinners."

" Save what ? "

" Sinners."

" Are you a sinner ? "

" Yes, I am a bad one."

" Worser than this guy ? Read der rest of 'er."

" Of whom I am chief."

" All right, if He kin save der chief of sinners, can't He save Dave Beach ? "

And He did.

" Whosoever " is found in more than one association.

1. The " whosoever " of PARTICIPATION in life (John iv. 13).

2. The " whosoever " of PRACTICE of sin (John viii. 34).

3. The " whosoever " of PARTNERSHIP with Christ (John xii. 46).

4. The " whosoever " of PERSECUTION (John xvi. 2).

5. The " whosoever " of PRAYER (Acts ii. 21).

6. The " whosoever " of PARDON (Acts x. 43).

7. The " whosoever " of PROTECTION (Rom. ix. 33).

WHY ?

" Why stand ye gazing up into Heaven ? "—Acts i. 11.

" Thousands wonder,
  Thousands ask :
Why the struggle,
  Why the task ?

" Why the burden,
  What the yoke ?
Is it all
  The devil's joke ?

" Why the bar,
  And why the bond,
If there's nothing
  There beyond ?

" Head and heart
Quarrel and cry ;
Head shouts : nothing !
Heart—you lie ! "

Many often put the questioning " why " in relation to the things of God, and their experience.

1. The Why of OUTLOOK. " Why do the nations rage ? " (Ps. ii. 1). Because they have nothing else to do ; or because they are envious of each other.

2. The Why of INLOOK. " Why art thou disquieted in me ? " (Ps. xlii. 5). Remove the cause of disquietude, and the worry will cease. It is the storm which creates the tumult of the sea.

3. The Why of ON-LOOK. " Why take ye thought (anxiety) ? " Worrying about present needs, and future possibilities will not help us to meet them (Matt. vi. 24-34).

4. The Why of SAD LOOK. " Why is thy countenance sad ? " (Neh. ii. 2, 3). Nehemiah's sadness led to " very great gladness " (Neh. viii. 17).

5. The Why of WRONG LOOK. " Why beholdest the mote in thy brother's eye ? " (Matt. vii. 3). We shall not see any mote in another's eye, if we get the beam out of our own.

6. The Why of UNCERTAIN LOOK. " Why gaddest thou about ? " (Jer. ii. 36). To gad means to have no certain place of dwelling.

7. The Why of No LOOK. " Why sit we here until we die ? " (2 Kings vii. 3). To sit still is to act ill. To have no purpose—not to see things rightly.

WITNESSING AND WARNING

" *Warning every man.*"—Col. i. 28.

When we realise that all about us are men who are dead in sin, and lost because of their rejection of Christ, we seem to be unmoved and almost indifferent. And if we should say that the preaching in the church is quite sufficient in the way of an invitation, my reply is that the unsaved people do not think it so. I remember a gentleman who became a member of my congregation whom I knew to be unsaved, and to whom I one day made a visit, telling him that I had made up my mind that I would never allow any one to enter my church and stay there for any length of time without I gave him a special invitation to come to Christ. I told him of his mother's concern and of his wife's anxious thought for his salvation, and when I asked him to come to Christ, his face suddenly paled and the tears began to run down his cheeks when he said : " This is the first invitation I have ever had to be a Christian. I had just about made up my mind that no one cared for my soul."

The Lord has saved us to witness to Him, and the power to do it is in the Holy Spirit (Acts i. 8).

1. WITNESS LOVINGLY, like Mary of Bethany (Matt. xxvi. 13).

2. WITNESS EARNESTLY, like Paul at Athens, when he saw the city given to idolatry (Acts xvii. 16).

3. WITNESS FAITHFULLY, as Samuel did to Saul, when he told him of his sin (1 Sam. xv. 23).

4. WITNESS PERSONALLY, like the Apostle when he told what the Lord had done for him (1 Tim. i. 16).

5. WITNESS SCRIPTURALLY, as Peter, who testified and witnessed to the sufferings of Christ (1 Pet. v. 1).

6. WITNESS CONSISTENTLY, like the one whom John commends, and of whom it could be said, " Who have borne witness of thy love " (3 John 6, R.V.).

7. WITNESS IN THE SPIRIT, so that it can be said of us, " God also bearing them witness with signs " (Heb. ii. 4).

WOMEN THAT HELP

" *The women whose hearts stirred them up.*"—Exod. xxxv. 26.

More than seventy years ago the King of Prussia, Frederick William III, found himself in great trouble. He was carrying on expensive wars, and had not money enough to accomplish his plans. But he knew that his people loved and trusted him, and he believed that they would be glad to help him. He therefore asked the women of Prussia, as many of them as wanted to help their king, to bring their jewellery of gold and silver, to be melted down into money for the use of their country. Many women brought all the jewellery they had, and for each ornament of gold or silver they received in exchange an ornament of bronze, or iron, precisely like the gold or silver ones, as a token of the king's gratitude. These iron and bronze ornaments all bore the inscription, " I gave gold for iron, 1813." These ornaments therefore became more highly prized than the gold or silver ones had been, for it was a proof that the woman had given up something for her king. It became very unfashionable to wear any jewellery, for any other would have been a token that the wearer was not loyal to her king and country. So the Order of the Iron Cross grew up, whose members wear no ornaments except a cross of iron on the breast, and give all their surplus money to the service of their fellow-men. How gloriously prosperous some of our missionary societies would become, if our people would only give their surplus jewellery and surplus money toward this God-honouring work of the world's redemption !

1. PRAISING WOMEN.—" All the women went after Miriam. . . . Sing ye unto the Lord " (Exod. xv. 20, 21).

2. POLITICAL WOMEN.—" All the women that were wise-hearted did spin " (Exod. xxxv. 25).

3. LISTENING WOMEN.—" Joshua read the law before the women " (Joshua viii. 35).

4. HONOURABLE WOMEN.—The elite of the Lord's own are the true nobility (Ps. xlv. 9).

5. BEHOLDING WOMEN.—Among those who viewed the sufferings of Christ were those who were said to be " Beholding afar off " (Matt. xxvii. 55).

6. PRAYING WOMEN.—Of the disciples who were endued with power at Pentecost, it is said, " They continued in prayer with the women " (Acts i. 14).

7. " HOLY WOMEN " are mentioned as those who are worthy of imitation (1 Pet. iii. 5).

WONDERFUL

" *His Name shall be called Wonderful.*"—Isa. ix. 6.

One can imagine with what intensity of feeling the Southerners would sing the well-known song :

> " Away down South in Dixie, away, away—
> In Dixie land, I'll take my stand,
> To live and die for Dixie land—
> Away, away, away down South in Dixie."

A modern writer represents a company singing it " before the War," by a number of people, young and old, at a house-party, and a Northerner being impressed by the pent-up feeling it expressed. One says to him of it, " A gleam of the current that is dammed up." The rejoinder brought forth is, " If the bank ever breaks what will happen ? " " A flood," is the reply.

Calvary's cross and cause inspires and evokes a greater passion, and makes the one who knows its fuel and flame to say, and sing :

> Upon the Cross of Calvary, away, away,
>   On Calvary's Cross I'll take my stand,
>   To live and die for Calvary grand,
> Upon, upon, upon the Cross of Calvary.

As we ponder the character of The Wonderful One, does it not kindle the passion, not only of patriotism, but of admiration for Him and devotion to Him.

He is " Wonderful."

W. Wonderful is His **W**ord.—" Thy testimonies are wonderful " (Ps. cxix. 129), exclaimed the Psalmist. They are wonderful in their power, in their promises, in their precepts, in their principles, in their purity, in their proffers, and in their peace.

O. Wonderful in His **O**ffering.—The Blood of Christ's Atoning Death is said to be " Precious " (1 Pet. i. 19). Precious because of Him who shed it, and because it is supernatural in its nature, satisfying in its atonement, unlimited in its procurements, powerful in its efficacy, sanctifying in its application, and eternal in its benefits.

N. Wonderful in His **N**ame.—For He is " Jesus " to save, " Christ " to anoint, " Lord " to govern, " Leader " to guide, " Captain " to conquer, " Bread " to feed, and " Shepherd " to tend (Acts iii. 6, 16 ; iv. 10, 12, 30).

D. Wonderful in His **D**oings.—In His acts of love, in His gracious ways, in His compassionate help, in His loving bestowments, in His wondrous miracles, in His helpful sayings, in His healing touches, and in His substitutionary work—He was, and is, wonderful (Exod. xv. 11.)

E. Wonderful in His **E**xample.—He is an Example in every way. In His lowly mien, in His sterling worth, in

His holy walk, in His gentle spirit, in His ardent zeal, in His resolute will, in His earnest work, in His loving ways, in His persistent purpose, and in His constant love—He is our Example (Phil. ii. 5-8).

R. Wonderful in His **R**iches.—We read of the " Riches of His grace," " The Riches of His glory," The Riches of His mercy, and " His unsearchable Riches." He is rich intrinsically, and not by bestowment. He is rich in Himself. No one enriches Him (Col. ii. 3 ; Eph. iii. 8, 16).

F. Wonderful in His **F**avour. — His favour passes all favour. It passes the favour of Ahasuerus towards Esther, Solomon towards the Queen of Sheba, David towards Mephibosheth, and Joseph towards his brethren (Zech. iii. 17).

U. Wonderful in His **U**nction.—As there was no preparation like the holy anointing oil, so the Spirit of Christ corresponds to all the Holy Spirit is. He is called the " Spirit of Christ," because they both correspond to each other (1 Pet. i. 8-13).

L. Wonderful in His **L**ove.—His love is eternal in its duration, exceptional in its manner, self-sacrificing in its death, substitutionary in its sacrifice, sympathetic in its service, helpful in its ministry, constant in its affection, and unchanging in its character (Ps. cvii. 8, 15, 21, 31).

WORD OF GOD : THE AUTHORITY

" *Where the word of a king is, there is power.*"—Eccles. viii. 4.

One has said, in calling attention to the fact that Romanism goes against the Word, " There is one Mediator between God and man, the man Christ Jesus, who gave Himself a ransom for all," says : " Catholicism sets up another authority over against the mind of Christ as it is in Scripture, and that authority is the priest. The ways in which Romanism has departed from New Testament truth are numberless—we have but to recall transubstantiation, purgatory, Papal infallibility, mariolatry, amongst many other heresies ; but at the root of them all lies this mighty perversion of the mind of Christ, which gives to the ordained priest powers by which he becomes a necessary mediator between God and man. Catholicism, whether Roman or Anglican, insists that there are two sorts of Christians—those who are the specially appointed channels of God's grace (the priests), and those who can only receive this grace by means of the priests (the laity). Some firms have special agents in various parts of the country, and refuse to supply their goods to the public except through these accredited agents. Catholicism teaches that God acts in this way, and that the priests are His sole agents. The New Testament, on the contrary, teaches that all men are alike before God, and He is ready and willing to supply grace according to need to any soul coming to Him. It was when Luther realised this, and saw that we are justified by faith, and not by the favour of priests, that Protestantism sprang mighty and armed into being."

There is one small word which is rendered " by " and " through " (the preposition " dia " with the genitive), which affirms beyond all contradiction, that all blessings come " by " and " through " Christ and His atoning death, not through a priest or any man.

1. SALVATION.—" I am the Door, *by* Me if any man enter in, he shall be saved " (John x. 9).

2. ACCESS.—" No man cometh unto the Father, but *by* Me " (John xiv. 6).

3. JUSTIFICATION.—" *By* Him all that believe are justified from all things " (Acts xiii. 39).

4. RECONCILIATION.—" Reconciled to God *by* the death of His Son " (Rom. v. 10).

5. JOY.—" Joy in God *through* our Lord Jesus Christ " (Rom. v. 11).

6. NEARNESS.—" Made nigh *by* the blood of Christ " (Eph. ii. 13).

7. PEACE.—" Peace with God, *through* our Lord Jesus Christ " (Rom. v. 1).

" WORK "

" *The people had a mind to work.*"—Neh. iv. 6.

" How long is it since you have worked ? " asked the chairman of the Prescot Bench recently of Thomas Ignatius Monk, accused of loitering with intent to rob the local parish church. " Work ! " exclaimed Monk. " The very word makes me shiver." Monk was committed for three months with hard labour.

There are seven references to work in Neh. iv.

1. AN ESSENTIAL QUALIFICATION.—Having " a mind to work " (ver. 6). When we have a mind to work, we shall work with a will.

2. AN ENEMY'S OPPOSITION.—The opposition was to " cause the work to cease " (ver. 11). Adversaries are sure to dog our steps if we work for the Lord.

3. AN INDIVIDUAL TASK.—" Every one unto his work " (ver. 15). Each doing his part is the secret of united action. Each at it, and all at it.

4. AN EARNEST LABOUR.—" My servants wrought in the work " (ver. 16). They did not look at it, they went at it.

5. A GOOD COMBINATION.—" Wrought in the work and ... held a weapon " (ver. 17). We need the sword to defend, as well as the trowel to build.

6. AN ESSENTIAL RECOGNITION.—" The work is great and large " (ver. 19). When we see what the work is, and what it requires, we rise with love and faith and earnestness to meet its requirements.

7. A HOLY CONFIDENCE.—" Our God shall fight for us. So we laboured in the work " (ver. 21). When God is at the back of us, we have a backing for anything.

" WORKS "

" Faith without works is dead."—James ii. 26.

Father Lorry, who was hurrying to catch the Dublin Express, overtook his Bishop, who was going to take the same train. " We've plenty of time," said the latter, pulling out his watch. " We've seven minutes yet, so we'll walk along together." They arrived at the station, however, just in time to see the train disappear. " Do you know, I had the greatest faith in that watch," said the Bishop. " What is faith without good works ? " returned Father Lorry.

James, in one section of his epistle, contained in chapter ii, uses the word " works " twelve times. The word signifies hard work, toil, doing things.

1. A QUESTION.—" Though a man say he hath faith, and have not works, can faith save him ? " (14). Saying without saintliness is a misnomer, for the faith expresses itself in likeness to Him.

2. A LONESOME FAITH.—" Faith, if it hath not works is dead, being alone " (17). A lonesome faith is a faithless faith, a tree without fruit, a profession without a possession, and a body without a soul.

3. A DOUBLE SHOW.—" A man may say, Thou hast faith, and I have works ; show me Thy faith without Thy works, and I will show Thee my faith by my works " (18). The one is a vain show, and the other is a vital one.

4. A VAIN FAITH.—" But wilt thou know, O vain man, that faith without works is dead ? " (20). A dead body is corrupt and corrupting, so is a faith without works.

5. A JUSTIFIED FAITH.—" Was not Abraham our father justified by works ? " (21). We are justified by faith in Christ's blood without works (Rom. iii. 28-31), but we justify our faith by our works.

6. A WORKING FAITH.—" Faith wrought with his works " (22). Faith and works are like the cogs in a cog-wheel, the one works with the other.

7. A PERFECT FAITH.—" By works was faith made perfect " (22). Faith perfects work, and work perfects faith. Thus the soul has two hands to perfect a complete body.

8. AN ILLUSTRATED COUPLET.—" Rahab . . . justified by works " (25). The red cord in her window was a sign of her faith, and her sheltering house to the spies, in her hiding of them, demonstrated her works (Josh. ii. 14, 24).

WORK : TO EVERY ONE GIVEN

" *He giveth to every man severally as He will.*"—1 Cor. xii. 11.

When God gives, He expects us to take ; when He commands, it is ours to obey ; and when He commissions us in service, it is ours to go.

Browning's poem on *The Boy and the Angel* pictures how

Gabriel had been sent down from heaven to take the boy's place as craftsman in a humble workshop :

> " And ever o'er the trade he bent,
> And ever lived on earth content.
> He did God's will ; to him all one,
> If on the earth or in the sun."

Here are some of God's commands, given by Paul, through the Spirit, to Timothy, in 2 Tim. ii :

1. A STRONG SON.—" Be strong in the grace " (ii. 1).
2. A FAITHFUL TEACHER.—" Commit thou " (ii. 2).
3. AN ENDURING SOLDIER.—" Endure hardness " (ii. 3).
4. A CONSIDERING HUSBANDMAN.—" Consider " (ii. 7).
5. A GOOD REMEMBRANCER.—" Remember " (ii. 8).
6. A DILIGENT WORKMAN.—" Study," " Be diligent " (ii. 15).
7. AN ALERT RUNNER.—" Flee " (ii. 22).
8. A DEVOTED FOLLOWER.—" Follow " (ii. 22).
9. A WISE AVOIDER.—" Avoid " (ii. 23).

WORLD AND THE CHRISTIAN

" They are not of the world, even as I am not of the world."
John xvii. 14.

" A Christian," says Mason, " has heaven in his eye, Christ in his heart, and the world under his feet." The world being under his feet, he cannot have the world in his feet.

The main question is, " What does our Lord say about the Christian and the world ? " In the seventeenth chapter of John's Gospel the believer is seen in a sevenfold relationship to the world.

1. THE BELIEVER IS TAKEN OUT OF THE WORLD.—" The men whom Thou gavest Me out of the world " (John xvii. 6). The whole force of this sentence is in the Greek preposition " ek," rendered " out of." It means to take clean out, as the children of Israel were brought out of Egypt. Following the Genesis of the new birth, there comes the Exodus of separation from the world.

2. THE BELIEVER IN THE WORLD, BUT NOT OF IT.—Christ says of His own, " These are in the world " (John xvii. 11). There is all the difference between the believer being in the world and the world being in the believer. The water in the ship will sink it, the ship in the water can sail over it.

3. THE BELIEVER HATED BY THE WORLD.—" The world hath hated them (ver. 14)." When the world can get on with us, and we can get on with the world, there is something wrong. Oil and water will not mix, and when they seem to, it is because there has been a shaking up by the hand of compromise.

4. THE BELIEVER KEPT FROM THE EVIL OF THE WORLD.— " I pray not that Thou shouldest take them out of the world, but that Thou shouldest keep them from the evil " (John xvii. 15). The place of separation is the place of power. If we go to Egypt for help, Egypt will soon deplete us and damage us too.

5. THE BELIEVER IS NOT OF THE WORLD.—" They are not of the world " (John xvii. 16). He is a pilgrim, a stranger in it. As a stranger he does not belong to it, and as a pilgrim he is passing through it.

6. THE BELIEVER SENT INTO THE WORLD.—" As Thou hast sent Me into the world, so have I also sent them into the world " (John xvii. 18). We are sent as witnesses, salt, and light to testify against the evil of the world, and to tell the world of a Saviour who can save from sin and sorrow.

7. THE WORLD BELIEVING ON CHRIST THROUGH THE BELIEVER.—" That the world may believe that Thou hast sent Me " (John xvii. 21-23). The life and love of the children of God is to convince the world of the being and love of the Saviour.

The tone and temper of the above words leave us in no doubt as to the will of the Lord in the believer's relationship to the world. If we are truly and wholly the Lord's we shall not want the world, and the world will not want us. When the Christian lies in the lap of the world of Delilah, he will surely be shorn of his locks of consecration ; and when the world gains an entrance into the being of the child of God, he will always find a leer of contempt on the face of the world, behind the mask of religiosity.

WORLD GROWING BETTER (?)

" *This know also, that in the last days, perilous*" (*fierce*)
" *times shall come.*"—2 Tim. iii. 1.

Some preachers say and sing :
" The world is growing better, no matter what they say,
The light is shining brighter in one refulgent ray.
And though deceivers murmur and turn the other way,
Yet still the world grows better and better every day."

Dr. W. H. Bates says that this chorus was sung with great enthusiasm by a concourse at a watering place after a characteristic discourse by a noted church secretary, a bishop " of some military and musical repute."

It is not what men say, or what they think, but what the Spirit says. The spoutings of men are not the sayings of the Spirit. Ponder the twenty-eight things that are said about men of the world, and the characteristics of the " Last days " in 2 Tim. iii. 1-13.

1. SELF-LOVERS.—" Men shall be lovers of their own selves " (2).

2. SINFUL COVETORS.—" Covetous." Greedy grab-alls to the hurt of others (2).

3. SELF-ADVERTISERS.—" Boasters " (2). Telling out about themselves.

4. INFLATED PROUDITES.—" Proud " (2). Blown out with self elation.

5. INSULTING ATHEISTS.—" Blasphemers " (2). Talking against sacred things.

6. SELF-WILLED ONES.—" Disobedient " (2). This is the essence of sin.

7. GRUMBLERS.—" Unthankful " (2). Complaining against God.

8. SACRELIGIOUS.—" Unholy " (2).

9. HARDENED.—" Without natural affection " (3).

10. UNRELIABLE.—" Truce-breakers " (3)

11. LIARS.—" False accusers " (3).

12. FEEBLE.—" Incontinent " (3).

13. DANGEROUS.—" Fierce " (3).

14. UNFRIENDLY.—" Despisers of them that are good " (3).

15. UNTRUSTWORTHY.—" Traitors " (4).

16. SWELLED HEADED ONES.—" Heady " (4).
17. PUFFED UP.—" High-minded " (4)
18. PLEASURE LOVERS.—" Lovers of pleasure " (4).
19. CONFORMERS TO SHOW.—" Having a form of godliness " (5).
20. CREEPITES.—" Creep into houses " (6).
21. INCAPABLE.—" Never able to come." (7).
22. OPPONENTS.—" Withstood " (8).
23. RESISTERS.—" Resist the truth " (8).
24. REPROBATES.—" Men of corrupt mind, reprobate " (8).
25. FOOLS.—" Their folly shall be manifest " (9).
26. BAD.—" Evil men " (13).
27. LEADERS-ASTRAY.—" Seducers " (13).
28. PROGRESSORS IN EVIL.—" Shall wax worse and worse " (13).

WORTHY ONE

" Thou art worthy to receive glory and power."—Rev. iv. 11.

St. Christopher vowed that he would give his loving devotion only to the strongest. So he first gave his service to the village lordling, then to the king. But finding that the king was afraid of the devil, he sought his company, which he found without difficulty. But seeing him turn pale at the sight of the cross, symbol of the greatest might in the universe, he gave his glad alliance unto God. What is the strongest, where is the highest ? We wish to seize upon the greatest for our development :

1. Because He is LOVING in Act (Gal. ii. 20).
2. Because He is COMPASSIONATE in heart (Matt. xv. 32).
3. Because He is SINLESS in nature (1 Pet. ii. 22).
4. Because He is HOLY in life (Heb. vii. 26).
5. Because He DIED for the worst (Rom. v. 8).
6. Because He is TRIUMPHANT in conflict (Heb. ii. 14).
7. Because He is the GOOD ONE in ministry (Acts x. 38).

Index

A

	PAGE
Accountability . . .	7
Alertness	7
All Israel	8
" All is well, since all grows better "	10
Angelic Ministry . . .	11
Anticipating Trouble . .	12
Atonement	13
Attractability of Personality .	14
Attractive Speaker . . .	15
Authority	16
A Whole Burnt-offering . .	16

B

Believer's Calling . .	17
Believer's Rights . . .	18
Be What You Are . .	19
Bible : What the Book Does .	20
Biter Bit	21
" Blessed " Ones . . .	22
Blessing Found Where Least Expected	23
Bloodless Gospel . . .	24
Blood of Christ . . .	25
Blood of Christ . . .	26
Blood of Christ : A Necessity .	27
Blood of the Lamb . . .	28
Book to put us Right . .	29
Business : The King's Business	29

C

Cause of the Trouble . .	30
Certainties	31
Certainties of the Faith . .	33
Cheerfulness . . .	34
Christ's Commands are His Enablings	35
Christ's Cross : Its Subjective Power	35
Christ's Death . . .	36
Christ's Indwelling . .	37
Christ's Message . . .	39
Christ's Resurrection is the Greatest Evidence of Christianity	40
Christ's Resurrection is the Greatest Exhibition of God's Power	41
Christ's Return . . .	42
Christ's Sayings . . .	42
Christ the Centre . . .	44
Cleansing	44

	PAGE
Cocoon Christians . . .	46
" Comforted with Nails " .	47
Coming of Christ . . .	48
Coming of Christ : What does it mean ?	49
Coming of the Holy Spirit .	50
Coming of the Lord . .	51
" Coming of the Son of Man "	53
Compromise	54
Conscience	55
Consistency	56
Corrupt Communications .	57
Creation declares the Creator .	58
Cries	59
Cross Endured : or A Cross, a Heart, and a Rose . .	60
Cross Forgotten . . .	61
Cross of Christ : Golden and Black . . .	62
Cross's Power to lift up . .	63
" Cut in "—in His hands .	63

D

Daily	64
Death of Christ . . .	67
Divine Healing . . .	69
Divinity of Drudgery . .	70
Doldrums	71
" Don't Pass the Cross " . .	72
Doubles	72
Drink : A Tramp's Testimony	74

E

Earnestness . . .	75
End of Life	76
Epitaph : John Wesley's .	77
Essential	78
Eternal Life	79

F

Fact of Christ . . .	80
Faith, Hope, and Love . .	81
Faith's Language . . .	82
Faith " spread abroad " .	83
" Five Alls "	84
Five : A Speaking Numeral .	85
Food versus Bones . .	86
Forgiving as Forgiven . .	87
Full Consecration . . .	87
Future Life	88
Future : What it Holds . .	89

G   PAGE

Getting Right with each other .   90
Giver of Victory   .   .   91
Giving : Christian giving   .   92
Gladstone's   Sayings   about
    Christ   .   .   .   93
Glorious Things   .   .   94
" God or Nothing "   .   95
God's Certain Acts   .   96
Good out of the seeming bad   97
Grace, Graces   .   .   98
Grasping Things   .   .   99
Greatest Work in the World   .   100

H

Hands   .   .   .   101
Hardness of Heart .   .   101
He alone is Worthy   .   102
Heart in the right place .   .   103
Heart of Gold   .   .   104
Heart : The Essential Thing .   105
" Helpmeet "   .   .   106
" He will do it "   .   .   107
Holy   Spirit's   Counteracting
    Work   .   .   .   107

I

Indifference .   .   .   108
Individuality   .   .   110
Integrity and Uprightness   .   111
Invisible made Visible   .   112
Isolation   .   .   .   113
Israel's Future   .   .   114
" Is your soul right ? "   .   115

J

Jesus, a Problem apart from
    Divine Revelation   .   116
Jew and the Gulf Stream   .   117
Jewish Prophecies   .   118
John's   Telling,   Tender,   and
    Trenchant   Touches   in   his
    Third Epistle   .   .   119
Joys : Coming Ones   .   120

K

Keep Off Satan's Territory   .   121
Knock at the Door   .   122

L

Lawlessness in the Pulpit   .   123
Laying up Treasure   .   125
Lazarus   .   .   .   126
Liberty by Slavery   .   127
Life Beyond .   .   128
Lifting Power   .   .   129
Light's Reflection .   .   130
Look and Pray   .   .   131

      PAGE

Lord's Requirements   .   .   133
Love's Attitude   .   .   134
Love's Ministry   .   .   135
Love's Traits   .   .   137

M.

" Made Radiant " .   .   139
Makings of the Lord   .   140
Man or Monkey ? .   .   141
Man who will Succeed   .   142
" Maranatha "   .   .   143
Mediator   .   .   .   145
Mistakes   .   .   .   146
" More," yea, " Much More ".   147
Mysteries   .   .   .   148

N

Name Above Every Name   .   149
Needs Met   .   .   .   150
" No Distinction of that sort
    there "   .   .   .   151
Not Ashamed of his Country .   152
" No Time for Criticism "   .   153
Not Yielded   .   .   154

O

" Obedience "   .   .   154
Obedience : Its Spirit   .   155
One Act may Lead to Many
    Consequences .   .   156
One : The Only One   .   157
" Only Unforgivable Thing " .   158
Opportunity and Ability   .   159

P

Palestine (Promised Land)   .   160
Palestine's Future .   .   161
Panacea   .   .   .   162
Paradoxes   .   .   .   163
Past and Present Tense .   164
Patience   .   .   .   165
Paul and the Philippian Jailor .   166
Paul's Afflictions   .   .   167
Peace Personified .   .   168
" Pearl Beyond all Price "   .   169
" Perfect Peace "   .   .   170
Personality Questioning .   172
Personal Knowledge   .   174
Personal Touch   .   .   175
Pick-up Man   .   .   176
Piteous Cry .   .   .   177
Places of Crisis   .   .   177
Places to Visit   .   .   178
Power of Trifles   .   .   179
Prayer   .   .   .   180
Prayer   .   .   .   181
Prayer : An Attitude   .   182

	PAGE
Prayer : Its Oughtness	183
Prayer : Its Privilege and Power	184
Prayer of Faith	185
Prayer : Richard Baxter's Testimony	186
Prayer that Prays : or an Alphabet of Prayerful and Personal Prayers	187
Prayer : The Greatest Ministry of All	188
Prayer : Three Kinds	189
Preacher's Theme	190
Presence Made a Difference	191
Proof of Discipleship	192
Put to Shame, or not	193

Q
Questions we Ask	194

R
Ready for Christ's Coming	196
Receptivity of the Christian Life	197
Recognised	199
Recognition in the Life to Come	199
Rejoicing Continually	200
Responsiveness of the Lord to Faith	202
Results : Faithful to the Lord, not looking for them	203
Rubbish	204

S
Sabbatism	205
Sacrifice	207
Saddening Sights	208
Saint : What is He ?	209
Salvation	209
Satan	210
Scripture's Claim	211
Scripture's Infallibility	212
Seeing Christ in Others	213
Seeking Ministry	213
" Self-sacrifice "	214
Separation	215
Separation keeps from Contamination	216
Seven Comings mentioned in John vi	217
Simplicity	218
Singing unto the Lord	219
Sinner's Right	220
Smoking and Habit	221
Snares	222

	PAGE
Some Contents of the Book	223
Something Sure and Lasting	224
Soul-less Man	224
Standing for God and the Right	225
Straw and Bricks	226
Substitution	227
Suffering for Christ	228

T
Taking the Place of Others	230
" Tell me what you know of Him "	231
Things God cannot do	231
" Tongue like a bell-clapper "	232
Traitor	233
Traits of a True Christian	234
Treasures in Christ	235

U
Unchanging One	236
" Under New Management "	237
Under the Juniper Tree	238
Unproductive heaps, productive	240

V
Virgin Birth	241

W
" Wake them up "	242
Watching	243
What is a Christian ?	244
What is Man ?	245
What is our Attitude to Christ's Coming ?	246
What the Lord is to His own	246
What Material are You Sending on ?	248
What's in a Name ?	249
What will He find ?	250
" Whosoever "	250
Why ?	252
Witnessing and Warning	253
Women that Help	254
Wonderful	255
Word of God : The Authority	257
" Work "	258
" Works "	259
Work : to every one given	260
World and the Christian	26·
World Growing Better ?	263
Worthy One	264